America Views China

AMERICA VIEWS CHINA

American Images of China Then and Now

EDITED BY

Jonathan Goldstein
Jerry Israel,
and Hilary Conroy

Bethlehem: Lehigh University Press
London and Toronto: Associated University Presses

Associated University Presses
440 Forsgate Drive
Cranbury, NJ 08512

Associated University Presses
25 Sicilian Avenue
London WC1A 2QH, England

Associated University Presses
P.O. Box 39, Clarkson Pstl. Stn.
Mississauga, Ontario,
L5J 3X9 Canada

The paper used in this publication meets the requirements of the American National Standard for Permanence of Paper for Printed Library Materials Z39.48-1984.

Library of Congress Cataloging-in-Publication Data

America views China : American images of China then and now / edited by Jonathan Goldstein, Jerry Israel, and Hilary Conroy.
   p.   cm.
  Includes bibliographical references.
  ISBN 0-934223-13-0 (alk. paper)
  1. China—Foreign public opinion, American. 2. Public opinion—United States. I. Goldstein, Jonathan, 1947– . II. Israel, Jerry.
III. Conroy, Hilary, 1919– .
DS706.A67   1991
951—dc20   89-85466
                                   CIP

PRINTED IN THE UNITED STATES OF AMERICA

Dedicated to

John F. Melby and Frank W. Gapp
Pioneers in the field of China reporting

and to

Colleagues at the John K. Fairbank Center
for East Asian Research
Bessere findet man nicht

Contents

Part III. Images of Contemporary China

Acknowledgments

While it would require a vast amount of space to thank each and every individual who made the production of this volume possible, the editors would like to express special gratitude to Paul A. Cohen of Wellesley College and the Harvard University Fairbank Center, who offered valuable criticism of earlier versions of this manuscript; to France H. Conroy, who assisted with the introduction; to West Georgia College History Department Chairman Albert S. Hanser, who provided teaching schedules that facilitated the completion of this volume; to the West Georgia College Learning Resources Committee, which twice funded some of the basic research for this publication; to John E. Ferling of West Georgia College and Sarah Lawall of the University of Massachusetts at Amherst, experienced anthologists who made numerous suggestions that speeded the production of this volume; to Darlene Bearden of West Georgia College, who retyped numerous versions of articles; to Eugene Wu, director, and the entire staff of Harvard-Yenching Institute Library, and to Charles Beard, director, and the entire staff of West Georgia College's Irvine Sullivan Ingram Library, which provided bibliographical assistance; and to Stephen H. Cutcliffe and the entire staffs of Lehigh University and Associated University Presses.

Introduction

HILARY CONROY

This volume was originally conceived as part of the "celebration" of the two hundredth anniversary of the beginning of direct United States trade with China in 1784 with the voyage of the *Empress of China*. But getting together the contributions took the editors more time than anticipated. We are now ready for public viewing, with one or two disclaimers. The first concerns the "science" of imagery. Despite our title we are not really into that, although we are aware of the arguments about it. Since Harold Isaacs published *Scratches on Our Minds: American Images of China and India,* in which he held up American misperceptions of Asia for all to see, the study of perceptions and images had indeed come a long way.[1] It was stimulated by Akira Iriye, beginning with his *Across the Pacific: An Inner History of East Asian–American Relations.*[2]

However, Iriye's very heavy emphasis on images, perceptions, and misperceptions as vital factors in international relations, especially Japanese-American, came in for heavy criticism along the way. This is vigorously argued in Herbert Bix's review article on Iriye's work entitled "Imagistic Historiography."[3] Bix argued that "imagistic historiography" misses the real causes of international problems. It focuses on little things, such as whether people see other people as they really are. It misses or avoids the real issues, such as who has how big a slice of the economic pie or which nation is grabbing land and exploiting its inhabitants. In short "imagistic historiography" misses the old, the *real* stuff of international rivalries and politics.

Then there has been the great controversy on "orientalism" generated by the book of that name by Edward W. Said.[4] In 328 pages of text and documentation, Said accused the whole oriental studies profession of various intellectual mistakes ranging from imperialism to sexism. Though his main concern was the Middle East, with Western mishandling of Arabic Studies predominantly

11

in focus, the implications for all Asian studies were sufficiently accusatory to elicit a full symposium of refutation in the *Journal of Asian Studies*.

This was despite the fact, as the editor noted, that *"Orientalism's* geographic concerns" lay "outside the domain of the *Journal*."[5] The *Journal of Asian Studies* is generally limited to the scholarly studies of East, Southeast, and South Asia, but does not include Western Asia. Said, himself, unfortunately for his argument against imperialism, Eurocentrically refers to this region as the "Middle East," a point made by South Asia specialist David Kopf in his contribution to the symposium.[6] Kopf criticizes Said in several ways. He takes issue with his statement, "Orientalism is—and does not merely represent—a considerable dimension of modern political-intellectual culture, and as such has less to do with the Orient that it does with 'our' Western world."[7]

Then he takes "historical Orientalism" from its beginnings with the formation of the Asiatic Society of Bengal at Calcutta in 1784, through the controversy surrounding Thomas B. Macauley's "Minute on Education" in the 1830s, and on to Jawaharlal Nehru's *Discovery of India,* written while Nehru was imprisoned by the British imperialists in the 1940s. And he finds that while Macauley's superior attitude toward Indian culture was indeed insulting, this angered the real British scholars of India, the true Orientalists, a fact that Nehru himself, dedicated nationalist though he was, knew and appreciated. Thus, Kopf answers: "Nehru and other Indian writers were in fact impressed with the Orientalists they knew of, whose contributions they used freely as building blocks in their own reconstruction of history."[8] He warns the reader that Said's *Orientalism* is "not a work of historical scholarship."[9]

Later on in the symposium, Richard H. Minear takes up "Orientalism and the Study of Japan." He is considerably more appreciative of Said's approach than Kopf and indeed finds that three leading Western scholars of Japan of successive generations from the 1890s to the present—Basil Hall Chamberlain, George B. Sansom, and Edwin O. Reischauer—*do* fit into at least some of Said's categories. He concludes that "Said has performed an important service for us all," for "even in the absence of overt Western domination, the attitudes manifested in the discourse of Japan seems to resemble closely those of Said's Orientalists."[10]

Another symposium concerned with *Orientalism's* attack on Orientalists was held at Princeton's Institute for Advanced Study in 1981. Its results were published under the title *As Others See*

Us.[11] Its editors, Bernard Lewis, Edmund Leites, and Margaret Case, were at pains to present all sides of the controversary, and to a large extent they succeeded. Thus Bernard Lewis compares westerners today to latter-day Ottomans, wherein "masked by the still imposing military might of the Ottoman Empire, the people of Islam continued until the dawn of the modern age the conviction of their own Immeasureable and Immutable superiority of their own civilization to all others."[12]

Leites in his article entitled "Philosophers as Rulers: the Literati in Early Western Images of Confucianism" observes that "the first Western image of China" was from the Jesuits who were "much impressed," but that later "Evangelical Christianity . . . no longer needs China to be a model of humane civilization." And in the United States "after Jackson" the mood was so anti-intellectual that Confucianism was considered absurd.[13]

Harold Z. Schiffrin gives special attention to Japan in "The Response and Reaction of East Asia to Its Scholarly Study by the West," his contribution to the Princeton symposium. He observes that Western writers who are highly critical of modern Japan, such as E. H. Norman and David Bergamini,[14] are more appreciated in Japan than in America.[15] This would indicate, if not prove, that Japanese studies "Orientalists" at least have not been "Imperialistic" in their approach to Japanese history.

Finally, Carl Steenstrup in his contribution to the symposium, entitled "Reflections on Orientalism," finds Said's book "deeply flawed and deeply disturbing." He thinks Said's "venom" is overdone and that Said "scolds indiscriminately" but that he has "forced Asianists to rethink their methodologies."[16]

In the light of all this, it is interesting that in his recent summary review of the causes of Japanese imperalism, Britain's senior Japanese history scholar, W. G. Beasley, pays little attention to imagery. The causes of Japanese imperialism, he concludes, were primarily economic ones stemming from modernization. Secondarily (though very importantly also), "there was a powerful strategic element in it, relating to the interests of what Schumpeter would call an atavistic military aristocracy."[17]

Perhaps the foregoing will help justify the decision by this volume's editors to try to avoid becoming mired in the controversies concerning imagery and orientalism. What we have sought here are basically innocent perceptions, but honest ones, unclouded by swirls of scholarly controversy.

As Professor Yen-p'ing Hao said in commenting on the papers presented at the American Historical Association session that originally inspired the development of this book: "Thus, the American images of China—or any other country for that matter—were conditioned partly by the objective situation in China and more importantly by the needs and experiences of Americans themselves. As time progressed, China appeared in different guises in the American consciousness. No wonder it is sometimes argued that the appropriate symbol of China is not the dragon but the color-changing chameleon." For this he cites Raymond Dawson's book entitled *The Chinese Chameleon: An Analysis of European Conceptions of Chinese Civilization.*[18] Hao further observes that "an image is the result of an interaction between the viewer and the view, with the viewer usually in command."

Before putting imagery aside, however, it should be noted that Lucian Pye, in his *Asian Power and Politics: The Cultural Dimensions of Authority,* attempted to catagorize Asian cultural traditions from Pakistan to Japan, at least as they affect politics and power in that vast area.[19] He felt impelled to do this, he says, partly because the mainstream of his own field of political science during the 1960s and 1970s had come to hold an untenable set of assumptions derived from dependency and development theories. The assumptions lumped Asia, Africa, and Latin America all together into something called the "Third World" or "Lesser Developed" countries. In fact, he argues, not only are the Asian countries very dissimilar to Africa and Latin America, they are very different from each other.

Pye then takes up various countries of East, Southeast, and South Asia to examine their similarities and differences. He finds in general that in East Asia three different varieties of Confucianism are still very much alive, helping to explain the varying degrees of success at modernization of Korea, Taiwan, and Vietnam (forms of "aggressive" Confucianism, chapter 3); China (with "an illusion of omnipotence," chapter 7), and Japan (a marvelously workable combination of "competition and consensus," chapter 6).

Under the heading "The East Psychoanalyzed," Lloyd I. Rudolph, political science professor at the University of Chicago, reviewing Pye's book for *The New York Times,* criticized the study on the grounds that it "resuscitates a psycho-cultural version of oriental despotism, a paradigm that has afflicted Western perceptions of Asia since Aristotle." And, he says, after Pye's first four chapter's "ruminate" on Asians as "races apart" the remaining chapters "offer accounts of 13 Asian countries replete with reductionistic appraisals of people and events and selective evidence that demonstrates the dominance of paternalistic authority and dependent relations from the Indian to the Pacific Oceans." He concluded that "Mr. Pye's version of Oriental despotism leaves one at a loss to account for national transformations in Asia over the last 40 years."[20]

The present author reviewed Pye's book more favorably. While admitting that Pye's "characterizations of the several Asian cultures and their power system products are, after all, stereotypical," I defined his analysis as "controversial in that excellent way of being stimulating, fascinating, thoughtful, and unlike most books by political scientists, immensely readable."[21]

A reverse, though not perverse, attempt at image-conscious discourse is that of Hitotsubashi (Japan) University's Tadashi Aruga, entitled "The Meaning of American History: Japanese Views." In general Aruga finds Japanese historians of the United States to have had a positive view of American history until the 1960s when, beginning with Yonosuke's Nagai's *Katai suru America* (Disintegrating America) there has been the opposite, although Akira Iriye writing for a Japanese audience sought to give reassurance of the "strength of American Liberalism."[22]

But the concern of our volume is American images of Asians, not their images of America, and a final word on the problem of being scientific about images is provided by Roger Pulver in his article entitled "Japan: A Key to Understanding the Western Mind." Starting with a few absurd quotations—e.g., Rudyard Kipling's "The Jap has no business savvy" and Charles Baudelaire's "The Japanese are monkeys"—he goes through Western images of Japan with a vengeance: "apt pupils" to "regimented conformists" to "industrial monsters," but socially made up of "female Madame Butterflys and male chauvinist samurai." All were very real in the American mind, and, Pulver argues, to a considerable extent were promoted by the Japanese government for entirely pragmatic reasons at various stages of Japan's modern history.

May I there leave "imagery" as, perhaps, a developing aspect of political and social science, but not one in which historians should attempt to impose too much order of analysis?[23]

In the essays that follow, we editors have allowed as much free rein as possible to our various contributors, whose handling of both approaches and impressions are quite diverse.

The four essays in "The Image is Formed" bring out both the positive and the negative in the earliest American attitudes toward China. They explore the "idealization" from fascination with Chinese art and culture, but also the increasing disdain as traders and missionaries got close up to the realities of a declining empire.

Raymond G. O'Connor opens by broadly considering "Asian Art and International Relations." He notes the traditional role that respect for Chinese aesthetics (particularly Chinese characters) played in gaining respect within East Asia. But if China was able to practice "aesthetic colonialism" in Korea, Southeast Asia, and in part Japan, this was far from the case when the West discovered the Middle Kingdom. Americans half-disparaged "the hideous shapes to which [the Chinese] pay devotion," half-found escapist amusement in a cult of "chinoiserie" that gave many Americans their first and only knowledge of distant China.

Jonathan Goldstein angles in more closely on the American public's first visual image of "the gateway" to China, which, both literally and ideationally, was Kwangtung province. He accounts for the "never-never land of cloudlike rocks, exotic plants and airy pavillions" that came to represent China for most Americans, based on the designs on canvas, glass, or wood that first traveled from Kwangtung to the United States. The early image omitted any hint of the squalor of Canton—at least until 1846, when the camera would arrive partially to displace the earlier representations.

With Jacques M. Downs's essay, the focus shifts to the "commercial origins" of American attitudes toward China in roughly the same period (1784–1884). Downs relates how, taking their "civil religion" with them, American merchants braved "a time in exile" in China as they represented their companies and sought quick fortunes—all the while trying not to sacrifice their integrity, an apparently difficult feat in China. It became even more difficult as the drug trade grew. Up until then, Downs finds American merchants to be "not racists, not imperialists," but perhaps "classists," respecting some Chinese while looking down on others; but as Americans, like the British, became involved in drug trafficing, the question arose, "What kind of people was it to whom it could be appropriate to sell narcotics?"

Concluding the first section, Murray Rubinstein studies the other early Americans in China, the missionaries, who first arrived in 1830. His focus is how they helped shape American opinion. These Protestants inherited a positive legacy of Catholic-Confucian mutual respect that dated back to Matteo Ricci in the sixteenth century, but the "guarded admiration" toward the Chinese of the first American missionaries turned by 1860 to contempt of these "perishing heathen." Rubinstein studies how the missionaries' images became the American public's images as the former acted as an early kind of "China watchers," keeping small-town America informed of the progress toward "the Christian opening of China." Since the project was doomed to frustration, the reports tended to be negative: human life as cheap, degraded, and godless; Confucianism as "empty humanism." The missionaries sowed the seeds of the idea that America could lead them out of all this—by force, if necessary.

Part II, "The Image Grows," picks up where Downs and Rubinstein leave off, with an essay by Raymond F. Wylie on the origins of official diplomatic relations arising out of both the needs of American merchants and the aggressive idealism of the missionaries. In fascinating detail, Wylie chronicles American diplomatic efforts from 1843 to 1857; not noble, but sometimes following the United States' own interests in championing a strong and open China. The commercial and missionary constituencies converged in wanting China to allow foreigners to operate freely and in wanting to head off British attempts to get privileged status. Therefore, United States policy vacillated between pushing for a strong, unified China to guarantee the open door and threatening to strike a deal with Great Britain to force "the rascally Chinese" to stop resisting Western commercial and Christian interests. The latter line of thinking got as far as a plan to seize Taiwan as an American base from which to "advance the cause of humanity, religion, and civilization." Approved by naval and diplomatic leadership, this plan was nixed by President James Buchanan as the states neared civil war.

Jonathan G. Utley's "American Views of China, 1900–1915," jumps to Theodore Roosevelt. In between had come the first sizable Chinese immigration, the influential Bret Harte poem "The Heathen Chinee," and the rapid awakening of Japan. Images of the Chinese portrayed violence and treachery in the wake of the Boxer Uprising. After the Boxers were completely crushed, these quickly gave way to images of frail, undisciplined, cowardly Chinese. Fears of "the yellow peril" were spawned, but not of an aggressive China: Japan's 43 million would provide the evil spearhead, and China's 426 million the waves to overwhelm white civilization. Progressive Era architects tried to move against such a dreaded eventuality by suggesting China could be saved by massive reform—rapid Westernization—turning the Chinese masses from "peril" to "market." And the 1911 revolution made them look like prophets, for a time.

Sandra M. Hawley turns to the role of popular culture in shaping the image, starting with "yellow peril" personified, Dr. Fu Manchu, and progressing to the still alien but more lovable Charlie

Chan. Just as images on glass and cloth had shaped the popular view of China a century before, so images in forty-nine films, growing out of six books and a comic strip, shaped the view in the first half of the twentieth century. In his adventures, set in exotic yet familiar Hawaii, Chan showed "intelligence, good humor, diligence, and loyalty." One Bostonian admirer remarked, "The Chinese are my favorite race . . . so clever and competent and honest among the lazy riff-raff of the Orient." Hawley sees Chan's somewhat sympathetic portrayal as a kind of necessary bridge between the malignant Fu Manchu and peasants who capture our hearts in Pearl Buck's writings in the 1930s.

Jerry Israel picks up with the changing image from the 1920s to the 1930s and 1940s, but from another perspective: the journalists' eye, from Carl Crow to Edgar Snow. He demonstrates how these two products of the Missouri School of Journalism, twenty years apart, inhabited in effect two different Chinas prophetic of the 1949 split: Crow the open door China of Shanghai's International Settlement; Snow, the "Red China" of Yenan. Crow, who came from missionary roots and doubled as a promoter of American products, wrote on the Chinese as common-sensical, loyal customers, tracing their upright philosophy back to "Master Kung." His China of businessmen, clerks, servants, and rickshaw boys had no "misery, wretchedness, poverty, or revolution;" Snow's China was the reverse. Although not a communist, Snow became convinced that only Mao could lead resistance to the Japanese whom Snow feared the most; he saw a chance for radical reform in China if the United States helped, Israel explains, but watched the chance go down the drain as Washington listened more to Patrick Hurley than John Stewart Service, more to Chiang Kai-shek than Mao Tse-tung.

Part III, "Images of Contemporary China," contains first-hand observations. Two "China hands" of the period in which Jerry Israel leaves off deserve mention before going on to the work of the contributors. Foreign service officer John Melby, whose unpublished memoirs were inspirational in the genesis of this volume, witnessed the parade of personalities that led to United States' misunderstanding of China in the 1940s. Melby recalls the flamboyant flier Claire Chennault, "obsessed with the notion that air power would defeat Japan" and totally dedicated to Chiang as he fashioned giant airstrips around Chengtu and Kweilin; and the sinister Milton "Merry" Miles, who worked with Tai Li, the most notorious of Chiang's secret police out of "Happy Valley" near Chungking. Both Chennault and Miles reported "directly to the White House." Later Miles and Tai Li would be the objects of a mass campaign staged by the Communists in condemnation of their ruthlessness. But as the most erratic of the misplaced personalities whom President Roosevelt selected as his "special representatives," Melby chooses Major General Patrick Hurley and writes as follows: "He [Hurley] arrived in China in early 1944 having not a clue as to where he was, with instructions to patch things up between Chiang and the Communists. . . . Journeying to Yenan first, he persuaded an astonished Chairman Mao Tse-tung to sign a Communist proposal he had written up himself for Chiang's consideration, which included an almost verbatim copy of the American Bill of Rights . . . Mao knew that Chiang would never accept it [and], when Hurley jubilantly returned to Chungking, he was greeted with ridicule. Reacting in embarrassment, he did his first flip-flop, angrily charging that he had been betrayed in the north." Later, Melby concludes, Hurley's invective would reinforce public suspicion against other American China hands, helping to spark the witch-hunt of McCarthyism.

The other China hand similarly involved in this volume's genesis, journalist Frank Gapp, recalls how the International Settlement in Shanghai began to crumble around him in August 1937. His ground-level account recalls both the bitter anti-Japanese sentiments of the period and China's nadir of haplessness and vulnerability—a scant twelve years before Mao would proclaim at the Gate of Heavenly Peace, "China has stood up." Gapp writes from the front: "Now refugees poured into the Settlement. . . . They came in hordes, and found shelter in alleys and nooks, and at night slept in the hallways of commercial buildings. . . Late in the afternoon a report came in that [a Chinese plane] had dropped several bombs accidentally on the very corner where I had been standing a few hours earlier—Nanking Road and the Bund."

Two and a half months later, Japanese General Iwane Matsui called a news conference. "He was blunt," Gapp recalls, saying simply "Now I am master of Shanghai." The Japanese authorities began censoring all mail, and confiscated an entire edition of *China Weekly Review* (Gapp was assistant editor) dealing with "the rape of Nanking." Japanese "ronin" entered the settlement and "seized prominent Chinese and took them back to Hongkew—they were never heard from again and the Settlement authorities were helpless to deal with the problem." A few years later, Matsui would be executed as a war criminal as the United States occupied Japan and the Communists took over China.

This brings in the 1950s and China-born Sinologist Paochin Chu's reflection, "American View of China, 1957–1982." When Chu arrived in New York on a cargo ship in 1957, he was wined and dined by the local pro-Taiwan faction; but it was the quiet meetings where he met Mrs. Edgar Snow, Felix Greene, and others working for United States–People's Republic of China (PRC) normalization that impressed him more. Yet it was not until the late 1970s and 1980s that he could talk publicly and positively about the PRC and not receive "stiff faces and frozen civility."

David B. Chan, who began his teaching career in a small Midwest college during the McCarthy era, also recalls how difficult anticommunism made the teaching scene until the 1970s. However, by 1979 an opposite problem has emerged: many of Chan's students and colleagues have become "euphoric" about "People's China," while Chan, who visits ordinary villages in his native Guangdong province, sees poverty, corruption, and hypocrisy. He concludes that our misunderstanding of China hasn't improved in the last quarter century, the pendulum has only swung toward the other extreme of adulation. Vividly contrasting his own raw experiences with the cooked-up sights and sounds of the model communes that other 1979 visitors were shown, Chan discusses the peculiar "inability to be objective about China," which has led the American perspective through one excess after another since 1784.

France H. Conroy's memoir, also of 1979, may be one of those excesses. His group of "progressive journalists" was hosted by the Propaganda Department of the Central Committee of the Chinese Communist Party. His left-insider's view of China during the spring of Democracy Wall and normalization provides a strong contrast to Chan's sobering reports, although Conroy, too, detects a negative side. Indeed his subsequent visits in 1985 and 1989 yield more problems, less optimism for any "new society," and questions as to whether Western-style solutions are really helping.

By the late-1980s, American China-watchers are supposed to have achieved a new maturity and objectivity, perhaps avoiding the pendulum swings of earlier eras. Have they? Several appraisals of China's economic progress reflect a healthy diversity of viewpoint in American imagery of China. Mark A. Plummer uses a reflection on Mao's tomb as a take-off point for a reappraisal of the PRC's four-decade history. He speculates as to how shocked the chairman would be were he to awaken: China back in the "primary state" of socialism, Deng Xiaoping in charge, Liu Shaoqi honored in his tomb's anteroom, his wife in prison, and Kentucky

Fried Chicken replacing protraits of Marx, Engels, Lenin, and Stalin in Tiananmen Square. Plummer reviews the changes from the Maoist 1950s to the pragmatist 1980s, then notes that China still officially adheres to Mao's "Four Cardinals Principles." It is as if communism in China, instead of being abandoned, is being handled in the same way as Mao's tomb: "closed for repairs."

Ramon H. Myers is more direct. Suggesting five standards by which to evaluate economic performance, he looks at China through hard social scientist's eyes. He compares the 1952–1978 and post-1978 periods. What he finds is a disappointing economic performance for the earlier period, then only modest improvement with post-1978 market reforms, not strong enough to pull out of a quarter century of stagnation.

With Jan S. Prybyla, what could be the latest pendulum swing is pushed further. China (mainland) was wrong; Taiwan "island China") right. The PRC needs to jettison altogether the idea of "one country, two systems," i.e., capitalist zones amidst "socialism with Chinese characteristics." What it needs is "capitalism with Chinese characteristics," which has been almost perfected by Taiwan and could, with difficulty, be transplanted. The PRC Soviet-type economic system, like others around the world, has irreparable systemic problems, from skewed growth to disincentives due to the neglect of consumption. Taiwan's dynamism, by contrast, has been remarkable, and seems now to be culminating in political liberalization.

Harry Harding ends on a more cautious note, getting back to the problem of rapidly changing images. He reviews the reports on China of the 1970s generation of American visitors—what was it that they liked so much?—and illuminatingly juxtaposes these reports next to the much more negative reports of the 1980s. He raises several questions: How much have the negative reports resulted from the demise of the foreign guest tour system and thus of creature comforts for the American visitors? Has it soured their mood as they send back reports, while having little to do with the Chinese people's welfare? Also, how much should Americans be hesitant to transport their own norms when evaluating another country? The 1970s observers were wary of this, the 1980s observers not. Harding suggests caution all around. Otherwise today's truth may again become tomorrow's myth.

To round out the volume, I try to step back to the broader perspective afforded by comparison: images of China versus images of Japan. Though originally there was no discrimination in the American mind, only the image of a generalized "Oriental type," as Americans began to distinguish, it seems that first one group then the other was in favor. The Japanese were "alternately admired and detested, but usually respected." The Chinese were "both loved and pitied, yet not generally admired or respected." From Perry's opening to the early twentieth century, it was generally the Japanese who evoked more positive descriptions: polite, hard-working, competent. But whenever Japanese ambition began to threaten Americans directly, the Japanese "virtues" seemed less positive; at such times the Chinese, submissive and needy but unthreatening, became the more attractive. By 1931, Japan's threatening side was dominant; fear turned to outright hatred during the war. But a few months into the occupation, a sudden reversal took place: Japan was suddenly nonthreatening, prone and needy; China, then showing courage and hard work but of the wrong political stripe, suddenly drew American resentment. The 1970s and 1980s would witness still another reversal. In general, however, Japan was respected for achievement, China pitied for tragic happenings.

This concludes the volume, but hardly this vast and fascinating topic. What have we left out? Quite a bit, which is why we direct readers to the substantial list of suggested readings. One very recent publication deserves mention here; and then two additional observations in closing, lest our last section, "Images of Contemporary China," leave too much the impression that America knows best.

First, the publication: it is called "Mutual Images in U.S.-China Relations" and is the product of a 1988 Woodrow Wilson Center symposium involving Michael Hunt, David Shambaugh, Warren Cohen, and Akira Iriye.[24] Its conclusion is quite similar to this volume's—that images have been ambivalent—but the symposium extends this to Chinese images of the United States. For example, David Shambaugh points out, "Chinese thought has always made a fundamental distinction between those who rule by benevolence *(wangdao)* and those who must rely on force to subjugate others *(badao)*." He adds, "In Chinese eyes, America has displayed both tendencies."[25] Akira Iriye in his concluding commentary suggests that "the storehouse of images" available in each country for perceiving the other doesn't change much, but some of the images are given "privileged status" at certain times, others at other times, depending on "the state of war, peace, or situations in between."[26] This is certainly supported by our own volume's findings.

Moving to what we may have left out, first we wonder if a truly "mature" image of China ought not to give more due to things Chinese, and in particular Confucianism, than our Part IV might indicate. Of course, Confucianism drew mostly criticism from missionary and business types alike until recently—excepting Ezra Pound, who in the 1920s developed an earthy, Yankee appreciation of it that we neglected to mention.[27] However, since 1972 scholarship has been emerging that indicts this dismissal of Confucianism as one-sided. Thomas A. Metzger's *Escape from Predicament: Neo-Confucianism and China's Evolving Political Culture*[28] and Roy Hofheinz and Kent Calder's *The Eastasia Edge*[29] have proposed that Confucianism may in the long run be more positive than negative in the socioeconomic sphere; while Herbert Fingarett's *Confucius: The Secular as Sacred*,[30] Tu Wei-ming's *Confucian Thought: Selfhood as Creative Transformation*,[31] and David L. Hall and Roger T. Ames' *Thinking Through Confucius*[32] find Confucianism promising as a post-modern religiophilosophy. We suggest, then, that a "mature" image of China today ought to include not only Westernization and market reforms as hopeful signs, but also the reanimation of the best aspects of the native value system.

Secondly, heeding Iriye's "storehouse" theory, we ask whether 1980s American interests (mostly material) have led to our hiding away one image of China that Americans knew well in the 1970s: China as Third World leader. Although certain regions of the mainland may be potential Taiwans, the PRC's staggering population and poverty makes it more like a Taiwan attached to an India. With world food, population, and resource problems heightening, the South versus North crunch seems still ahead; and China— unlike Taiwan, Hong Kong, South Korea, and Singapore—still looms as a natural leader of the South. At any rate, this seems like a good candidate for mainstream American observers' current blindspot,[33] and we editors leave these as open questions.

Notes

1. Harold Isaacs, *Scratches on Our Minds: American Images of China and India* (New York: John Day, 1958).

2. Akira Iriye, *Across the Pacific: An Inner History of East Asian-American Relations* (New York: Harcourt Brace, 1957); Iriye, *After Imperialism: The Search for a New Order in the Far East* (Cambridge: Harvard University Press, 1965); Iriye, *Pacific Estrangement: Japanese and American Expansion, 1897–1911* (Cambridge: Harvard University Press, 1972); Iriye, *Power and Culture: The Japanese-American War, 1941–1945* (Cambridge: Harvard University Press, 1981). See also Iriye, "Images and Diplomacy in Sino-American Relations,

in Michael Hunt, et al., "Mutual Images in U.S.-China Relations," *Occasional Paper No. 32* (Washington, D.C.: Wilson Center, Asia Program, 1988), 37–42.

3. Herbert Bix, "Imagistic Historiography," *Bulletin of Concerned Asian Scholars,* no. 3 (July–September 1975): 51–58.

4. Edward W. Said, *Orientalism* (New York: Pantheon Books, 1978).

5. Robert A. Kapp, "Editor's Note," *Journal of Asian Studies* 39 (May 1980): 463; Robert A. Kapp, ed. "Review Symposium: Edward Said's Orientalism," 481–517.

6. David Kopf, "Hermeneutics versus History," Kapp, ed. "Review Symposium," *op. cit.,* 496.

7. Said, *Orientalism,* 12; Kopf, "Hermeneutics versus History," 497.

8. Kopf, "Hermeneutics versus History," 496–506.

9. Ibid., 499.

10. Richard H. Minear, "Orientalism and the Study of Japan," *Journal of Asian Studies* 39 (May 1980): 507–17, especially 515–17.

11. Bernard Lewis, Edmund Leites, and Margaret Case, eds., *As Others See Us. Mutual Perceptions, East and West,* a special issue of *Comparative Civilizations Review,* nos. 13–14 (Fall 1985 and Spring 1986).

12. Ibid., 15.

13. Edmund Leites, "Philosophers and Rulers: The Literati in Early Western Images of Confucianism," in Lewis, et al., *As Others See Us,* 203–12.

14. Norman's study *Japan's Emergence as a Modern State* was first published by the Institute of Pacific Relations (New York, 1940) and was reprinted in John W. Dower, ed., *Origins of the Modern Japanese State* (New York: Pantheon, 1975). Bergamini's is *Japan's Imperial Conspiracy* (New York: William Morrow, 1971; Pocket Books, 1972).

15. Harold Z. Schiffrin, "The Response and Reaction of East Asia to Its Scholarly Study by the West," in Lewis, et al., *As Others See Us,* 253–65.

16. Carl Steenstrup, "Reflections on 'Orientalism' from the Angle of Japan-Related Research," in Lewis, et al., *As Other See Us,*52.

17. W. G. Beasley, *Japanese Imperialism, 1894–1945* (Oxford: Claredon Press, 1987), especially 258. See also Hilary Conroy, "Lessons from Japanese Imperialism," *Monuments Nipponica,* 21, no. 3–4, 334–45.

18. Raymond Dawson, *The Chinese Chameleon: An Analysis of European Conceptions of Chinese Civilization* (London: Oxford University Press, 1967).

19. Lucian Pye, *Asian Power and Politics: The Cultural Dimensions of Authority* (Cambridge: Harvard University Belknap Press, 1985).

20. *New York Times,* 9 February 1986.

21. American Academy of Political and Social Science, *The Annals* 488 (November 1986): 197–98.

22. Tadashi Aruga, "The Meaning of American History," *Hitotsubashi Journal of Law and Politics* 15 (1987): 1–11.

23. Said's *Orientalism* reared its ugly, or perhaps merely controversial, head again—at my own University of Pennsylvania—in 1988–89, when the Department of South Asia Regional Studies adopted "Orientalism and Beyond: Perspectives from South Asia" as the theme for its annual seminar series. Some of the seminar topics included: "Orientalist Empiricism" by David Ludden, "Castes of Mind" by Nicholas Dirks, "Affirmative Orientalism in India: Expanding the Boundaries of Said's Cultural Geography" by Richard Fox, and "Beyond Orientalism" by Ronald Inden.

24. *Occasional Paper No. 32* (Washington, D.C.: Wilson Center, 1988).

25. David Shambaugh, "Conflicting Chinese Images of America During the People's Republic of China." *Occasional Paper No. 32*, 21.

26. Akira Iriye, "Images and Diplomacy in Sino-American Relations," *Occasional Paper No. 32*, 39.

27. See Ezra Pound, trans., *Confucius: The Great Digest, The Unwobbling Pivot and the Analects* (New York: New Directions, 1969).

28. Thomas A. Metzger, *Escape from Predicament: Neo-Confucianism and China's Evolving Political Culture* (New York: Columbia University Press, 1977). See also the discussions in *Journal of Asian Studies* 39, no. 2 (1980).

29. Roy Hofheinz and Kent Calder, *The Eastasia Edge* (New York: Harper and Row, 1972).

30. Herbert Fingarett, *Confucius: The Secular as Sacred* (New York: Harper and Row, 1972).

31. Tu Wei-ming, *Confucian Thought: Selfhood as Creative Transformation* (Albany: State University of New York Press, 1985).

32. Roger R. Ames, *Thinking Through Confucius* (Albany: State University of New York Press, 1987).

33. See, for example, France H. Conroy, "China, the Soviet Union and the West; The Changing Ideological Terrain as a Factor in Pacific Community" in Roy Kim and Hilary Conroy, eds., *New Tides in the Pacific: Pacific Basin Cooperation and the Big Four* (Westport, Conn.: Greenwood Press, 1987), 99–124.

AMERICA VIEWS CHINA

Part I
The Image Is Formed

Asian Art and International Relations

RAYMOND G. O'CONNOR

This essay is a preliminary report on an investigation of one dimension of international relations, namely, the role of visual art objects in forming impressions of an alien people. Different cultures usually generate distinctive art styles, and art constitutes a method of communication that eliminates the intermediary, those whose reports on foreign lands tend to be colored by their own preconceptions or interests. Perceptions and attitudes can be important and, at times, decisive in determining relations between and among nations and peoples. The objects produced by the various societies have had repercussions of far-reaching consequences and have contributed to the misconceptions leading to misunderstanding and eventual conflict. My investigations have embraced the spectrum of non-Western art and its impact on opinion in diverse culture groups. In this essay my speculations will be confined to Asian visual output, for it possesses certain characteristics that differ from art originating in other parts of the globe.

The most common methods of intercultural contact have been trade, warfare, exploration, and inadvertance. Inadvertance, the lost mariner, may have been responsible for the transmission of Asian art to a portion of what became known as the "Western World," a transmission that is said to have occurred some three thousand years ago. Basing his contention primarily on trait or motive similarities between Chinese and pre-Columbian art, Paul Shao maintains that Shang Chinese voyagers visited Meso-America as early as the beginning of the Olmec culture, around 1200 B.C. Embracing the trans-Pacific diffusionist interpretation of the transmission of art styles, Shao also finds correlations in the art of China and that of the Mayans from about the third to the ninth centuries A.D.[1] Imitation may be the ultimate in flattery, although similarities of visual images are not conclusive evidence of outside influence. Academics have thrived on the

31

argument over whether human beings at certain stages of development tend to create similar art forms and myths, or whether they are borrowed from some other group, a single source as it were. But indigenous visual products were an early method of communicating what was unique in one society to another. The language barrier was overcome.[2]

Assuming that the trans-Pacific diffusionist theory is valid, any regular trade between these countries is unlikely, given the state of ocean transport and instruments of navigation. But trade was the great stimulus for contacts between Europe and Asia, trade in beautiful objects and eagerly sought condiments. Alexander's foray into India may not have been inspired by such crass motives, and the major impact of this venture may have been to provoke the creation of "graven images" of Hindu and Buddhist deities, with the prime example of Western influence being the Graeco-Roman Ghandaran sculptures of Buddha.[3] According to one source, "The antients [sic] made a notable distinction of [art] styles, into Laconic [an early Greek entity] and Asiatic," and "Orient" meant nations lying east of the Roman Empire.[4] Thus early categorizations and terms were conceived to reflect perspectives and torment subsequent classifiers of geographical space.

The first significant infusion of East Asian art into Europe apparently occurred in the first and second centuries A.D., when Rome at its height sought the elegant silks of China. Transported by caravan from Chang'an to Antioch on the Mediterranean along the tortuous "Silk Road," these fabrics appealed to the luxury appetites of the elite, and even some iron items were included in the cargo. On one occasion, the Roman Emperor Marcus Aurelius sent emissaries to the Chinese court. Trade between Rome and India was considerable but imports consisted largely of raw materials.[5] The effect of these interchanges on the attitudes of the respective civilizations toward each other is not clear. Trade was conducted by intermediaries, and the lack of direct contact, except for a few possible encounters, makes unlikely any consequential perceptions.

The land route between Europe and the Far East was virtually severed from the seventh to the eighteenth centuries by Islamic militant expansion. Arab seafarers mastered the sea route to China, sailing from ports in the Persian Gulf and hugging the coasts of what are now Iran, Pakistan, India, Sri Lanka, and Sumatra, and passing through the Strait of Malacca before reaching Canton. Arab visitors to China were awed by its art. A ninth-century Arab merchant wrote that "the Chinese may be counted among those of God's creatures to whom he hath granted, in the highest degree, skill of hand in drawing and in the arts of manufacture," and a fourteenth-century Arab visitor thought, "The people of China of all mankind have the greatest skill and taste in the arts." He concluded, "As regards painting, indeed, no nation, whether of Christians or others, can come up to the Chinese, and their talent for this art is something extraordinary.[6] Such praise reflected admiration for at least one dimension of Chinese civilization and revealed a degree of objectivity, for Muslim art was eclectic. It emerged as an amalgam of the styles that prevailed in the conquered countries and the folk crafts of those people who embraced the faith. But Islamic art came to have an identifiable character of its own that was imposed on many lands.[7]

The subcontinent of India fell prey to this cultural invasion with the Islamic occupation that began in the eighth century and burgeoned in the eleventh to the sixteenth centuries. India had long had contacts with the Middle East, from Iran to Egypt and Mesopotamia, due to favorable winds that simplified seaborn commerce.[8] Indian products included bronze and brass items, silks, cottons and leatherwork, and some transshipment occurred.[9] The Mogul Empire that ruled much of India for centuries not only introduced Muslim styles in art and architecture but destroyed much Hindu and Buddhist sculpture and painting, for depicting religious figures was anathma to the Muslim faith.[10] This destruction of indigenous art forms, forms that were symbols of existing religions, made this collision of cultures even more humiliating to the subjected Indians, and resulting perceptions continue to this day.

In East Asia the spread of Chinese art to Korea and Japan began before Buddhism came to those countries. Evidently the art of China was well received in both countries and created a favorable impression of the originating nation. This popularity and commonality of art styles aided in the unification of Korea and Japan by providing a bond to overcome factional rivalry, and it improved relations with their formidable neighbor.[11] The Three Kingdoms in Korea (57 B.C.–668 A.D.) gave tribute to Chinese rulers and imported religion as well as the arts and crafts of China.[12] One authority points out, however, that while some have considered Korean art merely a "provincial variation of Chinese art," the Korean "insistence upon communication by other than verbal, or written, means has tended to load the art forms with more than ordinary significance."[13] Although this "more than

ordinary significance" may have been lost on many outside viewers, it projected a version of the Korean ethos and esthetics that
helped foreign observers distinguish these peoples from those of
other East Asian cultures.

The full impact of Chinese and Korean art on Japan coincided
with the introduction of Buddhism to that country in the sixth
century, when scriptures and Korean Buddhist images were presented to the Imperial Court. Coming at a time when Japan was
being unified, the government welcomed and supported this infusion of culture, which further enhanced relations among the three
East Asian nations. "Among the reasons Buddhism was accepted
[in Japan] was its novel visual appeal," one writer contends, for
"Shinto lacked the philosophy to formulate an anthropomorphic
art."[14] When I visited Japan during the occupation and entered
the then Imperial Museum, a notice on the wall in impeccable
Spencerian English script asserted that there was no indigenous
art of Japan, that all of its art forms were borrowed. The notice
has long since disappeared, and the confession has been refuted
by evidence displayed in the now Tokyo National Museum and
elsewhere.

Korean and Japanese acceptance of Chinese art styles and symbols indicated a respect and admiration for what were regarded
as manifestations of a higher civilization, and promoted clear ties
among these nations. Yet Japan continued to have a virtual "love-
hate" attitude toward Chinese culture, a somewhat dialectical relationship associated in part with the language.[15] Although some
Japanese art is difficult to distinguish from that of China, Japanese
artists and craftsmen have made substantive modifications of foreign work and have created new media of expression. The visual
art of Japan well conveys its unique life and culture, and the
Zen images, often in the abstract, combine with the calligraphy
to express a non-Western spirit and way of thinking.[16]

The spread of Chinese art and Buddhism throughout East Asia
produced a similarity of art styles which, to many Westerners,
reflected what seemed to be one culture pattern and, therefore,
one classification of peoples. The art forms accompanying the
introduction of Buddhism into China, Korea, Japan, and other
Asian countries, offered a visual image of an alien culture that
written, oral, or doctrinal communication could not provide. Chinese merchants continued to distribute wares abroad, as they
had since at least the Han period (206 A.D.–220 A.D.), by land
and by sea. Consisting primarily of silks and procelains, they
were carried as far as the Philippines, where Sung items have

been found. A Chinese vessel sunk off the coast of Korea in the thirteenth or fourteenth century contained more than 13,000 ceramic pieces.[17]

"Through the medium of the Chinese written language," according to Professor E. G. Pulleyblank, "Chinese culture has extended beyond China to other East Asian countries—Korea, Japan, Vietnam—and has deeply influenced them, particularly but not exclusively at the level of high culture."[18] The esthetic quality of Chinese calligraphy had a great appeal even when the meaning of the characters was not known. The almost infinite variety of the various scripts permitted the calligrapher considerable latitude in self expression, and work of the masters was readily acknowledged and easily recognized. The "classical period" of Chinese calligraphy came during the "internationalist" T'ang dynasty (618–907 A.D.), whose rulers adopted the doctrine of "the empire is open to all" over that of "the empire belongs to one family," and relations with foreign lands and peoples were encouraged.[19] In 806 A.D. the monk Kukai brought esoteric Buddhism to Japan from T'ang China and founded the Shingon School, whose teachings were revealed in the mandalas, sculptures, temple implements, and paintings.[20]

But the enthusiastic reception of Indian and Chinese art by other Asian countries, and the consequent impact on relations among them, was not repeated by Westerners. Most Europeans were contemptuous of the native cultures of Asia, for the art did not meet their esthetic standards. The Jesuit Father Matteo Ricci, in China around 1600, noted "The Chinese use pictures extensively, even in the crafts, but in the production of these and especially in the making of statuary and cast images they have not at all acquired the skill of Europeans." Ricci concluded, "They know nothing of the art of painting in oil or of the use of perspective in their pictures, with the result that their productions are lacking any vitality."[21] Much of the Asian subject matter, usually representing "heathen" religious concepts, was repugnant to Europeans. The erotic Hindu sculptures, especially those of the Shiva "cult," offended Western sensibilities. The sexual act as a manifestation of ecstatic religious experience, as portrayed in Tantric Buddhism as well as in Hinduism, violated Christian precepts and, to Westerners, seemed to reveal a depraved, almost subhuman nature. The profound beliefs expressed by the artists and craftsmen through these visual objects were lost on the foreigners, who saw only the superficial and the obvious, without an awareness of, or even an interest in, the iconography. Europe-

ans were not offended by the portrayal of religious figures as
such, as were the Muslims. But they were offended by what was
depicted as religious and divine by this "pagan" society. Further,
Europeans were confused by what they saw as worship of "idola-
trous" images instead of the gods themselves.[22] Confronted by
displays of what they considered immoral and superstitious, Europeans questioned whether Asians could be treated as equals in
the world community.

The first direct contacts between Europe and Asia took place
in the thirteenth century when China, under the Mongol Yuan
dynasty (1260–1368 A.D.), opened its doors to the outside world.
Until then, the Near or Middle East had been "the meeting point
of western preconceptions and actual observations" of the Far
East.[23] But the reports of the first European travelers to China
itself tended to reflect the purpose of their particular mission.
Friar John de Plano Carpini and Friar William Rubruck, sent
by the Pope in the thirteenth century to investigate prospects
for conversion to Christianity, reported that conditions were favorable although they provided little additional information. The Venetian Marco Polo who followed was a trader, and while he did
describe the opulent court of Kublai Khan, the people, and the
countryside, his primary emphasis was on commercial opportunities.[24]

No significant exchange followed these preliminary contacts,
for when the Yuan dynasty was succeeded by the Ming in 1368,
China resumed a xenophobic stance. Increasing hostility between
the rising Ottoman Empire and Christian Europe in the fourteenth
and fifteenth centuries further interrupted European trade with
the Far East and prompted a desire to reach the "riches of Cathay"
by sea. Inspired by a variety of motives and aided by new technology, European oceanic enterprise found the route and exploited
this source of goods and condiments not available at home. The
first seaborn Chinese porcelains to come directly to Europe in
any quantity were brought by Vasco da Gama on his return from
his epochal voyage (1497–99). The Portuguese then enjoyed a
monopoly of this trade until replaced by the Dutch East India
Company, which carried porcelain to Europe in huge quantities,
as did the later British East India Company.[25] The nobility and
the rising middle class of Europe were avid consumers of the
elaborate ceramics and lavish skills that filled the holds of company
vessels. The image of Asia in the minds of these elites—those
who could afford the commoditees and who controlled the governments and economies of the more powerful European states—was

formed by these visual objects from the mysterious East that adorned the homes of the old and the new aristocracy.

Western customers began sending sketches of designs to be depicted on their porcelains, and the often quaint and childlike portrayals of Europeans and other Western-inspired subjects that came back from China titilated the Western gentry, who often made fun of them. Recently one authority wrote, "Among the most curious and interesting objects to be found in Chinese export porcelain are some amusingly naive figures depicting Europeans in costumes of the late seventeenth and eighteenth centuries."[26] Actually, terra cotta caricatures of foreigners had appeared as early as the T'ang dynasty and in no way indicated a lack of skill, merely a bit of humor lost on the Westerners.

Europeans and Americans did not share the Asian love of ceramics as a major art form—as not merely pretty and functional objects, but as a medium for conveying ideas and emotions, of expressing the ultimate in creativity by transforming clay through fire with skill and esthetic sensibility into a masterpiece to be caressed and enjoyed with ecstacy.[27] A seventeenth century Englishman wrote of seeing "prints of landskips, of their idols, saints, pagoods, of most ougly, serpentine, monstrous and hideous shapes to which they paie devotion: pictures of men, and countries, rarely painted on a sort of gumm'd *calico* transparent as glasse; also flowers, trees, beasts, birds &c; excellently wrought on a kind of sleve-silk very naturall."[28] While acknowledging technique of execution, this Englishman found some of the subject matter repellent and saw it as a reflection of a primitive society dominated by superstition. Moreover, the ethereal atmosphere, spatial relationships, and subtlety of line in Chinese painting, especially in the landscapes, was beyond Western comprehension. Conditioned by the lushness of the representational convention featured by the various continental schools, Westerners viewed this artistic output as mere sketches by untutored dabblers.

The products of East Asia first reached the Americas by what has been called "The longest uninterrupted commercial navigation line in history," the route plied by Spanish galleons from Manila to Acapulco that continued from 1573 until 1815. The Philippines were the entrepot where Asian and Spanish traders met, and silver became the medium of exchange for goods of the Orient.[29] Many of these items were transshipped from Mexico to Spain and helped form the European impression of East Asia, as well as having an impact in the New World.

The exotic nature of Chinese or pseudo-Chinese objects appealed to Europeans and became the vogue in the eighteenth century. Known as "chinoiserie," it spread from household items to architecture, and the fad reached the eastern portion of the United States where it developed fully in the early nineteenth century as a sort of "esthetic colonialism." American colonists received their first impressions of Asia from England, and the upper classes, especially those of New England and the middle colonies, copied the chinoiserie fashion. After the colonies gained independence, American ships ventured to the Far East without British restrictions. Carrying ginseng, furs from the Pacific Northwest, sandalwood from the Hawaiian Islands, and, later, opium from Turkey as mediums of exchange, American vessels brought home cargoes of Chinese products that found a ready market among all social classes. This direct exposure to the visual art and crafts of China gave Americans their first and, for many, their only knowledge of that distant land.[30] The image formed was one of a fantastic, uncivilized nation of strange people who lived on the opposite side of the globe, a fitting location for such a weird society.

Western perceptions of Asia were augmented by new art forms when Commodore Matthew Calbraith Perry and his "black ships" opened Japan to the world in 1854. Perhaps the first significant impression on Americans was made six years later when a Japanese delegation visited the United States to sign the Treaty of Amity and Commerce. Dressed in their elaborate robes and wearing swords—both examples of Japan's finest art work—the delegates exemplified the fantasy that parochial Americans associated with Asia.[31] But one Japanese art medium was received with enthusiasm by European avant garde painters, namely, the colorful woodblock prints, "ukiyo-e," often used for packing objects sent to the West. Public enthusiasm extended to Japanese decorative arts, and the term "Japonisme" joined chinoiserie to designate the rage for Asian art that swept the Western world in the nineteenth and twentieth centuries.[32]

Many Westerners found certain Japanese objects repulsive. The grotesque temple guardian figures, the hideous Bugaku and Noh masks, and the esthetic veneration of the Samurai sword gave the impression of a fierce, warlike society which seemed to glorify brutality and armed conflict. Much of Japanese painting, like the Chinese, distorted reality, and the bright colors of woodblock prints did not compensate for some of its subject matter. As James Michener observed, "No art of which we have record produced more sex pictures than ukiyo-e."[33] Obscenity, depravity, and fighting were characteristics many observers found in the art of Japan, characteristics that coupled with the "heathen" religious sculptures to reveal a nation with beliefs and aspirations wholly incompatable with those of the West. Public showings of Japanese and Chinese art at exhibits and international fairs that began in the mid-nineteenth century provided direct exposure to authentic examples of Asian creativity, although whether it evoked an understanding or even an interest in these countries is questionable. But a wider audience did view these visual objects first hand, and people of diverse classes in Europe and America were able to see evidence of these ancient civilizations. Reactions varied from a fascination with the objects representing these exotic lands to contempt and cultural condescension.

The nineteenth century Western interest in the novelty of Asian Art was accompanied by a devotion among collectors, connoisseurs, and museum curators to Asian art for its own intrinsic qualities. The scholary study of the techniques, objectives, and iconography of the art forms in authentic pieces, rather than the commercial export items, brought a new appreciation of these visual objects if not of the societies that produced them. Lavishly illustrated "coffee table" books appeared to interpret this strange art to the cognoscenti and bring its esoteric message to the cultural aristocracy. Old Chinese bronzes became the ultimate of collecting snobbery, and the sensuous appeal of exquisite jade pieces made them, along with the customary ceramics, highly prized in auction lots.

World War II brought Asia into Western perspective in a greater and more dramatic way than ever before. Subsequent political and economic developments have emphasized the role that Asian countries have played and continue to play in world affairs. Recent decades have seen the West hosting glamorous exhibits of art from Asian nations, at considerable expense to the host institution, to be witnessed by a substantial number of attendees. No doubt the motives of attendees were varied, as would be their reactions. Were they spurred by curiosity or understanding, a desire to make the inscrutable East more scrutable? Were they both fascinated and repelled, as had been earlier Westeners? And would viewing the ancient art of these countries provide clues to contemporary behavior? Cultural exchanges are designed to bring nations closer together, and art has been a factor in the dialogue between the cultures of East and West. But such exchanges may provoke a negative reaction. Art can express what words cannot, and these "images of the mind," so different from those of the Western world, reflect clashes in beliefs, values, and practices that, per-haps, can never be reconciled. The criteria for judging are simply antithetical.

This paper has tried to deal with one of the many factors respon-sible for creating an image of an alien people and the perceptions that emerged. Tentatively, it appears that Asian art has proved beneficial to relations between and among Asian countries. But the conceptualization of Asia through its art by the Western condi-tioned mind and eye has proved detrimental to relations between the two worlds of the East and the West.

Notes

1. Paul Shao, *Asiatic Influences in Pre-Columbian American Art* (Ames: Iowa State University Press, 1976); Paul Shao, *The Origin of Ancient American Cultures* (Ames: Iowa State University Press, 1983). See also Audrey McBain, "Reflections of Bronze Age China in Pre-Columbian American Art," *Arts of Asia* 14 (May–June 1984): 88–96.

2. Paul Tolstoy, "Diffusion: As Explanation and as Event," in Noel Barnard, ed., *Early Chinese Art and Its Possible Influence in the Pacific Basin* (New York: Intercultural Arts Press, 1972), vol. 3, *Oceania and The Americas,* 823–841. Tolstoy mentions "a contact inferred between cultures," 823.

3. G. B. Sansom, *The Western World and Japan: A Study in the Interaction of European and Asiatic Cultures* (New York: Knopf, 1951), 12; Dietrich Seckel, *The Art of Buddhism,* translated by Ann E. Keep (New York: Greystone Press, 1968), 29; David L. Snellgrove, ed., *The Image of the Buddha* (Paris: Kodansha International, 1978), 47. For Ghandara see ibid., 59–76.

4. *Oxford English Dictionary,* "style" quoting *Chambers Encyclopedia,* 1752 ed., and entry "Orient"; John Onians, *Art and Thought in the Hellenistic Age: The Greek World View, 350–50 B.C.* (London: Thames and Hudson, 1979); Robin Lane Fox, *Alexander the Great* (New York, Dial Press, 1974), 429.; Plutarch, *The Lives of the Noble Grecians and Romans* (New York: Modern Library, n.d.), 848.

5. Robert Erick Mortimer Wheeler, *Rome Beyond the Imperial Frontiers* (New York: Philosophical Library, 1954), 115–75; Michele Pirassoli-t'Serstevens, *The Han Dynasty,* translated by Janet Seligman (New York: Rizzoli, 1982), 126–27, 161; E. H. Warmington, *The Commerce Between the Roman Empire and India,* (2d ed., (London: Curzon Press, 1974). Among the imports listed by Warmington are animals and animal products, plants, minerals, and steel swords.

6. Quoted in Michael Sullivan, *The Meeting of Eastern and Western Art from the Sixteenth Century to the Present Day* (Greenwich, N.Y.: New York Graphic Society, 1973), 46.

7. M. S. Diamond, *A Handbook of Mohammadan Art,* 2d ed., (New York: Metropolitan Museum of Art, 1944), 7, 20.

8. Henrich Zimmer, *The Art of Indian Asia,* compiled and edited by Joseph Campbell, 2d ed. (Princeton: Princeton University Press, 1970), 1:42.

9. Richard Ettinghausen, "The Man-Made Setting: Islamic Art and Architec-

ture," in Bernard Lewis, ed., *The World of Islam: Faith, People, Culture* (London: Thames and Hudson, 1976), 60.

10. Basil Gray, ed., *The Arts of India* (Ithaca: Cornell University Press, 1981), 95–189; Stanley Wolpert, *A New History of India* (New York: Oxford University Press, 1977), 104–5.

11. Namio Egami, et al. *The Beginnings of Japanese Art* (New York, Weatherhill/Heibonsha, 1973), 62–63; "Introduction," *Art Treasures From Japan: Catalogue of Exhibit in the United States, 1965–1966* (n.p., n.d.), 19.

12. Takashi Hatada, *A History of Korea,* translated and edited by Warren W. Smith, Jr., and Benjamin H. Hazard (Santa Barbara, Calif.: ABC-CLIO, 1969), 23; Robert E. Fisher, "The Buddha Image in Korea," in Pratadapaditya Pal, et al, *Light of Asia: Buddha Sakyamuni in Asia Art* (Los Angeles: Los Angeles County Museum, 1984), 175.

13. Evelyn McCune, *The Arts of Korea: An Illustrated History* (Rutland, Vermont: Charles E. Tuttle, 1962), 19, 24.

14. J. Edward Kidder, Jr., *The Art of Japan* (New York, Park Lane, 1985), 42; Amy G. Poster, "The Buddha Image in Japan," in Pal, et al. *Light of Asia: Buddha Sakyamuni in Asian Art,* 183.

15. David Pollack, *The Fracture of Meaning: Japan's Synthesis of China From the Eighth Through the Eighteenth Centuries* (Princeton: Princeton University Press, 1986).

16. Tasuichi Awakawa, *Zen Painting,* translated by John Bestor (Tokyo: Kodansha International, 1970), 9, 17.

17. Chung Yango-mo, "Ceramic Wares Recovered Off the Coast of Korea," *Arts of Asia* 11 (July–August 1981): 105.

18. E. G. Pulleyblank, "The Chinese and Their Neighbors in Prehistoric and Early Historic Times," in David N. Keightley, ed., *The Origins of Chinese Civilization* (Berkeley: University of California Press, 1983), 411.

19. Howard J. Wechsler, *Offerings of Jade and Silk: Ritual and Symbol in the Legitimation of the T'ang Dynasty* (New Haven: Yale University Press, 1985).

20. Pierre Rambach, *The Secret Message of Tantric Buddhism* (New York, Rizzoli, 1979), 29.

21. Quoted in Sullivan, *The Meeting of Eastern and Western Art from the Sixteenth Century to the Present Day,* 48.

22. "In the early period of European explorations of Asia, travellers saw Hindu sacred images as infernal creatures and diabolic multiple-limbed monsters." Partha Mitter, *Much Maligned Monsters: History of European Reactions to Indian Art* (Oxford: Oxford University Press, 1977), vii. "The motive of a couple, often engaged in an overt sexual act, was employed freely on the external walls of a temple and is still regarded as an auspicious symbol." Pratapaditya Pal, *The Sensuous Immortals: A Selection of Sculptures From the Pan-Asian Collection* (Los Angeles, Los Angeles County Museum of Art, 1978), 81; "Tantra is a cult of ecstasy, focused on a vision of cosmic sexuality." Philip Rawson, *The Art of Tantra,* rev. ed. (New York: Oxford University Press, 1978), 7. Nor was eroticism absent in China. "The oldest manuals on Taoist sexual methods date from the Han period (206 B.C.–A.D. 220)." Michel Beurdeley, et al, *Chinese Erotic Art,* translated from the French by Diana Imber (New York: Chartwell Books, 1969), 7.

23. June Taboroff, "Orientalists," *Aramco World Magazine,* November–December 1984, 27.

24. Leonardo Olschki, *Marco Polo's Precursers* (Baltimore: Johns Hopkins University Press, 1943), 6, 38–39; *The Travels of Marco Polo, The Venetian,* revised from Marsden's Translation and edited with introduction by Manuel Komroff (New York: Boni & Liveright, 1926).

25. Jorge Graca, "The Portuguese Porcelain Trade with China," *Arts of Asia* 7 (November–December 1977): 45; Elinor Gordon, "Concerning a Number of Apprehensions," in Elinor Gordon, ed., *Chinese Export Porcelain: An Historical Survey* (New York: Universe Book, 1977), 13–14.

26. Joseph T. Butler, "Chinese Porcelain Figures of Westerners," in Gordon, ed., *Chinese Export Porcelain: An Historical Survey,* 90.

27. Cecile and Michel Beurdeley, *A Connoisseur's Guide to Chinese Ceramics,* translated by Katherine Watson (New York: Leon Amiel, n.d.), 6–7. The Jesuit Father Joao Rodrigues wrote increduously of "a kind of earthenware bowls . . . which is prized beyond all belief" by the Japanese. Quoted in *They Came to Japan: An Anthology of European Reports on Japan, 1543–1640* Compiled and annotated by Michael Cooper (Berkeley: University of California Press, 1965), 261.

28. P. J. Marshall and Glyndwr Williams, *The Great Map of Mankind: Perceptions of New Worlds in the Age of Enlightenment* (Cambridge: Harvard University Press, 1982), 86. Also see 86–87, 172–73 for English perceptions.

29. Patricia Justiniani McReynolds, "Asian Ivories in Mexico and the Galleon Trade," *Arts of Asia* 13 (July–August 1983): 100–103.

30. George H. Danton, *The Culture Contacts of the United States and China: The Earliest Sino-American Culture Contacts, 1784–1844* (New York: Columbia University Press, 1931). See especially 18, 29.

31. The cultural myopia was reciprocated. See Masao Miyoshi, *As We Saw Them: The First Japanese Embassy to the United States, 1860* (Berkeley: University of California Press, 1979).

32. Siegfried Wichmann, *Japonisme: The Japanese Influence on Western Art in the 19th and 20th Centuries* (New York: Harmony Books, 1981), 6, 8.

33. James A. Michener, *The Floating World* (New York, Random House, 1954), 202. "Japanese mythology is surprisingly rich in the number of its references to acts of creation, courtship, sexual intercourse, defloration, and feats of magic." Michael Czaja, *Gods of Myth and Stone: Phallicism in Japanese Folk Religion* (New York: Weatherhill, 1974), 205. "Right-minded Europe at that moment only saw it [erotic Ukiyo-e] as a demonstration of sin which braved taboos and smacked of heresy, whereas it was not at all out of the ordinary for the Japanese." Gabriele Mandel, *Shunga: Erotic Figures in Japanese Art,* translated by Alison L'Eplattenier (New York: Crescent Books, 1983), 5.

34. Geoffrey Hudson, "The Historical Context of Encounters between Asia and Europe," in Raghavan Iyer, ed., *The Glass Curtain between Asia and Europe* (London: Oxford University Press, 1965), 60–61; "Incomprehension reaches tragic proportions in the confrontation of the Western tradition with the civilizations of Asia." Denis Sinor, ed., *Orientalism and History,* 2d ed., (Bloomington: University of Indiana Press, 1970), introduction, xv.

Cantonese Artifacts, Chinoiserie, and Early American Idealization of China

JONATHAN GOLDSTEIN

Introduction

This essay is an attempt to describe the early American visual image of what Professor Murray A. Rubinstein has termed "the gateway," Kwangtung province in the eighteenth and nineteenth centuries.[1] Kwantung and its component anchorages, especially the city of Canton, Whampoa, Lintin, and Macao, were not only literally but also ideationally the gateways for early American access to China. In those two centuries Kwangtung craftsmen emblazoned images of China on artifacts that were exported to Europe and America. Upon reaching American shores many Chinese motifs influenced domestically manufactured artifacts. The altered designs on these artifacts are known generically as chinoiserie. Both Chinese images and American versions are historically significant because from approximately 1786 to 1846 Kwangtung was the only part of China to which Americans had commercial access. The visual image of China produced in Kwangtung therefore became a significant component of the American visual image of all China.

This paper focuses on the nature of the visual image of the gateway. A more ambitious task not attempted here would be to assimilate early American visual imagery of China with nonvisual input. Those two components contributed to an overall early American impression of the Middle Kingdom. An even more ambitious task would be to explain how broadly based attitudes and impressions came to affect United States governmental policy toward China and toward Chinese immigrants to the United States. These broader historical concerns are referred to in my book *Philadelphia and the China Trade*. This essay explores some simi-

larities between early American and subsequent visual images
of China, but does not attempt to specify the relationship between
early images and later attitudes and policy.

In 1785 the Baltimore-built and New York and Philadelphia–
financed *Empress of China* initiated an ongoing Sino-American
trade entirely in United States ships.[2] The material culture of
the early American China trade came to the fore in numerous
bicentennial exhibits held in 1984 and 1985, in concurrent publications, and in lectures.[3] The commemorative exhibits included and/
or depicted artifacts from China and Western representations of
them. The exhibits and events also publicized baronial stateside
residences with interiors and sometimes exteriors wholly or partially constructed in what was considered Chinese style, occasionally with Anglo-Chinese gardens alongside. From this material
culture some generalizations can be drawn about the early American image of "the gateway."

Scholarship That Informs Our Understanding of China Trade Material Culture

Before proceding with those generalizations, one should credit
the many scholars who laid the intellectual underpinning for our
understanding of the material culture of the China trade. Peter
Marshall, Glyndwr Williams, Philip Curtin, and Jay Botsford scru-
tinized the general impact of non-Western art on European society.[4] Laurence P. Roberts specifically examined the impact of
Chinese and other East Asian and Pacific artistic influences on
Europe.[5] Patrick Conner's *Oriental Architecture in the West* discussed Persian, Egyptian, Moorish, and Chinese influences on
American architecture.[6] Clay Lancaster devoted a series of publi-
cations first appearing in the 1940s to the specific influence of
Chinese forms on American architecture.[7]

In the dozen years immediately preceding the 1984–85 exhibitions, H. A. Crosby Forbes and Carl L. Crossman continued
the pioneer scholarship of Clay Lancaster. Forbes and Crossman
documented and analyzed the imagery of "China" and "Chinese"
on handicrafts imported to early America. Forbes' history of Chinese export silver, his published article, and exhibitions he arranged for Milton, Massachusetts' China Trade Museum revealed
images of China upon "vast quantities of export wares" imported
into early America. According to Forbes, "the artisan community
at Canton with its porcelain and enamel painters, its painters in

oils and watercolors, its weavers and embroiderers, its silversmiths and other metal workers, its carvers, gilders and cabinet makers, produced more goods, of consistently high quality and good taste, in greater variety over a longer period of time, than any other artisan community the world has ever known."[8] Crossman, conducting his research simultaneously but largely independently of Forbes, documented additional instances of the introduction of Chinese motifs in early America. In his book *The China Trade,* in several articles, and in exhibitions he mounted at the Peabody Museum of Salem, Massachusetts, Crossman demonstrated how Chinese people, landscapes, flora, fauna, and historical and mythological scenes were depicted upon stone, shell, metal, horn, ivory, glass, clay, wood, paper, and fabric and thereby "entered" early American homes. According to Crossman, millions of yards of Chinese silk, much of it elaborately decorated with Chinese floral motifs, reached the United States in the nineteenth century, along with hundreds of thousands of decorated fans and thousands of sets of chessmen, each man painstakingly carved from white or red-dyed ivory.[9]

Forbes and Crossman concluded that the image of China on Chinese-made artifacts was often created in a bucolic manner. A refined, elegant, and often mythical China bore little semblance to reality. Nevertheless, it was those images that became part of the American impression or understanding of what China was.

Archaeological research has provided additional data on the presence of decorated Chinese export objects in early American homes. Digs in Philadelphia's Society Hill district and at Colonial Williamsburg have unearthed numerous types of Chinese export porcelain in varied socioeconomic contexts: rich homes, poor homes, tavern sites. These artifacts indicate that the China trade was not only a commerce in finer decorative arts but in less expensive popularly consumed artifacts. The China trade affected and influenced all classes and was not the sole province of the elite.[10] Archaeological evidence is especially important when one takes into account that the importation of China trade goods to the colonies up to 1784 was to some extent illicit, over and beyond those commodities transshipped from Great Britain. Quantities of porcelain and other goods were smuggled in from St. Eustatius in the Dutch West Indies and elsewhere. Understandably, such transactions were rarely noted in documents.[11]

While many China trade artifacts have been unearthed in Pennsylvania and Virginia and others have been studied and publicized by Forbes and Crossman, an even more extensive array of such objects was displayed in the 1984–85 gallery exhibitions. The exhibits corroborated the revelations of Forbes and Crossman, reconfirmed by archaeological evidence, that Kwangtung artisans were not only competent but versatile. In addition to producing high-quality porcelain and silk of their own native styling, they developed a vigorous industry duplicating Western-style objects and designs from prototypes. By 1750, enamelling workshops were moved from remote Ching-tê Chen to the port city of Canton, far more accessible to westerners. At Canton, Western monograms, crests, and pictorial etchings could be readily reproduced on ceramics. Designs from prints were copied on canvas or glass in Canton by the end of the eighteenth century. Canton carpenters used both native and imported woods in their reproduction of prototypes.[12]

The popularity of Chinese designed and replicated goods in early America may have derived from the fact that such products were decorated in a fashion widely different from what was common in the early American marketplace. The American taste for Chinese goods appears to have coincided with and perhaps been inherited from European upper classes. The exotic seems to have held a charm for Americans and Europeans alike. The fascination was at least partially rooted in dissatisfaction with dominant baroque and classical modes. In art and in social behavior, one means of relieving the monotony of classicism was the introduction of novel customs like tea drinking with its refreshingly outlandish sets of imported ornaments. Americans further enlivened classical motifs in their homes with the introduction of imported Chinese wallpapers, artifacts, and European chinoiserie that created a romantic illusion of China. Examples of Chinese objects can be found in virtually all James River manors in Virginia of the eighteenth and first half of the nineteenth centuries, as well as in merchant homes of Philadelphia, Providence, Boston, Salem, and Newburyport of the same era.[13]

Americans, as has been already mentioned, did not restrict themselves to imported Chinese products or to European chinoiserie in their efforts to satisfy a longing for the romantic and exotic. Concurrent with the importation of Chinese goods and European chinoiserie artifacts, two distinct forms of cultural borrowing occurred in the development of decorative arts in America and were reflected in the 1984–85 exhibits. There were attempts to domestically manufacture objects with Chinese designs. And efforts were undertaken not only to decorate the inside of American structures, but also to construct a building's entire exterior in the Chinese style.

Influence of China Trade Artifacts on European and American Decorative Arts

With respect to American-produced chinoiserie, the 1984–85 exhibits revealed that American artisans began to graft onto their products either Chinese designs or European romanticizations of them. This stylistic development was prevalent in American furniture, silver, textile, and wallpaper production. Lithography and watercolor painting produced documents depicting Chinese people and Chinese-style buildings. In each case the trends were not particular to one geographical region of the United States and appear to have been nationwide.

The catalog for the 1985 Peabody Museum of Salem exhibit "After the Chinese Taste" documented the influence of Chinese forms and surface decoration on American furniture makers, including an imitative lacquered surface decoration known as "japanning." This term was a misnomer in that most of what japanners were copying came from China. Japanned furniture from England first appeared in American markets in the 1690s. Since New York and Boston seem to have been the most important markets for these foreign products, it is not surprising to find that they were also the cities where American japanned furniture was mainly produced.[14] Distinct images of Chinese were painted up and down a tall japanned pine clock made in Boston about 1750 by Gawen Brown, and across a Baltimore armchair of Renshaw and Barnhard of approximately 1805.

Like japanned products, early American silver, textiles, and wallpaper bore imaginary Chinese figures and imagery. Lithographs and watercolors faithfully depicted real Chinese and Chinese-style structures. Chinese floral motifs encircled some of S. Kirk and Sons' Baltimore-made silver mustard pots, waste bowls, tea services, candlesticks and coffee pots. This decoration seems to have been directly inspired by almost identical design found on Chinese export silver. The Peabody Museum catalog traced much of this inspiration to the influence of Jean-Baptiste Pillement (1728–1808), who published *A New Book of Chinese Ornament* in 1755. Pillement's "Chinese" motifs appeared on the English printed wallpaper in the Jeremiah Lee Mansion, Marblehead, Massachusetts, 1768, and on the American printed wallpaper in General Henry Knox's home in Thomaston, Maine.[15]

Perhaps the most impressive Chinese figure in early American iconography was done without reference to Pillement. This was the large mezzotint of the Hong merchant Houqua seated amid the palatial grandeur of his villa. It was engraved by John Sartain of Philadephia, allegedly after a portrait made in Canton.[16]

Pagodas, those unmistakable "Middle Kingdom" motifs, were interspersed with sailing ships and New England–style churches on a jacquard coverlet of about 1840. Pagodas were featured in the Philadelphia lithography of Lucas and Newsam and watercolors by David Kennedy and Benjamin Evans. The tower also appeared, perhaps as a result of Pillement's inspiration, on a Ford and Tupper silver kettle of 1825. It was shown rising next to a Philadelphia family's monogram.[17]

Grandiose Buildings in the Chinese Style

It was in architecture where the pagoda motif specifically, and the style of chinoiserie in general, found its most grandiose expression. As with so many other aspects of the history of taste, eighteenth and nineteenth century Americans followed the China-loving fancies of their European cousins. By the end of the seventeenth century, Europeans had erected their first Chinese-style monument, the "Trianon de Porcelain," at Versailles. In 1761, a 163 foot tall pagoda was erected in London's Kew Gardens. The number of Chinese landscapes and garden pavilions increased in Europe following publication of Thomas Chippendale's *Gentleman and Cabinetmaker's Directory* in England in 1754.[18] This book appears to have stimulated the use of Chinese forms on woodwork decoration both inside and outside of early American buildings.[19] Examples of the usage of Chinese exterior architectural forms, as opposed to artifacts around the house, included the University of Virginia colonnades; the Valcour Aimé pagoda in Louisiana; a painted pagoda in the garden at "Mt. Pleasant," Philadelphia; John Notman's Mount Holly, New Jersey, "Chinese Cottage"; and John R. Latimer's Wilmington, Delaware, manor.[20] Far and away the most grandiose Sinitic structures were the domiciles of returning China traders Andreas van Braam Houckgeest and John P. Cushing, and the commercial property erected by Peter Browne. No discussion of the impact of Chinese fashions in early America would be complete without at least a brief description of these three structures.

Andreas van Braam Houckgeest's residence, "China's Retreat," was built in Croydon, Pennsylvania, in 1796 and was a landmark on the west bank of the Delaware River until its destruction in 1970. It was topped by a small pagoda and wind bells, while indoors was a seventeen-figure Chinese diorama, which included pagodas, bridges, ponds, streams, trees and human figurines. Chinese house servants maintained the residence, and the imported furnishings included over two thousand drawings of China. The total effect of this romantic recreation was perhaps best summarized by Philadelphia publisher Moreau de Saint-Mèry, who wrote, after a visit to "China's Retreat":

> The furniture, ornaments, everything at Mr. Van Braam's reminds us of China. It is impossible to avoid fancying ourselves in China while surrounded by living Chinese and by representations of their manners, monuments, and arts.[21]

John Perkins Cushing's "Belmont," was constructed in Watertown, Massachusetts, in 1834 and ran a close second to "China's Retreat" in terms of its ability to create the illusion of China. Not only did John P. Cushing surround himself with Chinese servants and house furnishings. He also erected greenhouses with rare Chinese fruits and trees, including the first gingko trees imported to the United States. Boston legends describe the hospitality at Belmont, where "annual Fourth of July parties featured Chinese firecrackers and fireworks, crystallized ginger and mechanical toys."[22]

Perhaps the most complete adaptation of Chinese architectural style in North America was the hundred-foot high pagoda with Chinese pavilion and garden constructed in Fairmount Park, Philadelphia, in 1827 and 1828. This creation, sometimes referred to as "The Temple of Confucius," was the inspiration of Philadelphia attorney Peter Browne. The tower was an exact replica of a Canton pagoda familiar to Western visitors. Browne's "Pagoda and Labyrinth Garden," as the complex was also known, probably combined refreshment facilities and botanical displays with some sort of entertainment, all of which blended to give patrons the illusion of being transported to China.[23]

The evidence of imported artifacts, chinoiserie and architecture reveals that, as early as the mid-eighteenth century, American colonists were imitating their European cousins in attempting to create their own romantic visions of Cathay. They had erected villas, gardens, amusement parks, and other public displays that were at least partially Chinese in appearance or contents. As in Americans' adoption of small-scale Chinese-style artifacts, the usage of large-scale displays was nationwide and undertaken by some of the most distinguished early American designers.

There was one final process by which a romanticized visual image of China was transmitted: through the so-called "museums of Chinese curiosities." These creations may be partially considered the product of a genuine American interest in things Chinese. Like other forms of material culture, some of these museums were also inspired by commercial motives. Although advertised as "edifying" collections, these displays also served to amuse and titillate onlookers. Returning China trader Nathan Dunn opened his "Chinese Museum" to the Philadelphia public in 1839. Over one hundred thousand Americans paid to see Dunn's assemblage of gaily costumed Chinese mannequins arrayed beneath silk banners and lanterns. Over 50,000 copies of his *Descriptive Catalogue* were sold in the first few months of the exhibit. Dunn wished to capitalize on European receptivity toward romanticized and idealized images of China and the Chinese. Consequently, in the early 1840s he moved his display to London, where it was installed in a pagoda that John Notman had specifically designed for Dunn. Also in the 1840s, John Peters, a member of Caleb Cushing's United States diplomatic mission to China, set up a second Chinese museum in Philadelphia, later moving it on to Boston. Also a money-making institution, Peters' museum offered an "extensive view of the Central Flowery Nation." It appears to have been even larger than Dunn's, containing sixty full-size figurines to Dunn's fifty-three.[24]

The original and longest-lived of the "cabinets of curiosities" was that of the East India Marine Society of Salem, Massachusetts, established in 1799 and now the Peabody Museum of Salem. Originally a repository for artifacts collected by Salem sea captains, the "cabinet" featured, like the other museums, mannequins in Chinese attire. Nineteenth-century accounts record amusement and entertainment as viewers' impression of the display. One onlooker described the collection as a "subject of wonder."[25] Another saw it as a "source of amusement to visitors of all classes."[26] A third recalled that it was

> an experience to step from the prosaic street of New England into that atmosphere redolent with the perfumes of the East. That arcade of sitting and standing figures became real friends of mine. Mr. Blue Gown and Mr. Queer Cap must be greeted whenever I went to the Museum.[27]

Conclusion: An Early American Vision of "The Gateway"

To that viewer and other early Americans the museums, villas, parks, gardens, and smaller decorative objects offering visual images of China possessed a "mysterious attraction." Fairy-like beings cavorted—on porcelain, furniture, carvings, textiles, and paintings—in a never-never land of cloud-like rocks, exotic plants, and airy pavilions. Where, in this romantic vision of Cathay, was the poverty, squalour, stagnation, starvation, exploitation, and misery also part of the real China? The popularity of "Chinese" objects in early America tells us as much about ourselves as about China. The material culture of the old China trade is evidence that a fantasy world could be conjured up through commercial interest and could become part of an American conception of China. Westerners essentially made the decisions about what was borrowed and worked into the American image of China.

No attempt has been made here to deal with an American visual image of China after the mid-nineteenth century. In 1846 the first Sino-American treaty went into effect and significantly increased American access to China. Our conceptions of China changed as many gateways, or trading ports, opened in addition to Canton. However, one final thought can be offered concerning post-1846 imagery. The mid-century introduction of photography to China offered Americans an alternative to the romantic vision suggested by earlier artisans. It was not so much the process of photography as the way it was used. Tourists and news photographers thronged a widely opened China and snapped scenes that denied the earthly paradise pictured on saleable decorative artifacts. These scenes were reproduced in private collections of photos, in mass-marketed stereopticon cards and, most widely, in the printed mass media.[28] Although Western woodcuts had occasionally communicated unpleasant Chinese scenes to Americans before the mid-nineteenth century, it was the mid-century development of mass media techniques in the United States, especially the high-speed, steam-driven "pulp" media press, which made possible swift dissemination of photographs of explicitly unpleasant subject matter previously omitted from most romantic decor.

The romantic vision of China has not been totally displaced by the camera for it continues to be evoked by Chinese and American artisans today. These image makers are subsidized by a flourishing trade in "Chinese" art items, at Chinatown curio shops and Friendship Stores. However, since the mid-nineteenth century, the romantic image of China on artifacts has had to coexist with the stark reality of photography, which can vividly depict the harsh life of another China.

Notes

1. Professor Rubinstein used the term "the gateway" in connection with the October 31, 1987, Mid-Atlantic regional Association for Asian Studies panel "Visions of the Gateway: Western Perceptions of Kwangtung Province in the Eighteenth and Nineteenth Centuries." The panel was held at Lehigh University, Bethlehem, Pennsylvania, and was chaired by Professor Rubinstein. The author wishes to thank Peter Pih of West Georgia College, Jane Leonard of the University of Akron, and William Sargent of the Peabody Museum of Salem for criticism of this paper and Darlene Bearden, Beth Beggs, and Lisa Chase of West Georgia College for secretarial assistance.

2. On *The Empress of China* voyage, see Jonathan Goldstein, *Philadelphia and the China Trade, 1682–1846: Commercial, Cultural, and Attitudinal Effects* (University Park and London: Pennsylvania State University Press, 1978), and Philip Chadwick Foster Smith, *The Empress of China* (Philadelphia: Philadelphia Maritime Museum, 1984).

3. In 1984 and 1985, ten *Empress of China* commemorative museum exhibitions were mounted, numerous related publications were issued, and lectures were held in the eastern United States. Among larger museums, the Philadelphia Museum of Art (PMA) hosted the exhibit "Philadelphians and the China Trade, 1784–1844." The PMA and the Philadelphia Maritime Museum sponsored an exhibit entitled "The Canton Connection: Ships, Captains and Cargoes." An illustrated catalog was published by the PMA of the objects in both PMA exhibits. The Peabody Museum of Salem, Massachusetts, shortly after its 1984 merger with the Milton, Massachusetts, China Trade Museum, mounted the exhibits "Directly from China: Export Goods for the American Market, 1784 to 1930" and "After the Chinese Taste: China's Influence in America, 1730–1930," with illustrated catalogs for each exhibit. Also in 1984, exhibitions at least partially focused on early Sino-American trade in New York City at the Museum of the City of New York, the American Museum of Natural History, and the Berry-Hill Galleries, and in Washington, D.C., at the National Portrait Gallery. Smaller museums also commemorated the *Empress* bicentennial: the Searsport, Maine, Penobscot Maritime Museum and Atlanta's High Museum of Art held small exhibits of China trade artifacts. The High Museum additionally sponsored a "Patterns of Trade" public lecture series with presentations by China trade scholars Arlene Palmer Schwind, Philip C. F. Smith, and Ross E. Taggert. Jean Gordon Lee, *Philadelphians and the China Trade 1784–1844* (Philadelphia: Philadelphia Museum of Art, 1984); Philadelphia Museum of Art brochure "China Trade," 1984; Ellen Paul Denker, *After the Chinese Taste: China's Influence in America, 1730 to 1930* (Salem, Mass.: Peabody Museum of Salem, 1985); Christina H. Nelson, *Directly from China: Export Goods for the American Market, 1784–1930* (Salem, Mass.: Peabody Museum of Salem, 1985); "China's Trade Mark: An Exhibit," *Washington Post,* 6 April 1984; Margaret C. S. Christman, *Adventurous Pursuits: Americans and the China Trade 1784–1844* (Washington, D.C.: National Portrait Gallery, 1984); David S. Howard, *New York and the China Trade,* (New York: New-York Historical Society, 1984); "High Museum of Art (Atlanta) January Schedule," 1985.

In addition to the museum exhibitions, at least one scholarly symposium was held to celebrate the bicentennial of Sino-American trade relations. The panel "The Cultural Dimensions of American-Chinese Relations, 1784–1984" was held at the Society for Historians of American Foreign Relations (SHAFR) Tenth Annual Meeting, Washington, D.C., 2 August 1984. Letter, William H. Becker to SHAFR membership, 16 January 1984, and conference program.

The *Empress'* voyage was also commemorated in January 1984 when Chinese Premier Zhao Ziyang visited Washington, D.C. The premier recalled the pioneering voyage in his speech at the official ceremonies. *USA Today,* 22 February 1984.

4. Peter Marshall and Glyndwr Williams, *The Great Map of Mankind: Perceptions of New Worlds in the Age of Enlightenment* (Cambridge: Harvard University Press, 1982); Philip Curtin, *The Image of Africa: British Ideas and Action, 1780–1850* (Madison: University of Wisconsin Press, 1964); and Jay Botsford, *English Society in the Eighteenth Century as Influenced from Overseas* (New York: Octagon, 1965).

5. Laurance P. Roberts, "The Orient and Western Art," in Arthur E. Christy, ed., *The Asian Legacy and American Life* (New York: John Day, 1942).

6. Patrick Conner, *Oriental Architecture in the West* (London: Thames and Hudson, 1979), chap. 12.

7. Clay Lancaster, "Oriental Forms in American Architecture 1800–1870," *The Art Bulletin* 29, no. 3 (September 1947): 183–93; and Lancaster, "Oriental Influences in American Architecture" in *The Oriental Impulse in America* (Williamsburg, Va.: Colonial Williamsburg, 1969). Lancaster specifically described the Chinese impact in "The Chinese Influence in American Architecture and Landscaping," *Nineteenth Annual Washington Antiques Show 1974* (catalog), 33–36, 92–99.

8. H. A. Crosby Forbes, "The American Vision of Cathay," in *Nineteenth Annual Washington Antiques Show 1974* (catalog), 49, 51–54; H. A. Crosby Forbes, John Devereaux Kernan, and Ruth S. Wilkins, *Chinese Export Silver, 1785 to 1885* (Milton, Mass.: Museum of the American China Trade, 1975).

9. Carl Crossman, *The China Trade* (Princeton: Pyne Press, 1972), 192, 206, 244. See also: Crossman, "China Trade Paintings on Glass," *Antiques* 95 (March 1969), 376–82; Crossman, "The Rose Medallion and Mandarin Patterns in China Trade Porcelain," *Antiques* 92 (October 1967): 530–36; Crossman, "Chinese Export Porcelain and Other Objects of the China Trade 1785–1840," in *The Oriental Impulse in Early America* (Williamsburg, Va.: Colonial Williamsburg, 1969), 11-13; Crossman, *A Design Catalog of Chinese Export Porcelain for the American Market* (Salem, Mass.: Peabody Museum, 1964).

10. Excavations at Colonial Williamsburg and Philadelphia have revealed substantial Chinese porcelain in eighteenth-century contexts. Shards with elaborate overglaze-decorated floral patterns, particularly pink *famille rose* coloration, have been found on tavern sites and property of craftsmen and shopkeepers in Williamsburg. On the other hand, crudely or simply decorated pieces have been unearthed in Philadelphia, especially at a dig nicknamed "Franklin's trash pit." Such cheap varieties were often imported for their value as ballast on tea ships, and became weekday dishes for lower social and economic classes. Barbara Liggett, *Archaeology at Franklin's Court* (Harrisburg, Pa.: McFarland, 1973); Ivor Hume, *Pottery and Porcelain in Colonial Williamsburg's Archaeological Collections* (Williamsburg, Va.: Colonial Williamsburg, 1969).

11. Even on those few occasions when mention does occur, such as in smug-

glers' correspondence, rarely is a distinction drawn between a genuine Chinese item such as porcelain and imitation wares simultaneously produced in such European factories as Delft, Bow, Worcester, Liverpool, or Caughley. A similar vagueness appears in legitimate documents. Benjamin Franklin, for example, referred to the first appearance of "China" in his house about 1730, but it is unclear from his reference whether he meant genuine porcelain from China or imitation. Letters: Thomas Richè to George Clifford, 18 September 1762; to Q. Hodshon, 7 October 1762, Historical Society of Pennsylvania, Philadelphia, Richè Letterbooks, 1750–71; Benjamin Franklin, *The Autobiography of Benjamin Franklin,* edited by Leonard Labaree, Ralph Ketcham, Helene Boatfield, and Helene Fineman (New Haven: Yale University Press, 1964), 145.

12. Forbes, "American Vision," 53; Claire LeCorbellier, *China Trade Porcelain* (New York: Metropolitan Museum, 1974), 7–8; Crossman, *China Trade,* 117, 221–22; Hume, *Pottery,* 39–40.

13. B. Sprague Allen, *Tides in English Taste (1619–1800)* (New York: Pageant Books, 1958), 1:234; Lancaster, "Chinese Influence"; Hugh Honour, *Chinoiserie* (London: J. Murray, 1961); Crossman, *China Trade,* passim.

14. Denker, *Chinese Taste,* 3.

15. Denker, *Chinese Taste,* 4–5, 14–15, 37; Dorothy Rainwater, "House of Kirk: America's Oldest Silversmiths," *Spinning Wheel,* October 1965, 11; *Samuel Kirk and Son: American Silver Craftsmen* (pamphlet).

16. Goldstein, *Philadelphia,* 38, illustration opposite p. 36.

17. Forbes, *Chinese Export Silver,* passim; Rainwater, "Kirk," 11; *Kirk* (pamphlet).

18. Lancaster, "Chinese Influence"; Honour, *Chinoiserie,* passim; Crossman, *China Trade,* passim.

19. Denker, *Chinese Taste,* 5–7; Lancaster, "Chinese," 92–93; Lancaster, "Oriental Forms," 183–93; Conner, *Oriental,* 173–74.

20. *South Carolina Gazette* (Charleston), 1 April 1757; A. J. Downing, *A Treatise on the Theory and Practice of Landscape Gardening* (New York and London: Wiley and Putnam, 1841), 345; Joan Thill, "A Delawarean in the Celestial Empire." (M.A. thesis, University of Delaware, 1973), 271–77; Denker, *Chinese Taste,* passim.

21. Harold Eberlein and Cortlandt Hubbard, *Portrait of a Colonial City: Philadelphia, 1670–1838* (Philadelphia: Lippincott, 1939), 478; William Birch, *The Country Seats of the United States,* no. 19 (Springfield, Pa.: W. Birch, 1808); Andreas van Braam Houckgeest, *Voyage de l'Ambassade de la Compagnie des Indes Orientales* (Philadelphia: M. L. E. Moreau de Saint-Mery, 1797), 1:iii–xvi; Ruth Seltzer, "The Best of Two Old River Houses," *Evening Bulletin* (Philadelphia), 10 December 1957, 58; Marion Rivinus and Katharine Biddle, *Lights Along the Delaware* (Philadelphia: Dorrance, 1965), 71; Edward Barnsley, *History of China's Retreat* (Bristol, Pa.: Bristol Printing Comany, 1933); William Davis, *The History of Bucks County, Pennsylvania* (Doylestown, Pa.: Democrat Book and Job Office Print, 1886), 133; William Birch, "Autobiography," Society Miscellaneous Collection, Historical Society of Pennsylvania, Philadelphia; Janet Thorpe, "Chinoiserie in America with Emphasis on the Van Braam Houckgeest Collection," (term paper, Institute of Fine Arts, New York University, May 1964), 14–16; M[argaret] Jourdain, "The China Trade and Its Influence on Works of Art," *Apollo* 34 (November 1941): 111. A watercolor painting of "China's Retreat" by Birch is in the Library Company of Philadelphia.

22. Lancaster, "Chinese," passim; Forbes, "American," 51–52.

23. William Chambers, *Designs of Chinese Buildings* (London: published for the author, 1757), plate V; *Old Landmarks and Relics of Philadelphia* (Philadelphia: R. Newell & Son, 1876); Ellis Oberholtzer, *Philadelphia: A History of the City and Its People* (Philadelphia: S. J. Clarke, 1912), 2:198; Lancaster, "Chinese," 34, 93.

24. Enoch Wines, *A Peep at China, in Mr. Dunn's Chinese Collection* (Philadelphia: Printed for Nathan Dunn, 1839), vi–viii; Forbes, "American," 52–53; Casper Souder, *The History of Chestnut Street* (Philadelphia: *Sunday Dispatch,* 1858), 148–49; Henry Shinn, *History of Mount Holly* (Mt. Holly, N.J.: privately printed, 1957), 157; Hummel, "Dunn," 39. See also John Peters, *Miscellaneous Remarks upon the Chinese* (Philadelphia: G. B. Zieber, 1847); Forbes, "American Vision. 53.

25. *Essex Register* (Salem, Mass.), 9 October 1826. There were also several American Indian figures.

26. James Buckingham, *Eastern and Western States of America,* (London: Fischer, 1842). 1:270–75.

27. Caroline King, *When I Lived in Salem, 1822–1866* (Brattleboro, Vt.: S. Daye Press, 1937), 29–30.

28. William Hunter, *The 'Fan Kwae' in Canton before the Treaty Days* (London: Kegan Paul, Trench, 1882), 113; Crossman, *China Trade,* 46; Forbes, "American Vision," 55.

The Commercial Origins of American
Attitudes toward China, 1784–1844

JACQUES M. DOWNS

The major concerns of early American politics were problems of foreign relations. In fact, down to the First World War, the United States' primary interest in its relations with most other countries was commerce. Trade figured very importantly even in our relations with Britain, France, and Spain, and who else but merchants and missionaries knew anything about Asia, Africa, the Pacific, Latin America, or the Mediterranean?

It is therefore remarkable that so few diplomatic historians of the era have consulted mercantile records. Until the late nineteenth century, our only official representatives in large areas of the globe were commercial consuls—traders who happened to be living in countries where the U.S. needed agents. Most consular business was maritime (i.e., commercial). Our commercial archives bear abundant testimony to the vital importance of foreign trade in our development as a nation. Unless historians show more interest, these records are likely to be destroyed. Although business records can be a vitally important source of data for early American history, they are rapidly being lost. In the last decade several collections have been fed into the incinerator.

These commercial letters and record books give one a special perspective on the preeminently mercantile origin and thrust of American policy. Our relations with China, as with many other nations, began as something private and commercial—a special interest, which more or less imperceptibly became the national interest. Even the missionaries—the largest noncommercial group of Americans in China—at first accepted attitudes not far different from those of traders. In large part, these attitudes ultimately became policies that were the basis of America's approach to China for many years. Early in this century Tyler Dennett wrote that modern American policy in Asia is largely a body of precedents which have accumulated from decade to decade since the close of the war of the American Revolution. These precedents have a remarkable consistency due in large measure to the unchanging geographical and slowly changing economic and political conditions under which American trade with Asia has been conducted.[1]

We usually condemn the influence of special interests in the making of policy, and rightly so, but were merchants' views any different from those of the rest of the country? Or, more realistically, did anyone else care? If, as seems probable, the rest of the country was largely unconcerned, are we raising subversive questions about the ability of a democracy to conduct foreign relations?

As businessmen, Canton traders thought like businessmen. They were "economically rational." They had traveled halfway around the globe, with large amounts of other people's property under their fiduciary control. Business had to be first in their loyalties. Anything else would have been unethical. Their correspondence and memoirs are full of reaffirmations of this theme. Commonly, in a commercial letter, a merchant mentions an event, then assesses its effects on the market and on his own business. To twist a banal quotation attributed to Calvin Coolidge, "The business of Canton was business." To be sure, noneconomic motives existed, but economic self-interest remained a powerful drive. In China, as elsewhere, this drive was reinforced by the traders' view of their primary duty—to preserve, and if possible, to increase the property with which they had been entrusted.

Thus Canton traders tended to favor, to oppose, or to be indifferent to the Opium War, the abolition of the "Canton system," or the establishment of diplomatic relations with China, as they saw these events affecting trade, especially their own. There may be a direct line of development from Robert Bennet Forbes's famous refusal of Captain Elliot's appeal to join the British in abandoning Canton in 1839 to late-century railroad leaders' defense of antisocial corporate policy by reference to managements' duty to its stockholders.[2] The reasoning was the same in both cases, and precedent can be as important in business as it is in diplomacy or law. They were concerned that financial trust should not be sacrificed to other considerations, whether of honor, patriotism, the long-run benefit of the community, or sometimes even of morality and legality.

The mercantile residents had come to Canton for only one reason. They were single-minded men, there to make a fortune and take it home as soon as they possibly could. They regarded their stay in China, however comfortable, as a time of exile, for which they expected to be very well compensated. In fact, the average stay was about seven years from arrival to retirement for a well-connected young man fortunate enough to get himself placed in one of the four big companies. In seven years, most could earn $100,000, a substantial fortune at that time. As always, the moral problem was how to accomplish this admirable end without compromising one's integrity. The exploitive mercantile attitudes that Rutherford Alcock and Louis Mallet of the British Foreign Office cited in later years were very similar to the views of many Americans in this early period.[3] All intelligent men knew and some deplored what the drug trade was doing to China, but the traders managed to overlook it. Yet these men were not monsters; they were sincere, earnest, often sensitive, Christian gentlemen.[4]

The traders were also not racists. To be sure they held the lowest class of Cantonese in contempt, but they disdained the lower classes elsewhere as well. Moreover, they often had great respect for at least some aspects of Chinese culture, as the furnishings of their homes testify. To Ch'ing officials, they offered the grudging respect that accompanies fear, and many were close to Chinese merchants. It is only remotely possible that the ferocity of California mobs in the late century originated in the disparaging words of early China traders.[5] Traders' attitudes were complex. The opium trade itself was a creator of hard attitudes, but one also finds considerable sympathy for the Chinese in the correspondence of drug merchants. Then, of course, there were people like the partners of Olyphant & Co., who were very outspoken against the opium trade and were pillars of the China Mission. Their views were indistinguishable from those of the missionaries. Yet somehow all of these people agreed on most of the important elements of United States commercial policy.

The American expatriate community's opinion was more important to American relations with China than the corresponding British China-coast opinion was to British diplomacy. Unlike Britain, the United States had no corps of intelligent, professional, civil servants with a clear conception of the national interest. Historian Nathan Pelcovits has depicted the struggle for control of policy between these wise British bureaucrats and the ignorant, selfish, and feckless old China hands. Because they were well-placed, well-informed, and logical, British civil servants were able to produce a sensible policy after the Opium Wars had made it unavoidable.[6] In Jacksonian America, "rotation in office" produced no counterpart to these sagacious British statesmen. For many years our old China hands met no real resistance to their simple, often self-serving demands.

Later in the century, missionaries would create a somewhat different concept of American national interest in China, but in those early days merchants and missionaries pulled together.

American governmental inertia operated against the early adoption of any official China policy. The dispatch of the Cushing mission came in response to community demand, and the resultant treaty gave the Canton resident merchants and missionaries more rights and privileges than they had dared hope for. The United States was very lucky that there was as yet no cry for "extended sovereignty." While British merchants tended to be commercial imperialists, most Americans still held true to the anti-imperial ethic of their revolution. Indeed, most of the American commercial correspondence of that period condemns the British for attacking China, for barbarities during the war, and ultimately for their empire itself. By and large, American merchants thought the British traders who called for a "forward policy" headstrong, greedy, bloodthirsty, and very foolish.[7] The English newspapers, the *Canton Press* and more especially John Slade's *Canton Register* served to alienate the resident Americans by their intemperate stand. Nevertheless, some younger American merchants and at least one senior trader, Joseph Coolidge (who had been manhandled by Chinese soldiers), agreed with the British on the necessity of punishing the Chinese. It is interesting to note the ambivalence of old opium traders like Warren Delano and Augustine Heard, who sympathized with the Chinese, while reiterating the belief that China had to be taught a lesson. As the war dragged on and Commissioner Lin's isolation of the foreign community receded into the past, more and more Ameicans expressed opinions like Heard's:

Whatever faults the Chinese may have . . . bad treatment of commercial foreigners is not one of them & they appear to . . . me to have the right side of the question in their quarrel with the English.[8]

Still later, he commented more pointedly:

The Chinese have been severely punished and I think most unreasonably dealt with. They have been obligated to relinquish the policy that has guided them for centuries and promise everything that their invaders required.

He then predicted that the time would come when the Chinese would throw off this foreign "yoke."[9]

Possibly American altruism toward China may not have been the legacy solely of the missionary movement. Some credit belongs to the merchants and to their ideology—that "civil religion" in which Americans of that era took such pride. There may also have been some sympathy toward China among the British civil servants that Pelcovits mentions, such as Frederick Bruce and Robert Hart. Both influenced Anson Burlingame, the U.S. minister to China who was also to lead China's 1868 diplomatic mission to the United States and Europe. Without that influence, Burlingame might be hard to explain.[10]

Another fact emphasized by the commercial correspondence is that most treaty-port institutions were developed in old Canton before the war. The treaties made it possible to spread these institutions up the coast. In this chain of communities, appeared people from Canton—both Western and Chinese—who replicated the practices and attitudes of the old system. It took the experience of another decade and another war to create an entirely new order. Even then, many of the elements of that new order were holdovers from old Canton. The Cohong could not survive, and the foreigners had to be given a hand in the governance of the new ports. But the Cohong had been moribund for many years anyhow, and the foreigners had managed to exert considerable influence even during the life of the old Canton system.

But what about the opium trade itself, that "long-continued, systematic, international crime?" This question is so entangled with whatever subject one addresses in early Sino-American relations that it is hard to treat any other subject independently. Historian Michael Greenberg's statement that the traffic in Indian opium to China was *probably the largest commerce of the time in any single commodity* [sic]"[11] is only marginally stronger than the *Hunt's Merchants Magazine's* assertion a century earlier that the amount paid for the drug was "probably the largest sum given for any raw material supplied by one nation to another," except for American cotton exports to Britain.[12] By the late 1830s, opium was the basis of East-West commerce. It balanced the payments and was the economic foundation of the Canton foreign community. Anyone who traded to China without bringing in silver from abroad was somehow implicated. Even the missionaries who cashed their drafts; accepted transportation up and down the coast; and received mail, contributions, and other types of support from opium traders, benefitted from the drug traffic and therefore sustained it in some degree. Everyone needed it. Commercial records give special emphasis to this illegal commerce and more particularly to aspects of the question frequently overlooked by historians who have not used commercial records. For example, although they may employ quotation marks, traditionial historians refer to the Opium War's "opening" of China. If the conflict did, indeed, "open" China, it did so in a very special sense. Even a cursory study of the trade makes one acutely aware that, commercially speaking, China was already "open." Other goods had followed opium to Lintin and the other "outside anchorages," until that "outside" business often exceeded the legitimate commerce at Canton. Moreover, as the coastal trade developed, the same dynamic began to operate elsewhere. The Opium War merely legitimated what the opium trade had already accomplished.

It has been argued that the really new element following the war was Hong Kong, a foreign possession on the coast. Yet Macao had been there for nearly three hundred years, and anyway, from the perspective of the smugglers, Hong Kong was merely a more secure, dry-land version of Lintin. Even before the war, Hong Kong had been one of the "outside anchorages," especially during typhoon season. The first European buildings on the island were godowns for goods that could not go upriver. The crown colony quickly became the best smuggling base in Asia. Just as Chinese duties and regulations had driven the trade to the outside anchorages, so new restrictions encouraged the trade to abandon Canton for the free port of Hong Kong. The treaty-ports served much the same purpose, and all were located near coastal smuggling stations.

Opium may have been the catalyst in Chinese-American relations just as it was in the trade. According to some accounts, the Americans disliked the British during the early years of the trade. Britain was still the traditional national enemy then. Americans fought her twice in the first forty years of their existence. British commanders in the Eastern seas were incredibly arrogant during the maritime wars of the first fifteen years of the century. Americans and Chinese were sometimes forced to support each other during this turbulent era in the face of some remarkably cavalier actions of British naval officers. Apparently only once, during the *Lady Hughes* incident of 1784, did Americans join hands with their transatlantic cousins against the Chinese, and that alliance was very brief.[13]

The opium trade changed all this. Some supercargoes noticed that there was a perceptible cooling of Sino-American friendships during the 1820s and 1830s, the period of explosive growth in the drug trade.[14] Opium was involved in every incident involving diplomatic action by the American consul. The *Lydia,* 1815, the *Wabash,* 1817, and the *Emily* were all opium vessels. Although Swisher has argued that in the second of these cases, Americans were treated to a demonstration of swift, honest Chinese justice,[15] why should they have appreciated it? A growing number of them were drug smugglers, and Chinese justice was mobilizing against them. Only a few years afterwards, an American seaman was judicially strangled and his ship ordered out of the river. The cumulative result of these confrontations was to divide the Americans from the Chinese and to bind them to their former enemies.

To take part at all in the Indian drug trade, Americans had to cooperate with the British, and the brotherhood of drug traffickers in the growing community of the foreign ghetto muted the hostility between them. As this illegal trade increased, the Americans as well as the British became increasingly aware of Chinese law. No one is more conscious of the rigors of the law than a criminal, and many traders of both nationalities were on the wrong side of Chinese justice—hence Canton's English publications' frequent discussion of the advantages of legalizing the opium trade and of introducing extraterritoriality into China.

When the Americans left the opium trade, their brief reconciliation with the British came to an end. Effective enforcement seems to have changed American sentiment. When the government's anti-opium campaign reduced demand so substantially that it made the trade both less profitable and more odious, Russell & Co., the largest American firm, abandoned it. The partners in the firm began speaking of the narcotics business as "disreputable," just as their fathers had suddenly seen the immorality of "trafficking in human flesh" when the international slave trade was outlawed in 1808.[16] Implicit in the traders' belated recognition of the dishonorable nature of opium dealing is the idea that they had known it all along. They noted as much in their memorial to Congress in 1839.[17] Russell & Co. did not reenter the traffic until the British expedition had crushed the Chinese policing system, and Wetmore never sold the drug again. Merchants were always conscious of their reputations. As Thurman Arnold was to show in a somewhat different context a century later, a threat to a businessman's reputation can be a most effective means of obtaining his obedience to the law. But as long as they could get away with it, and as long as the trade paid so handsomely, traders could ignore their consciences and the denunciations of missionaries.

For the Chinese, opium was simply the issue. When the Elliots first met Ch'i-shan at Taku, all the latter wanted to talk about was opium.[18] As Tan Chung has pointed out, what produced the Opium War was "the opium trade offensive against China and the increasing Chinese protest against it."[19] Had it not been for the drug commerce, it is conceivable that East-West relations might have continued much as they had for the previous fifty to seventy-five years. And yet, the drug traffic could not have been abandoned without seriously dislocating world commerce. Without opium, the China trade certainly could not have continued on anything like the volume of the previous quarter century. But to China, opium was an unmixed evil, and it is difficult to imagine any alternative to the course the Ch'ing government adopted. The drug was corrupting the Chinese people, demoralizing its soldiery, draining its specie, and raising the cost of living. It was undermining the authority of the Manchu government, the integrity of its finances, and even what has come to be called its credibility. From the Chinese standpoint, the massive expansion of the trade was indeed an offensive, conducted not by a single nation, but by all sea-borne foreigners.

Given the difficulties involved—a long coast with many islands and inlets, the technical superiority of even private foreign vessels (and their arms) over anything the Chinese navy could put on the water, the obsessive demand for the narcotic, and the corruption of the lower levels of the mandarinate—Ch'ing officials probably did about as well as they could. From 1837 onward, police vigilance increased so markedly that Western boats, using the storeships as a base, had to deliver the drug themselves. The reluctance of the Chinese to attack foreign craft made them safer than the old smug boats, most of which had already been seized and broken up. Even the junk trade was curtailed by the government's enforcement drive. As William Jardine himself wrote shortly before his departure for home,

> The present persecution of Opium dealers & Opium smokers is not much more severe than on some previous occasions; but it pervades every province throughout the Empire, a circumstance never before known to have occurred.[20]

The question of legalization was a red herring. Even granting the traders' ignorance of Chinese politics, it is hard to see what inducement they thought legalization could have held for China. Probably few thought much about it at all. Everyone was aware of the pernicious effect of the drug on the Chinese economy and government, and the physiological results of addiction were common knowledge. The opium trade was just too damaging for China to permit it to continue, much less to legalize it.

Governor Teng's campaign was so effective that Elliot feared the trade would fall into the hands of the worst elements in China (a prophetic concern). Smoking had been cut drastically. Jardine estimated that a three-fourths cut in consumption had taken place by the end of 1838, and he predicted that if the campaign were to continue for a year, the reduction would become permanent.[21] China had eliminated most of the Chinese dealers and brokers. The "scrambling dragons" were gone, but westerners had replaced them. If China was serious about stopping the opium trade, the next step had to be some measure against the foreigners directly. Here was the development that drug traders had often acknowledged would eliminate the trade—effective enforcement of the law and the elimination of demand. No one had ever claimed that foreigners had a right to compel China to accept opium. What else could China have done? The question was now simplified: were the British ready to acknowledge that the Chinese were sovereign in their own country, even if that recognition meant great and permanent damage to the world commercial and banking system? By 1839, clearly that price was too high. Opium's economic value, as Fairbank has said "outweighed its moral turpitude."[22]

No traders at this time could have been ignorant of this situation. For a modern historian to change the name of the conflict to the "First Anglo-Chinese War" is an evasion. It was an *opium* war. One can understand the Chinese sense of outrage. Not only was the conflict fought for a depraved goal, but it continued a commerce and a way of life as insulting as it was injurious to China. An opium merchant had to define his market in a special way. What kind of people was it to whom it was appropriate to sell narcotics? How could the proud Chinese bear to watch the transformation of the golden ghetto of the old Canton system into a exclusive suburb dominated by a foreign, commercial elite? Moreover, now the foreign enclave was spreading along the coast to the treaty-ports. To these foreign footholds, Chinese were admitted only on the foreigners' terms—i.e., subservience. Fairbank's use of the ricksha to symbolize the culture of the treaty-ports is striking.[23] It was indeed a hybrid creation—Western bicycle tires and Chinese effort, but it was more than that: It employed superior Western technology to convert the Chinese into a beast of burden for the white man . . . and for money.

Notes

1. Tyler Dennett, *Americans in Eastern Asia* (New York: Macmillan, 1922), 3–4. Earl Swisher says that from 1844 to 1860 "most of the problems of the period are traceable in the trade and in so far as a policy was formulated during the period, that policy grew out of the experience of the American traders." "The Character of American Trade with China, 1844–1860," in Kenneth W. Rea, ed., *Early Sino-American Relations, 1841–1912* (Boulder, Colorado: Westview Press, 1977), 133–34. See also Caleb Cushing's statement quoted in "The Treaty of Wanghia," in Rea, ed., *Early Sino-American Relations*, 83.

2. "I replied that I had not come to China for health or pleasure, and that I should remain at my post as long as I could sell a yard of goods or buy a pound of tea. . . ." Robert Bennet Forbes, *Personal Reminiscences*, 2d ed. (Boston: Little, Brown 1882), 149–150. Thomas Cochran, *Railroad Leaders* (New York: Russell & Russell, 1965), 202–17. See especially George H. Watrous' statement (p. 214), "After all your first duty and mine also is to the property with which we are respectively connected and we have no duty or right, even to sacrifice that for anything or anybody."

3. Nathan Pelcovitz, *Old China Hands and the Foreign Office* (New York: American Institute of Pacific Relations, 1948), passim. As one British Shanghai resident noted to Sir Rutherford Alcock: "In two or three years at farthest I hope to realize a fortune and get away . . . and what can it matter to me if all Shanghai disappear afterwards in fire or flood? You must not expect men in my position to condemn themselves to prolonged exile in an unhealthy climate for the benefit of posterity. We are money-making, practical men. Our business is to make money, as much and as fast as we can—and for this all modes or means are good which the law permits." John K. Fairbanks, *Trade and Diplomacy on the China Coast, 1842–1854*, one-volume ed. (Cambridge: Harvard University Press, 1964), 161, n.c.

4. See my article, "Fair Game: Exploitive Role-Myths and the American Opium Trade," *Pacific Historical Review* 16, no. 2 (May 1972): 133–49.

5. *Pace* Stuart Creighton Miller, *The Unwelcome Immigrant* (Berkeley & Los Angeles: University of California Press, 1969).

6. Pelcovitz, *Old China Hands*, p. 19ff.

7. There are many sources for this generalization. Probably among the most easily available are the Heard Papers at Baker Library, Harvard Business School, Boston Mass., the Delano Papers at the Franklin D. Roosevelt Library, Hyde Park, New York, and the "Russell & Company" Papers at the Library of Congress. For a surprising testimony from an unlikely source, see Paul Sieman Forbes, "Journal," 10 May 1841, Forbes Papers, Baker Library. Yet all American residents were offended by Lin's isolation of the foreigners, and some were dismayed by the surrender of the opium, but thereafter—paradoxically—most tended to approve of Elliot's measures.

8. Augustine Heard to George Hayward, 10 May 1842; Heard Papers, Baker Library.

9. Augustine Heard to A. F. Seebohm, Hamburg, 11 May 1843, Heard Papers, Baker Library.

10. David Anderson, "Anson Burlingame, American Architect of the Cooperative Policy." *Diplomatic History* 1, no. 3. (Summer 1977): 242 ff. Although Anderson seems to believe that the influence of Burlingame was greater on Bruce than vice versa, he makes it clear that the two men were on very close terms. Burlingame wrote to Seward just before Christmas. 1843, "My colleagues are

all my warm friends," (p. 243). I think one may assume that influence worked in both directions.

11. Michael Greenberg, *British Trade and the Opening of China, 1800–42* (Cambridge: Cambridge University Press, 1951), 104.

12. *Hunt's Merchants' Magazine* 3, no. 6 (December 1840): 471.

13. Josiah Quincy, *The Journals of Major Samuel Shaw* (Boston: William Crosby and H. P. Nichols, 1847), 186–195. Shaw's letters to General Henry Knox are even harsher on the English than are the edited *Journals*. See Knox Collection, Massachusetts Historical Society.

14. B. P. Tilden, "Father's Journals," 3d voyage (3 September 1835), Peabody Museum, Salem, Massachusetts, 2:89.

15. Earl Swisher, "Extraterritoriality and the Wabash Case," *American Journal of Internal Law* 45 (1951): 564–71.

16. Downs, "Fair Game," 145, n. 31.

17. "Memorial of R. B. Forbes and Others," House Exec. Doc. no. 40, 26th Cong., 1st sess. The petition seems to have been the work of Warren Delano. See his letter to Frederick A. Delano, 18 May 1839; Delano Papers.

18. James Matheson to John Thacker, London, 1 October 1840, James Matheson's Private Letterbook, Jardine Matheson Archive, Cambridge.

19. "Interpretations of the Opium War (1840–42): A Critical Appraisal," *Ch'ing-shih wen-t'i* 3, supplement 1 (1977): 44.

20. To Jamsetjee Jejeebhoy, Bombay, 1 January 1839, William Jardine's Private Letterbook, Jardine Matheson Archive.

21. Ibid.

22. Fairbank, *Trade and Diplomacy,* 133.

American Board Missionaries and the Formation of American Opinion toward China, 1830–1860

MURRAY A. RUBINSTEIN

In 1830 the general American attitude toward the Chinese was one of guarded admiration, but by 1860 it had shifted to one of contempt. American missionaries in China played a part in bringing about this change. Their writings and their speeches convinced many Americans that the Chinese were "perishing heathen." This paper will examine missionary commentaries and explore how they were related to the processes of attitude changes from 1830 to 1860.

Missionary perceptions of China and the impact of such perceptions have been dealt with by Raymond Dawson and Stuart Creighton Miller. In *The Chinese Chameleon,* Dawson examined a variety of missionary images and suggested that nineteenth-century Protestant missionaries helped to negate the positive image of China, which earlier Catholic missionaries had popularized.[1]

Dawson's canvas was a large one, a virtual history of Western images of China. Stuart Creighton Miller worked on a smaller canvas; his book, *The Unwelcome Immigrant,* was an examination of nineteenth-century American images of China.[2] Miller intended to show that the negative image—which missionaries, merchants, and diplomats created and which the American media popularized—was accepted by many Americans who then became convinced of the cultural inferiority of the Chinese. Both of these books were essentially image studies. They were examinations of how missionaries and other Westerners saw the Chinese and described them in private reports and in published books and articles. Miller was the more ambitious in his attempt to link image with action—to demonstrate that American acceptance of the hostile image produced anti-Oriental sentiment and restricted immigration.

An image is only a part of the communications process. It is a message that is sent from one individual or group to another. A missionary image does not occur in a vacuum; it can be examined only within the context of a total communications system. Miller examined the media, which served as the carriers or transmitters of the image but did not focus upon the way the image was received. He assumed that the public read the newspapers and accepted the image of China these papers presented. Communications systems are closed environments, however, which consist of sources, messages, channels, receivers, and effects.[3] One should study the entire system to be able to understand the specific problems of effect and impact. This is the aim of my examination of the way the missionary image of China was transmitted to the American audience.

Three distinct groups were integral parts of the communications network that was created to transmit the missionaries' image of China. The first was the mission itself, which served as the source of the message. The second was the board, which acted as gate-keeper and edited the missionaries' image. The final group was the American Protestant public, who received the image and reacted to it.

The South China Mission of the American Board was the source of information and images. The mission began its operations in 1830 in the port of Canton. The members of the mission, Elijah Coleman Bridgman, David Abeel, Samuel Wells Williams, Peter Parker, Edwin Stevens, and Samuel Brown, worked hard to create a base for a large scale missionary enterprise. They first studied the Chinese language. With the language at their command, they translated tracts, prepared gospel and Bible lessons, established schools, operated clinics, distributed books and pamphlets, and preached to the Chinese of Canton and Macao. They also set up an English language press and published materials for the Western community of South China and for the American public. The missionaries considered theirs to be a "mission of preparation."[4]

When war came in the wake of the Sino-British conflict over opium, the missionaries moved to safer quarters at Macao.[5] They returned to Canton in 1841 before the signing of the Treaty of Nanking.[6] In the next few years, the missionaries expanded the American Board presence in China by helping to establish mission stations at Foochow, Amoy, Ningpo, and Shanghai.[7] The South China Mission did not expand during this second period in its history, which coincided with the Treaty Port Era (the years 1842 to 1860). It was a time of confrontation between Chinese and Western communities. Riots and outbreaks of anti-Western hostility were common.[8] The South China missionaries continued to work along lines established in the 1830s.[9] They lobbied for a Christian opening of China (i.e., a time when missionaries could feel free to roam China at will, spreading the good word) and they operated as China watchers, keeping the board and the American public aware of conditions on the huge continent.[10] They wrote letters, prepared formal reports, and kept personal and institutional records. They published books, pamphlets, and magazines about the China scene. These materials contained information and insights that were extracted by the board and reworked, eventually forming a distinct missionary image of China.

Personal letters from the missionaries to the board's Foreign Secretary were the most common communications. The missionaries had been told to send back information. Bridgman, the first American missionary to China, was informed, "It will be desirable that you make as full communications respecting the character, condition, manners, and rites of the people, especially so far as these things are affected by religion."[11] He and Abeel, his companion during the first years in China, wrote many letters that gave the board detailed pictures of conditions in Canton.[12] The next year, 1831, Bridgman was alone, yet he found time to continue sending home long descriptive letters.[13] Later missionaries also wrote home frequently. Some described their day-to-day lives, while others dealt with their specific activities.[14] Stevens and Williams often wrote about excursions they had gone on and sights they had seen.[15] The letters formed a rich reservoir of material that could be tapped by those wishing to understand China and by those who wished to make a case for further Christian expansion in East Asia.

The missionaries also wrote detailed reports. In 1836 they organized a formal mission, elected officers, and decided to prepare detailed, carefully structured statements, which they planned to send to the board twice a year, in May and September. They then summarized the work of the previous six-month period in a long letter ending with a demand for additional missionaries and more funds.[16] By the 1840s the semi-annual meetings became impractical and were replaced by full-scale annual conclaves held in September, the beginning of the trading season. The reports of these meetings reached the United States three months later, in late December.[17] During the 1850s the missionaries changed their procedure again. They decided to meet in May so that the annual report they prepared could be accompanied by a budget request that would reach America in August. The board would then be able to use the South China Mission's annual report in its own annual report. This procedure was followed for the rest of the decade.[18]

These mission reports were historically significant documents. They contained descriptions of each type of activity and summarized both accomplishments and problems. They also indicated the state of mind of each member of the mission.[19] Finally, they contained brief descriptions of China and the Chinese that gave the board a sense of what the people were like. The reports were materials the board could use for future planning as well as for publicizing the work of the mission.

The missionaries also sent the board their diaries and journals. Bridgman and Abeel were the first of the journal keepers. Bridgman's contained information on his trip to China and his first years at Canton.[20] Abeel's dealt with his journeys to Southeast Asia.[21] In the mid-thirties, Stevens, Williams, and Parker kept similar daily records. Stevens's was an account of his expeditions along the China coast. Williams's dealt with his voyage to Japan.[22] Parker wrote detailed descriptions of his operations in the Opthalmic Clinic in Canton.[23] The missionaries as a body also kept a journal for the mission. This was begun in the mid-thirties and was kept for the next sixty years.[24]

The missionaries also provided the board with published materials that had been printed on the mission's presses at Canton and later at Macao. A number of works were prepared during these decades. Among them were *A Chinese Christomathy in the Canton Dialect* (Macao, 1844), *Easy Lessons in Chinese* (Macao, 1842), *Chinese Topography* (Macao, 1844), *A Chinese Commercial Guide* (Macao, 1844, and Canton, 1848), and *A Tonic Dictionary in the Canton Dialect* (Canton, 1856).[25] These works were written for the Western merchants in Canton. Copies of each book were also sent to America and served to introduce some Americans to Chinese language, literature, and the particulars of the China trade.

The Chinese Repository was the most important work the board missionaries published in China. Its editor was Bridgman and its publisher was Williams, but other missionaries and laymen contributed articles and information.[26] The first monthly issue of the magazine appeared in 1832, and the last was printed in 1851. During the first two years the format was quite rigid. Each issue contained specific sections on set topics, and missionary affairs were emphasized, though the missionaries had stated the secular nature of the magazine.[27] A looser format was adopted in 1834, and the only fixed section was the last one, entitled "Journal of Occurences." Although the magazine covered a wide range of subjects, Sino-Western confrontations were the dominant concern. Over three hundred articles discussed the diplomatic situation and problems related to trade.[28] There were also background articles dealing with such subjects as history, geography, politics, and society.[29] The missionaries were also keenly interested in the language and literature of the Chinese. Ninety separate articles on these topics were listed in the full index Williams prepared in 1852.[30] Religious matters were dealt with at length. Over two hundred pieces appeared on such subjects as the medical mission, the book translation effort, the Morrison Education Society, and the Ultra Gangetic missionary enterprise.[31] Paganism, the indigenous religious structure, was also studied, and a variety of articles on Buddhism, Confucianism, and Taoism were included in the *Repository*.

The missionaries wrote letters and reports to keep the board informed of their progress and to make the board aware of the problems they faced. Published material that was sent to the board had a wider audience. The missionaries were providing their superiors with detailed background material to help them understand the full extent of the challenge posed by China.

Each missionary had his own individual perception of China and this perception could be seen in his letters. Each missionary could also articulate his own vision in articles and books. Some did so during this early period. David Abeel, who had his journal published, was one of these.[32] Others, such as Williams, preferred to wait until their particular visions had crystalized.[33] Still others never defined their visions in their lifetimes; it was done by those who memorialized them. Bridgman and Parker were in the latter category.[34] But many missionaries were too busy dealing with the day-to-day business of running a mission to define their impressions, leaving this task to the members of the board's Prudential Committee.

The transmission mechanism was the mails. Missionaries had friends in the Western communities who were sympathetic to the cause of Christian expansion. These merchants—D. W. C. Olyphant was the most accommodating[35]—took the missionaries' letters, journals, and publications with them and had them delivered to board headquarters. The foreign secretary wrote his replies, and the messages were sent back to China by merchant vessel. The time involved in this exchange of letters was over six months, a lapse that explains one cause of mission-board tensions.[36]

The American Board played the role of "gatekeeper" in this communications network.[37] The American Board of Commissioners for Foreign Missions was the first American society to fund, organize, and direct the work of American Protestant missionaries in foreign countries. A group of conservative Congregationalist ministers had established the Board in 1810, in response to a letter from a group of students at the Andover Seminary. These students volunteered to serve as missionaries if a coordinating society were set up to support them. The ministers answered the students by establishing the Board.[38] Two years later the Board had collected sufficient funds to send the first small group of students as missionaries to India. In 1830, the year the South China Mission began to function, the Board's officers could point with pride to the establishment of mission stations in India, the Sandwich Islands, the Levant (the Mid-East), and among the Cherokee Indians of Georgia.[39]

The Board fitted Perry Miller's definition of bureaucratized benevolence.[40] In the years from 1830 to 1860 it organized and directed an ever-growing number of missions. Its China enterprise expanded. Stations in other areas were established.[41] The Board raised funds for the support of this far-flung benevolent empire. Auxiliary societies set up in its first decades provided a steady source of funds, year after year.[42] And the Board acted as propagandist for the cause of missions. It ran a publishing house that produced upwards of eighty thousand books and pamphlets per year.[43]

Though Presbyterians and members of Dutch Reformed churches had supported enterprises during the first three decades, the Board was Congregationalist at heart. It was theologically conservative—orthodox trinitarian was the formal term—and its leaders stressed concepts such as Millenarianism, Active Benevolence, and Obedience to Christ's Last Commandment. Each of these ideas had been worked out by Jonathan Edwards and had been further developed by Edwards' disciple, Samuel Hopkins. New England School theologians, men such as Timothy Dwight of Yale, had helped found the Board.[44] The Board's missionaries believed they were working to bring the millenium closer by converting the heathen peoples of the non-Western world. The Board tried to promote the work of its missionaries by informing its supporters in the American churches about conditions in the outside world and describing the efforts of its dedicated, self-sacrificing missionaries. Before the Board officers could publish their messages, however, they had the task of editing and excerpting volumes of material. In so doing, they acted as gatekeepers.

Gatekeepers is a term used by Kurt Lewin to describe those editors of midwestern newspapers who chose stories for their newspapers from the many items coming into their press rooms on the news service wires.[45] Those officers of the Board who edited and prepared the *Missionary Herald* and other Board publications served in that role. They had vast amounts of material at their disposal, as anyone who works with the Board's archives soon discovers. They had to sort and extrapolate this material and fit it into a magazine of about forty pages per issue. In their desire to create a climate of interest in China as a mission field, rather than to develop one particular and distinctive image of China, they chose colorful, emotion-provoking material that often pictured the Chinese at their worst. The suffering and hardship of the "perishing heathen" was depicted again and again in the pages of the *Herald*.

Various types of South China Mission materials were chosen for inclusion in the periodical. The *Respository* was often used as a source of articles. Bridgman's introductory article from the first issue of that magazine was printed, and the *Herald* editors noted the importance of the new Canton-based publication. In that same year an article on geography and a description of Canton were published in the *Herald*.[46] In 1834 more articles on geography and others on such topics as Buddhism and Chinese printing[47] were taken from the missionaries' magazine. The 1835 volume of the *Herald* included two *Repository* articles: one on Robert Morrison, the London Missionary Society missionary to China, and one on Chinese grammar. The *Herald's* editors continued to make use of the *Repository* during the last years of the decade, but took fewer articles with each passing year. By the 1840s the Board and the missionaries argued over the importance of the *Repository*[48] as a source of articles. The Prudential Committee eventually refused to publish *Repository* articles, and turned instead to the unpublished material the missionaries sent home—journals, personal letters, and formal reports.

The missionaries' letters and journals appeared in the Board's magazine. Formal letters were particularly valuable because of their standardized formats and their comprehensive coverage of the mission's activities. A semi-annual report first appeared in the May 1838 issue of the *Herald*.[49] The *Herald* for March 1840 contained another such report, one that had been written in the first months of the opium crisis.[50] During the war years, the editors made use of the letters of individual missionaries to give their readers a feel for the events.[51] After the war they used the more formal letters. A report by Williams was included in the May 1845 *Herald,* and one by Bridgman appeared in January 1847. A report on missionary efforts during the Taiping Rebellion was printed in the December 1857 *Herald.*[52]

The *Herald's* editors chose mission materials carefully. They wished to demonstrate certain themes, such as the unusual mix of degradation and elightenment that the missionaries found in China. They wished to defend the use of military force against a blindly despotic heathen state. They wished to show that the Chinese were intelligent and would accept the word of Christ if the message was announced clearly and frequently. They also wished to show that the missionaries were flexible enough to use a variety of methods in their enterprise. No one image of China emerged in the pages of the *Herald.* Instead, a sort of mosaic was created out of the scattered bits and pieces of the missionary writings and publications.

The *Missionary Herald* was originally called the *Panapolist.* It became the *Panapolist/Missionary Herald* in the second decade of the nineteenth century, and finally the *Missionary Herald* in the 1820s. Between 1830 and 1860 twenty-two thousand copies of the *Herald* were distributed each year. It averaged about four hundred fifty pages per year over this span. From 1830 to 1845, each yearly volume contained four hundred eighty pages, while in the following fifteen years, from 1846 to 1860 the number of pages per yearly volume gradually dropped to about four hundred.[53] Changes in layout of the magazine reduced the number of pages but increased the content.

The format changed little from year to year. The first and longest section of each issue contained reports from the various mission fields. Letters, reports, and journals from many mission stations were used in this section. The second section was devoted to domestic matters. A third section contained information about the work of other mission societies, while a fourth was given over to brief notices and snippets of information about the missions. The fifth section was a listing of financial contributors to the Board for a given month. Next to each name was the amount the individual or the group had given. The Board used the fifth section to give recognition to those who actively supported the cause of missions. This, then, was the *Herald* as it would appear to a reader in the 1830s, 1840s, or 1850s.[54] It was, in its own way, an average readers' window to a world he would probably never see.

The missionaries and the Board had means other than the written word for reaching their public. Networks linking missionary and the home public were developed. These new networks involved the spoken word. They linked preacher with congregation, and lecturer with audience. Missionaries often returned to the United States. Some came back to retire from their fields; others, to recuperate from serious illness. Some, like Williams, Bridgman, and Parker, simply wanted to take a furlough. Whatever the reasons for their return, each had an opportunity to speak directly to an American audience, and many found themselves in demand as speakers. The furloughs of two members of the South China Mission demonstrate this interpersonal network.

Peter Parker returned to the United States in December 1840 and went back to South China in the fall of 1841. He spent the months of his furlough in almost ceaseless activity. Three days after he landed in New York, he spoke at the Tabernacle Church. Edward V. Gulick, Parkers's modern biographer, noted that Parker "was chagrined to find that he spoke poorly" and suggests that the missionary "was undoubtedly still groping for a readjustment to America." He further suggests that "his culture shock must have been accompanied and compounded by nervousness over the new role of itinerant propogandist."[55] In the months that followed, Parker seems to have conquered his nervousness; for he spoke before groups of clergy and friends in New Haven, before a congregation in Washington, D.C., and before members of the Senate and the House at the joint session of Congress. Early the next year, he went on a series of short engagements to Philadelphia, New York, and New Brunswick. He married in late March and spent his honeymoon on the lecture circuit. His bride had to listen to her husband talk about China in New Haven, Springfield, and Framingham. One of his most impressive performances was before the Medical Association of Boston, where he spoke at a heavily attended special meeting.[56] He then spent a few months in London, and when he returned to the United States, was reunited with his bride. Soon thereafter he arranged their passage to China.

Samuel Wells Williams left China in late 1844, and for the better part of the next year, he made his way slowly toward Europe and America. For the adventurous Williams this was a grand time; his letters to family and friends reflect his wonder and excitement.[57] He reached New York in October in 1845 and immediately found himself the center of attention, as had been his friend Parker before him. He spent the next year traveling through the states of the Northeast and the Midwest. He found that people wanted to hear him speak, and he soon organized speaking tours that took him to many cities. His personal account book for the years 1844 to 1848 provides information about his itinerary, as well as insight as to his parsimony and attention to detail. In early 1846 he traveled to his family home at Utica and then made visits to Cleveland, Oberlin, Buffalo, Rochester, and Geneva and Rome, New York. Later in the year he visited New York City, Washington, D.C., and Plattsburgh, New York.[58] His son and biographer, Frederick Wells Williams, described his father's tours. It was his opinion that "there success was considerable, owing both to his extended and accurate knowledge of the subject and the general interest which the recent war and opening of the country had excited in the minds of all intelligent persons."[59] A son is not an unbiased observer, especially a son who succeeds his father as professor of Chinese studies at a major university. But there is some evidence to support Frederick Wells's assertion. A letter written to Samuel Wells Williams by a number of prominent citizens of Rochester demonstrates the interest the missionary had excited.[60]

Williams's lectures were so well organized that the missionary printer and his associates thought they could be easily turned into a valuable book. Williams spent the better part of his next year in America reworking these lectures and then looking for a publisher. He found one only when some of his merchant friends agreed to defray the costs of publication.[61] The book was Williams's magnum opus, *The Middle Kingdom,* a work generally recognized as the most influential Western text written on China during the nineteenth century.[62] In this instance the spoken word became the written word, and even more Americans were able to learn about China.

But just what was the missionary board image of China? There was no single image, for each missionary had his own vision of China. It was this personal vision that was conveyed in the missionary letters and lectures. And a composite image began to emerge. China was described as a beautiful land that had been despoiled by its inhabitants. The countryside was scenic and sometimes spectacular. The cities and the villages were just the opposite. The villages were collections of filthy hovels. The cities were decaying areas with walled inner centers and sprawling outlying suburbs. City streets were winding and narrow passages through which flowed a flood of human traffic. The missionaries, it seems, could never become comfortable with the sheer numbers of Chinese. Their reiterated use of the flood metaphor indicates their discomfort.

The Chinese themselves were portrayed as a superior type of "perishing heathen." Missionaries wrote about the Chinese love of education, their concern for the family, their belief in the essential goodness of man, and their stress on morality and proper conduct. Then these American Protestants went on to present the negative qualities of the nation. The Chinese were notorious gamblers, destroying their families with their love of games of chance. They were a lascivious, depraved people who treated their women with contempt.

These flaws in the Chinese character, American readers learned, stemmed from the hollow nature of Chinese religion. There was no belief in God, and by Western missionary standards, no morality. As might be expected, the religious structures the Chinese had developed came in for the harshest criticism. Confucianism was an empty humanism. Taoism was a form of philosophical gibberish that had degenerated into superstitious nonsense. Buddhism was an imported, effete from of paganism. Even worse, in the missionaries' view, was the Chinese combination of all three of those religions into one amalgam that they called the San Jyau, the Three Teachings.

This, then, was the missionaries' China, a beautiful land of stinking, crowded cities, populated by learned but corrupt and degenerate heathens.

But what of the missionaries' audience? How did the messages from the missionaries and the board affect the American public's regard for China? I have described the two elements in two interrelated communications systems. Now is the time to deal with the receiver of those communications and to consider their effect.

The audience itself was a segment of the American public composed of church leaders and church members. In Elmo Roper's scheme of concentric circles of influence, the church leaders would be categorized as the "lesser disseminators" while their congregations would be termed "participating citizens." Beyond them lay the outermost circle of the "politically inert."[63] The American public had been attuned to religious currents and was constantly made aware of those waves of religiosity associated with the Second Great Awakening. Ray Allen Billington has shown how this public was reached during the decades of the Protestant Crusade.[64]

The missionary effort was aided by audiences already conditioned to this crusade and its accompanying anti-Catholic and antiforeign demonstrations. But to say that the shift in American attitudes toward China—from comparative ignorance colored by romance to shocked and disparaging pity—was simply a side effect of the Protestant Crusade does not fully explain the reasons and the manner of the change.

The explanation I propose is that the missionaries sent the board volumes of material containing multiple images of China. The board reviewed that material and extrapolated more defined images of China. They presented this version to the church leaders, the "lesser disseminators" and the "participation citizens" in the pages of the Missionary Herald. In so doing, they created an interest in missions and in China. They also convinced those readers who could be convinced by the opinions of distinguished clergy that China was a rather terrible place populated by an intelligent but morally corrupt heathen citizenry. When the missionaries came home, they spoke to the congregations who had read about China. They talked about the land, the government, the people. They discussed language, culture, land, religion. They tried to be sympathetic, and later protested that they were trying to correct erroneous impressions.[65] They also naturally tried to make a case for expansion of the mission effort. Parker talked at length about medical missions, while Williams discussed the work of the mission press in what must have been exhausting detail. The sermons they preached and the lectures they gave reinforced that view conveyed in the Missionary Herald and the Chinese Repository.

Joseph T. Klapper's discussion of the use of different media was directed toward modern situations but his conclusions are applicable here. He concluded that the use of one type of media, reinforced by face-to-face contact, proved to have a decided effect upon the target audience.[66] I hypothesize, then, that the missionary image thus affected a change in American attitudes; but only when the printed word was reinforced by the spoken word, presented in the lectures and sermons of missionaries home on leave. There are two types of evidence that can be brought to bear in support of this thesis. One is literary evidence: letters and journals that describe audience response or reaction. The letter from citizens wrote: "Believing that the lectures would be both interesting and profitable to our fellow citizens, we would respectfully request that you deliver the same course in Rochester."[67] There was a similar letter from Caleb Cushing, the American diplomat who negotiated the Treaty of Wanghsia. Cushing commended Williams on his decision to engage in a lecture tour and assured him of the value of the effort.[68] Cushing and the good citizens of Rochester were "lesser disseminators." They recognized the privilege of being able to hear informative lectures delivered by an expert, and felt that public opinion could thus be influenced. A second type of evidence of this image manipulating is the contribution list included in each issue of the *Missionary Herald.* A preliminary study of those contribution lists for the period 1830 to 1860 indicates that in those months when the missionaries were in America, contributions from the citizens visited did increase.[69] Letters from the missionaries to the board during this period and from missionaries to friends and audiences at home support this financial evidence.[70] Edward V. Gulick's analysis of Parker's lectures focused upon missions but supports my argument about the impact of the speeches. He stated: "Their [the public's] reception of his message also says a good deal about them. Whereas the very idea of missions had been repugnant to Americans of an earlier generation, missions were now widely acceptable. . . ."[71] One might add that the idea of missions was acceptable because the American public was now familiar with mission work on publications like the *Herald,* and this familiarity intensified when the missionaries came home to address their public.

The change in American attitudes toward China occurred as Americans grasped the missionary image of China as it was conveyed in Board and mission publications, restated and amplified by returning missionaries. South China missionaries presented the public with written and spoken images that played an undeniable part in shaping the attitudes of that audience.

Notes

1. Raymond Dawson, *The Chinese Chameleon* (London: Oxford University Press, 1967).

2. Stuart Creighton Miller, *The Unwelcome Immigrant* (Berkeley: University of California Press, 1969).

3. Studies of communications networks are included in the following: Reed H. Blake and Edwin O. Haroldsen, *A Taxonomy of Concepts in Communication* (New York: Hastings House, 1975); F. Gerald Kline and Phillip J. Tichenor, eds., *Current Perspectives in Mass Communication* (Beverly Hills, Calif.: Sage Publications, 1972); Wilbur Schram and Donald F. Roberts, ed., *The Process and Effects of Mass Communication* (Urbana: University of Illinois Press, 1972); Charles S. Steinberg, ed., *Mass Media and Communication* (New York: Hastings House, 1972); Allan P. Pred, *Urban Growth and the Circulation of Information*

(Cambridge: Harvard University Press, 1973). Studies of the effects of communication include the following: Carl I. Hoveland, Irving Janis, and Harold H. Kelley, *Communication and Persuasion* (New Haven: Yale University Press, 1953); Elihu Katz and Paul Lazarfeld, *Personal Influence* (Glencoe, Ill.: Free Press of Glencoe, Inc., 1955); Joseph T. Klapper, *The Effects of Mass Communication* (Glencoe, Ill.: Free Press of Glencoe, Inc., 1960).

4. This first phase of the Board's mission is covered in the following: Peter Ward Fay, *The Opium War* (Chapel Hill: University of North Carolina Press, 1975); Paul A. Cohen, "Christian Missions and Their Impact," in John K. Fairbank, ed., *The Cambridge History of China, vol. 10, Late Ch'ing, 1800–1911 Part 1* (London: Cambridge University Press, 1978), 543–90; Kenneth Scott Latourette, *A History of Christian Missions in China* (London: Society for Promoting Christian Knowledge, 1929), 209–81. It is examined in some detail in Murray A. Rubinstein, "Zion's Corner" (Ph.D. diss. New York University, 1976).

5. Frederick Wells Williams, *The Life and Letters of Samuel Wells Williams, Ll.D.* (New York: G. P. Putnam's Sons, 1889), 118.

6. Bridgman to Anderson, 5 April 1841 in A.B.C. 16.3.8, vol. 1a. The South China Mission correspondence is contained in the collection of materials on the American Board of Commission for Foreign Missions that is housed at the Houghton Library, Harvard University in Cambridge, Massachusetts (hereafter abbreviated as A.B.C.). The series used in the preparation of this essay were A.B.C. 16.3.8, A.B.C. 16.3.11, and A.B.C. 2.01, vol. 1–20.

7. "Journal of the South China Mission," in A.B.C. 16.3.11; Clifton Jackson Phillips, *Protestant America and the Pagan World* (Cambridge: Harvard University Press, 1969), 195–98.

8. The Sino-Western confrontation is examined in Frederick Wakeman, Jr., *Strangers at the Gate* (Berkeley: University of California Press, 1966). The classic work study of the treaty-ports is John King Fairbank, *Trade and Diplomacy on the China Coast* (Cambridge: Harvard University Press, 1953). The American role in diplomacy is examined in Te-kong Tong, *United States Diplomacy in China, 1844–60* (Seattle: University of Washington Press, 1964).

9. "Journal of the South China Mission," A.B.C. 16.3.11. The Journal is a detailed record of events prepared by the members of the South China Mission. It is an excellent brief introduction to the mission's history.

10. The American Board lobbied for the rights of Christians, and the missionaries took an active role in diplomatic affairs. See Frederick Wells Williams, *Life and Letters,* chaps. 8–10, and Tong, *United States Diplomacy,* chaps. 13–16.

11. Prudential Committee to Elijah Coleman Bridgman, "Letter of Instructions," A.B.C. 2.01.

12. Two such letters are Bridgman to Evarts, 21 Oct. 1830, A.B.C. 16.3.8, vol. 1., and Bridgman to Evarts, 13 Nov. 1830, A.B.C. 16.3.8, vol. 1.

13. Bridgman, "Journal," 25 Feb 1831, A.B.C. 16.3.8.

14. These letters are in A.B.C. 16.3.8, vol. 1, 1a, 2. Some examples are: Bridgman to Anderson, 17 Jan. 1832, A.B.C. 16.3.8, vol. 1.; Williams to Anderson, 27 Feb. 1834, A.B.C. 16.3.8, vol. 1.; Parker to Anderson, 21 June 1836, A.B.C. 16.3.8, vol. 1.; Bridgman to Anderson, 19 Feb. 1846, A.B.C. 16.3.8, vol. 2.; Boney to Anderson, 20 May 1858, A.B.C. 16.3.8, vol. 2.

15. Two examples are Stevens to Anderson, Nov. 1835, A.B.C. 16.3.8, vol. 1., and Williams to Anderson, 29 Nov. 1836, A.B.C. 16.3.8, vol. 1.

16. South China Mission (Bridgman) to Anderson, 7 April 1836, A.B.C. 16.3.8, vol. 1, was the first of these reports. Some other examples are: South China

Mission to Anderson 24 April 1837, A.B.C. 16.3.8, vol. 1.; South China Mission to Anderson, March 1838, A.B.C. 16.3.11.

17. The first of this type of annual report was Parker to Anderson, 1 Sept. 1846, A.B.C. 16.3.8, vol. 2.

18. The initial end of season annual report was Williams to Anderson, 1 June 1855, A.B.C. 16.3.8, vol. 2.

19. An example is "Annual Report, 1849," South China Mission to Anderson, Dec. 1, 1849, A.B.C. 16.3.8, vol. 2.

20. Elijah Coleman Bridgman, "Journal," A.B.C. 16.3.8, vol. 1.

21. David Abeel, "Journal for 1830–1831," A.B.C. 16.3.8, vol. 1.

22. Edwin Stevens, "Journal of Expeditions, 1835, 1836," A.B.C. 16.3.8, vol. 1., and Samuel Wells Williams, "Journal of Expedition to Japan," 1837, A.B.C. 16.3.8, vol. 1.

23. Excerpts of Parkers' journals were used by George B. Stevens in his biography of the missionary physician. See George B. Stevens, *The Life, Letters, and Journals of the Rev. and Hon. Peter Parker* (Boston: Congregational and Sunday School Publishing Association, 1896). The modern study of Parker's career is Edward V. Gulick, *Peter Parker and the Opening of China* (Cambridge: Harvard University Press, 1973).

24. South China Mission, "Journal," A.B.C. 16.3.11.

25. These titles are listed in Alexander Wylie, *Memorials of Protestant Missions to the Chinese* (Shanghai: Presbyterian Mission Press, 1867), 71, 78–79.

26. *The Chinese Repository,* 20 vol. (Canton, 1832–51).

27. *The Chinese Repository,* vol. 1 (1832–1833), vol. 2. (1833–34).

28. *The Chinese Repository,* vol. 20 list of articles, xxv–xxxviii.

29. *The Chinese Repository,* vol. 20 list of articles, ix–xix.

30. *The Chinese Repository,* vol. 20 list of articles, xxii–xxv.

31. *The Chinese Repository,* vol. 20 list of articles, xliii–liii.

32. David Abeel, *Journal of a Residence in China and the Neighboring Countries from 1829–1833* (New York: J. Abeel Williamson, 1836).

33. Samuel Wells Williams, *The Middle Kingdom* (New York: Charles Scribners Sons, 1848).

34. Eliza J. Bridgman, *The Life and Labors of Elizah Coleman Bridgman* (New York: A.D.F. Randolph, 1864); Stevens, *Life/Parker.*

35. D. W. C. Olyphant was a New York merchant who ran a trading concern in Canton. He was one of a small group who requested that the American Board send missionaries to China. He provided Abeel and Bridgman with passage to Canton and housed them. Over the years he helped the South China Mission in other ways such as underwriting the cost of *The Chinese Repository.*

36. The dialogue between the South China Mission and the American Board is examined in Rubinstein, "Zion's Corner," chap. 9.

37. George A. Donahue, Phillip J. Tichenor, Clarice N. Olien, "Gatekeeping: Mass Media Systems and Information Control" in Kline and Tichenor, eds., *Current Perspectives,* 41–69.

38. James A. Field Jr., *America and the Mediterranean World* (Princeton: Princeton University Press, 1969), 84–86.

39. Board activities in this period are examined in Phillips, *Protestant America,* chaps. 2–4.

40. Perry Miller, *The Life of the Mind in America* (New York: Harcourt, Brace, and World, 1965), chap. 2.

41. Phillips, *Protestant America,* chap. 6.

42. Rufus Anderson, *Memorial Volume of the First Fifty Years of the American Board of Commissioners for Foreign Missions* (Boston, 1861), 178–84.

43. These figures are an average of the yearly statistics published in *The Missionary Herald* in the years from 1830 to 1860.

44. The best introduction to the New England School is in Sydney E. Ahlstrom, *A Religious History of the American People* (New Haven: Yale University Press, 1972), chap. 25.

45. Donahue, Tichenor, and Olien, "Gatekeeping," in Kline and Tichenor, eds., *Current Perspectives,* 41–69; Blake and Haroldsen, *Taxonomy,* 109–10.

46. *The Missionary Herald* 29 (1833): 72–74, 144–45.

47. *The Missionary Herald* 30 (1834): 189–91, 234–37.

48. Rubinstein, "Zion's Corner," chaps. 9, 10.

49. South China Mission, "Semi-annual Report," *The Missionary Herald* 34 (1838): 169–71.

50. South China Mission, "Semi-annual Report," *The Missionary Herald* 36 (1840): 81–82.

51. For example; Bridgman, "Letter," *The Missionary Herald* 37 (1843): 471–73; Bridgman, "Letter," *The Missionary Herald* 39 (1843): 119–20; Pohlman, "Letter," *The Missionary Herald* 41 (1845): 52–53.

52. Williams, "South China Mission Report," *The Missionary Herald* 41 (1845): 155–57. Williams, "South China Mission Report," *The Missionary Herald* 53 (1857).

53. The averages for page-per-volume were arrived at after page counts and tabulations of *The Missionary Herald* for the years 1830 to 1860.

54. This is the format of a typical issue of *The Missionary Herald*. Each yearly volume contained two special issues. In the January issue a review of the work done at each mission station was published. In November was published an account of the Board's annual meeting.

55. Gulick, *Peter Parker,* 96.

56. Ibid., 97–101.

57. Samuel Wells Williams to William Frederick Williams, 20 March 1845, folder 1845, box 1, "Williams Family Papers," Manuscript Division, Sterling Library, Yale University, New Haven. Samuel Wells Williams to Elijah Coleman Bridgman, March 12, 1845, folder 1845, "Williams Family Papers."

58. Samuel Wells Williams, "Account Book for Expenses," 1844–48, box 22, "Williams Family Papers."

59. Williams, *Life and Letters,* 146–47.

60. Citizens of Rochester, New York, to Samuel Wells Williams, March 1846, folder 1846, box 1, "Williams Family Papers."

61. Williams, *Life and Letters,* 155–60. The details concerning the writing and publication of *The Middle Kingdom* are to be found in folder 1847, box 1, and folder 1848, box 1, "Williams Family Papers."

62. William J. Brinker, "Commerice, Culture and Horticulture: The Beginnings of Sino-American Relations," in Thomas Etzold, ed., *Aspects of Sino-American Relations Since 1784* (New York: Franklin Watts, 1978), 13–14.

63. Elmo Roper, "Forward," in Elihu Katz and Paul F. Lazarfeld, *Personal Influence* (Glencoe, Ill.: Free Press of Glencoe, 1955), xvii–xix.

64. Ray Allen Billington, *The Protestant Crusade* (New York: Macmillan Company, 1938).

65. Samuel Wells Williams, "Introduction," *The Middle Kingdom* (New York: Charles Scribner's Sons, 1848).

66. Klapper, *Effects of Communication,* 106–12.

67. Citizens of Rochester, New York, to Samuel Wells Williams, March 1846, folder 1846, box 1, "Williams Family Papers,"

68. Caleb Cushing to Samuel Wells Williams, 26 Jan. 1847, folder 1847, box 1, "Williams Family Papers."

69. "List of Contributors," *The Missionary Herald* 25–56 (1830–1860).

70. For example: Williams to Mrs. Harriet Wood, 10 Aug. 1844, folder 1844, box 1, "Williams Family Papers."

71. Gulick, *Peter Parker,* 101–2.

Part II
The Image Grows

American Diplomacy in China, 1843–1857: The Evolution of a Policy

RAYMOND F. WYLIE

In recent years scholarly attention has focused on Sino-American relations in the postwar period and especially on the process of normalization of ties since 1979. This is not surprising, since to many it seemed that the United States and China were in effect "getting to know" each other after a lengthy period of Cold War hostility. In this context, the diplomatic record of the mid-nineteenth century is both interesting and relevant to the present age. It was during the period from 1843 to 1857 that the United States and China first entered into official diplomatic relations with each other. This was a period of experimentation for both countries, but by 1857 American policy toward China had been set for many years to come. The earlier period, then, provides a valuable historical perspective on Sino-American rapprochement in the 1970s and 1980s.

Most historians concerned with this subject accept the years 1844–1860 as the correct periodization, the logic being that these two years (1844 and 1860) represent the operative dates of the Treaty of Wanghsia and the Treaty of Tientsin (signed in 1858) respectively.[1] These two years are certainly of critical importance in the history of Sino-American relations, but they do not appear to delineate a definite period in the evolution of United States policy toward China. The decision was taken by Washington in 1843 to establish formal diplomatic relations with China. This was the important date, and the treaty that followed in 1844 was merely the result of that decision. Similarly, the second treaty, of 1858 (1860), was the result of an important decision that had been taken by Washington in 1857. So, from the point of view of the evolution of U.S. policy toward China, and this is the point of view taken here, 1843 and 1857 are the years that delineate one period from another. Prior to 1843, the United States really did not have a policy toward China; from 1843 to 1857, it worked to establish one; and the policy decided upon in the latter year served as a guide for ensuing decades.

Ignoring minor themes, there appear to be three main issues that faced American statesmen concerning relations with China during the period under discussion. One was policy making. What policy should the United States adopt toward China, and how should this policy be adapted to meet the requirements of a rapidly changing situation? Another concerned U.S. relations with the European powers active in Asia, especially Great Britain. Should the United States follow Britain's lead, cooperate with her, maintain a position of neutrality, or even go so far as to oppose her in the Far East? The final problem involved the actual implementation of American policy toward both China and the European powers. Were the State Department, the diplomatic and consular services, and the navy adequate to the new responsibilities involved in maintaining official relations with the world's largest empire? These were the three main problem areas successive U.S. administrations had to deal with during this early period in Sino-American relations. In this chapter, I wish to examine how the United States dealt with these crucial issues from 1843 to 1857, years which in retrospect stand out as the formative period in the evolution of United States policy toward China.

U.S. Policy Making

American-Chinese relations originated in commercial intercourse between the two nations and remained at that level for many years. After the Revolution of 1776, Americans were eager to seek new markets abroad, and trade with China appeared to hold much promise for the future. As members of the British empire, the American colonies had been excluded from Asian trade by the monopoly of the British East India Company, but after independence they were free to seek trade wherever they wished. And so in 1784 Robert Morris and others financed the voyage of the *Empress of China* from New York to the Chinese port of Canton. For the next half century the China trade fluctuated, but in general it remained profitable enough to permit its continuation. These early American merchants had only a commercial interest in China. Provided the trade was left undisturbed, they were reluctant to become involved in political developments along the China coast.

While the first American merchants had set out for China in 1784, it was not until 1830 that they were joined by their missionary brethren, who came to preach the gospel and, at the same time, propagate Western culture. The missionaries soon grew restive under the restrictions placed on their work by the Chinese authorities, and they tended to support any measures that would lead to greater freedom of action. They sincerely believed that China, faced with the challenge of the Western Christian nations, must either "bend or break." Nor did they shink from the possible use of force to achieve their aims. As David Abeel, a leading American missionary of the period, put it, "God has often made use of the strong arm of civil power to prepare the way for his own kingdom."[2] Given this frame of mind, the missionaries tended to support Britain's policy of armed coercion against China to "open" the empire to the Western powers. The missionaries' aggressive attitude was given greater significance by the fact that many of them came to occupy places of importance in U.S. diplomatic and consular services in China. Dr. Peter Parker, the outstanding missionary in the diplomatic service during this period, actually served a term as commissioner.

In spite of this pioneering effort on the part of merchants and missionaries, the U.S. government did not show a great deal of interest in China. Before 1815, American merchants at Canton had petitioned Congress requesting the appointment of a salaried consul and other diplomatic personnel, but the request had been ignored. In spite of this general lack of interest, in 1822 President James Monroe gave a letter addressed to the emperor of China to an American merchant, and John Quincy Adams, as secretary of state, addressed a letter to the governor-general of Kwangtung province. It is unknown, however, whether either letter was accepted by the Chinese authorities.[3] President Andrew Jackson was personally interested in the China trade, which he mentioned in his annual message of December 1831. In 1832, moreover, the U.S. government authorized the Edmund Roberts expedition to the Far East for the purpose of securing treaties with several Asian powers and protecting the interests of American merchants in that area. The Roberts expedition was a sign of the slowly awakening interest of the U.S. government in Asian affairs, but this interest was not to find concrete expression until the Opium War of 1839–42.

"Meanwhile," writes Tyler Dennett, "American policy in the Far East merely meant the policy of the Americans at Canton . . . [who] had but one desire—to keep the trade open to Americans on terms as favorable as, or more favorable than, those enjoyed by their competitiors who were chiefly British."[4] (Thus it was that the United States' later "Open Door" policy toward China (1899–1900) originated in the attitude of the early American merchants engaged in the China trade.) However, these practical men of commerce were faced with the immediate problem of how to keep the "door" open in the mid-nineteenth century, thus ensuring their participation in the trade. There were three possible alternatives: to rely on the United States to keep the door open, to cooperate with Britain for the same purpose, or to look to China itself to maintain equality of trade for all foreign nations. The merchants put little faith in the first alternative because their own government did not exhibit much interest in the China trade, and in any case the nearest U.S. naval base was on the Atlantic coast, the other side of the world. Cooperation with England was equally out of the question for two reasons. In the first place, the British were the Americans' chief competitors in the trade, so they could hardly be expected to defend the Americans' position. Second, Anglo-American relations had been unstable since the Revolution of 1776 and were further exacerbated during the War of 1812. Minor clashes between British and American ships in the China seas were frequent in the decades prior to 1840. During these disputes, lack of adequate naval protection forced many American captains and merchants to appeal to the Chinese authorities to protect their rights within Chinese territory and coastal waters. On 14 October 1805, for example, American merchant-consul Edward Carrington wrote to Captain Ratsey of H.M. Brig *Harrier:* "Should the demand which I have made to you not be complied with, I shall make a formal representation and appeal to the Chinese Government of this unprecedented and outrageous violence against the rights of nations."[5]

This practice of appealing to the Chinese authorities for protection from the British led eventually to the policy of encouraging a strong and unified China as the best guarantee that the "open door" would be maintained. Allied with this was a strong desire on the part of the Americans to disassociate themselves in the minds of the Chinese from the more aggressive behavior of the British. Although this positive attitude toward Chinese authority declined somewhat after 1820, it was still noticeable at the time of the Opium War. In the March 1843 issue of *Hunt's Merchants' Magazine*, a writer (referring to the opium trade) maintained that "China has a perfect right to regulate the character of her imports."[6] And one of the leading China merchants described

Britain's action against China as "one of the most unjust wars ever waged by one nation against another."[7] When Imperial Commissioner Ch'i-ying indicated to Commodore Lawrence Kearny in 1842 that American merchants were to be given the same trading privileges as the British, most of the merchants at Canton felt their policy of respecting the authority of the Chinese government had been proven sound.

Due to the lack of government interest in China and the late arrival of the missionaries on the scene, the American merchants at Canton played the major role in the early stage of Sino-American relations. These merchants were encouraged by circumstances to formulate a fairly well-defined policy toward China: maintenance of an "open door" with respect to trade, promotion of a unified and strong China as the surest means of keeping the door open, and disassociation from Great Britain. Merchants were appointed to serve as U.S. consuls at Canton, their opinions were sought on all aspects of the Far Eastern scene, and they were the only Americans to maintain fairly close and constant contact with the distant Chinese empire. It was not surprising, then, that the China policy of the American traders at Canton was in time to become the China policy of the U.S. government itself.[8]

The transformation of the American merchants' policy toward China into official government policy was the direct result of the Opium War of 1839–42. By the end of the 1830s American interest in China had broadened considerably—trade was progressing steadily, the growth of the cotton industry stimulated dreams of a huge Chinese market, and returning missionaries had been actively disseminating knowledge about China and the Chinese. Presidents Martin Van Buren, William Harrison, and John Tyler all watched the Opium War with interest, and Peter Parker (on home leave during 1840–42) had many interviews with them. At this time, the general opinion in the United States was that the Anglo-Chinese war was "another item in the sad catalogue of [British] outrages on humanity."[9] In a lecture to the Massachusetts Historical Society in December 1841, John Quincy Adams ventured to justify the British attack on China, but he was decidedly in the minority.[10]

With war in the offing, a group of agitated American merchants at Canton had petitioned Congress on 25 May 1839 with a three-point request: limited cooperation with Britain and other nations to force the Chinese to sign a treaty, the appointment of an official agent to negotiate a commercial treaty with China, and the dispatch of a naval force for the protection of American lives and property.

But in early 1840 a group a China merchants in Boston and Salem, far removed from the scene of action and correspondingly cooler headed, delivered a counter petition to Congress warning against any hasty action that might antagonize the Chinese and damage the trade. They suggested that only a naval force be sent, without power to interfere in the war or to negotiate with the Chinese. Congress agreed and sent Commodore Lawrence Kearny to China, and no further action was taken.[11]

On 30 December 1842, after the news of the signing of the Anglo-Chinese Treaty of Nanking had been received, President John Tyler requested Congress to approve the dispatch of a resident commissioner to China to attend to both commercial and diplomatic affairs. After a lively debate, Congress gave its approval on 3 March 1843, calling for the appointment of "a citizen of much intelligence and weight of character" whose compensation would correspond to "the magnitude and importance of the mission."[12] The most articulate opposition to sending a mission to China was expressed by Senator Thomas H. Benton, who remarked in the House on 8 March 1843 that China was "not within the system, or circle, of American policy" and that therefore "we have no need of a minister to watch and observe her conduct."[13]

President Tyler's request to Congress for a mission to China is a milestone in the development of Sino-American relations. It should be duly noted, however, that the decision to send a mission to China was the direct result of the Opium War and the Treaty of Nanking, and not of internal American developments. As Tong Te-kong points out, neither major political party favored any particular policy toward China, and U.S. diplomacy in China was virtually independent of domestic politics.[14] Had there been no Anglo-Chinese war, the American merchants engaged in the China trade would probably have been content to continue the trade on a nontreaty basis. But fearing that Britain was going to acquire a privileged trading position as a result of the war, the American merchants put pressure on their government to negotiate a treaty with China assuring them of the same trading rights as were accorded the British. Washington's action on this matter was also encouraged by Peter Parker, who felt that the missionary effort in China would fare better under the aegis of a formal treaty. And so the Cushing mission was dispatched to inaugurate official diplomatic relations between these two Pacific nations.

Establishing diplomatic relations with China was one thing; maintaining them on a satisfactory basis in the ensuing years was quite another. In these early years of the republic the machinery of diplomacy was still relatively primitive and not adequate to its responsibilities. This was certainly true with respect to the management of Sino-American relations. During the period 1843–57, none of the U.S. presidents (with the exception of James Buchanan) was well informed about or interested in China. With this presidential lack of interest, more power was vested in the secretaries of state, but here the situation was scarcely better. This period was one of tremendous instability in the State Department, during which the secretaryship changed hands no less than eight times, or thirteen times if the ad interim appointments are included.[15] And most of the individual secretaries were too preoccupied with domestic politics, European and South American diplomacy, and personal presidential ambitions to devote much time to developments in China.

Nor was the Department of State itself adequate to the tasks it was called upon to perform. During this period the State Department contained seven bureaus, and Chinese affairs were placed under the charge of the second of the three clerks assigned to the diplomatic bureau. But the department was very small in relation to its responsibilities; in 1849 Secretary John M. Clayton reported that his department was staffed by twenty-four clerks, one regular and two assistant messengers, two extra clerks, seven packers, and a laborer. In August 1856 the department was reorganized to include a total of fifty-seven persons, but during the period under consideration it remained "smaller than a first-class United States consulate at the present time [1964]."[16]

Considering the inadequacy of the State Department and the apathy of the secretaries of state, it is not surprising that much power devolved on the individual commissioners who went to China. In fact, they were invested with a great deal of "discretionary power," which ambassadors to European capitals would seldom have enjoyed. For instance, Secretary William L. Marcy wrote to Commissioner Humphrey Marshall on 7 June 1853: "As it is impossible to anticipate here what will be the condition of things there, no specific instructions in regard to your official conduct can be given. Your own judgment must be your guide as to the best means to accomplish the desired object."[17] This vesting of discretionary power in the hands of individual commissioners was no doubt also due to the slowness of communications between the United States and China at this time, but it hardly made for effective diplomacy. This is even more true when we consider the fact that all but one of the commissioners had no previous experience in diplomacy, that none had much previous knowledge of China, and that they rarely stayed in China for more than a year.

The insufficiency of U.S. diplomatic machinery with regard to China is equally apparent in the organization of the consular service. Until 1854, when regular salaried consuls began to be substituted, all American consuls in China were merchant-consuls; that is to say, merchants first and consuls second. The appointment of a merchant-consul was considered to be a local responsibility and the State Department was often ignorant of even the names of its official representatives. The inadequacy of the consular service is strikingly illustrated in the observation of Charles William Bradley upon his arrival at Amoy as United States consul in 1849. Bradley noted that the British consulate there consisted of "a Consul, Vice Consul, First Assistant, Second Assistant, Interpreter, Assistant Interpreter, Medical Attendant, Chinese Writer, Linguist, and many minor servants . . . and of a vessel of war from that government being constantly stationed in the harbour. . . ." Embarrassed by his own modest establishment (i.e., himself), Bradley consoled himself by appointing his son, Charles W. Bradley, Jr., to the position of vice consul.[18]

Confusion over jurisdiction between different branches of the government also hindered the development of effective diplomacy in China. For instance, the commissioner, the secretary of the legation and the different consuls all worked and reported independently to the State Department, and this led to numerous clashes between the different officials.[19] But the most important area of friction concerned the relationship between the commissioners to China and the commodores of the U.S. naval squadron in the China seas. United States naval vessels had been active in Asian waters since the early years of the nineteenth century; in the absence of any official diplomatic officers, however, they had been under the direct control of the Department of the Navy. But lack of coordination between the State Department and the Navy Department often hindered the effective implementation of policy.

The Beginnings of Diplomacy

Before discussing the record of U.S. diplomacy in China during the years 1843–57, some attempt should be made to bring into focus the Americans' image of themselves and their attitudes toward their two chief "antagonists," China and Great Britain. American self-confidence had been building for years, but it was in the 1840s that this confidence found expression in the concept of "Manifest Destiny." In their drive to the Pacific, Americans wanted to accomplish more than the mere occupation of territory; they wanted to introduce civilization to barbarous lands. Caleb Cushing, later the first U.S. commissioner to China, shared this desire. In a speech to the House of Representatives in 1838, he expressed the hope that when the settlers should reach the Pacific, they would "carry along with them the laws, education, and social improvements, which belong to the older states . . . worthily fulfilling the great destiny reserved for this exemplar American Republic."[20]

Given this self-image, it was perhaps inevitable that more imaginative Americans would not regard the Pacific Ocean as putting a natural limit to the "great destiny" of the republic. On the contrary, in 1850 William H. Seward described the Pacific as a beacon, inviting the United States "to extend the sway of peace, of arts, and of freedom, over nations beyond the seas, still slumbering under the mingled reign of barbarian superstition and unalleviated despotism."[21] This civilizing mission was happily combined with a mission more prosaic but equally close to the hearts of many Americans—unfettered trade. And so it was that an expanding and evangelical America came face to face with China, the oldest existing empire in the world. Americans had a mission, both Christian and commercial, and they were not going to be deterred by Chinese lack of interest and hostility. As an officer of one of the opium clippers remarked, "We were fully prepared for a brush with the rascally Chinese and determined not be put out of our course by one or two mandarin boats."[22]

Toward the British the Americans had an ambivalent attitude; they recognized England as the seat of Anglo-Saxon civilization, but at the same time they were suspicious of her intentions and resentful of what they considered her Machiavellian methods. But in spite of their reluctance to resort to the use of force to further their interests in China, most Americans were not prepared to be excluded from the privileges that Britain might acquire at the cannon's mouth.[23] The British Foreign Office was well aware of this and in fact pursued a deliberate policy of trying to unite all of the Western powers dealing with China into a "common front" vis-à-vis the Chinese. As an inducement, the British offered equal participation in whatever privileges their action might secure; that is to say, the British were quite willing to maintain the "open door" in China.[24] This British strategem proved effective and "it became ingloriously, yet very profitably, the role of the United States pacifically to follow England to China in the wake of war, and to profit greatly by the victories of British arms."[25]

On 8 May 1843 Caleb Cushing was appointed United States commissioner to China and given the full powers of envoy extraordinary and minister plenipotentiary. His mission had one main purpose, as Secretary of State Daniel Webster pointed out in his instructions to Cushing: to make a treaty "such as has been concluded between England and China." The fundamental principle underlying the proposed treaty was that American interests would be best protected by recognizing China as a sovereign power and concluding a formal treaty based on the equality of the two nations. In addition, Webster told Cushing to establish clearly the difference between Great Britain and the United States and to assure the Chinese that the United States, unlike Britain, had no colonial ambitions in Asia. Thus Webster spelled out the three key concepts in early U.S. policy toward China: desire for equality of trade, respect for Chinese sovereignty, and disassociation from Great Britain.[26]

By the time Cushing arrived in China in 1844, however, the primary aim of his mission had already been accomplished. As part of his general policy of appeasement following the Opium War, Imperial Commissioner Ch'i-ying had already secured approval from the emperor to grant the Americans the same trading privileges as had been accorded the British. There has been some controversy as to whether Commodore Lawrence Kearny actually extracted the "most-favored-nation" promise from Ch'i-ying as early as 1842, but there seems little doubt that the policy was formulated independently by the Chinese themselves.[27] In any event, the Chinese believed that the granting of equal trading privileges without discrimination in favor of any one nation might serve to restrain other nations from resorting to force for the obtaining of concessions.[28]

As to U.S. recognition of Chinese sovereignty, Cushing's attitude was rather ambivalent. On the one hand, he suspected Ch'i-ying of regarding China as superior to the United States and expressed the hope that the Chinese official would "see the evident propriety of adhering to the form of national equality."[29] On the question of China's jurisdiction over Americans who committed crimes in China, on the other hand, Cushing was careful to get the Chinese to grant the privilege of extraterritoriality. That is, American citizens who committed crimes in China were to be tried and punished by their own courts and own laws, and not those of China. This was a rather serious infraction of China's sovereignty, but Cushing was quite firm on the issue.[30]

After concluding the Treaty of Wanghsia on 3 July 1844, the first of the United States' "unequal treaties" with China, Cushing left for home. He reported to the secretary of state: "I recognize the debt of gratitude which the United States and all other nations owe to England, for what she has accomplished in China. From all this much benefit has accrued to the United States."[31] This is very interesting, for in a speech to the House of Representatives on 16 March 1840, Cushing (referring to the Opium War) had attacked "the base cupidity and violence which have characterized the operations of the British individually and collectively in the seas of China. . . ."[32] Cushing's change of heart represented an attitude that was to become prominent in later U.S. diplomacy in China: If British aggression endangered American interests in China, the United States was hostile to Britain; but if this same aggression were to promise an improvement in America's position in China, Britain could count on at least the United States' moral support.

This point of view was clearly expressed by Alexander Hill Everett, Cushing's successor as commissioner to China. Shortly after Everett's arrival in China in October 1846 (a protracted illness had delayed him), the British attacked Canton in an attempt to secure the right of entry within the city walls. The new U.S. commissioner feared that this attack on Canton was the first step in a long-range plan by British to dominate, and even possibly annex, all or part of the Chinese empire. As Everett had received few instructions from the State Department, he drafted a lengthy report to Secretary James Buchanan outlining his ideas on a proper policy toward China. British domination of China, he argued, would upset the Western balance of power and "seriously endanger the independence of even the most powerful [of the Western states], including the United States." Therefore, Everett concluded, Russia, France, and the United States all had a direct interest in "preventing the Chinese empire from being swallowed up in that of Great Britain, or even from coming more immediately under her influence."[33]

This being the case, these three nations should come to an agreement as to the nature of the present crisis in China, define their interests as clearly as possible, and then decide upon a common course of action. If adequate agreement were reached, the three powers could then undertake "a temperate, but, at the same time firm and serious appeal to Great Britain . . . and induce her to reconsider her projects against the independence of the Celestial Empire." There was even reason to believe, Everett wrote, that such action "might secure the independence of China for an indefinite future period. . . ."[34] Unfortunately, Everett died soon after drafting this proposed policy, and the issue was not given much attention in Washington. Besides, the Anglo-Chinese imbroglio quickly subsided, and American fears as to British intentions were put to rest for the time being.

After Everett's untimely death at Macao, the site of the United States legation, John W. Davis was appointed to replace him. Davis was given few specific instructions as to U.S. policy toward China and he himself did not feel inclined to formulate his own ideas to any great extent. Nevertheless, Davis's term in China is noteworthy for two reasons. Davis arrived in China in August 1848, just when an important change was taking place in Chinese policy toward the Western powers. After the Opium War, Ch'i-ying and Huang En-tung had carried out a policy of appeasement to curb Western belligerence. But after the British attack on Canton in 1847 indicated that London was not to be put off by appeasement, Peking swung in favor of a "hard line" of nonintercourse with the Western nations. Accordingly, Hsü Kuang-chin and Yeh Ming-ch'en were dispatched to Canton to handle China's relations with the various Western powers, and a policy of virtual nonintercourse was put into effect immediately. Indeed, Tong Tekong has written of Hsü and Yeh that "in reply to foreign requests, they simply wrote a few lines if they cared to reply at all."[35] As a result, successive United States commissioners had great difficulty in contacting high Chinese officials, and the desirability of adopting a "more aggressive" policy in dealing with the Chinese became increasingly apparent to the Western powers.

The second development of importance during Davis's term was the establishment of U.S. consular courts in accordance with the terms of the grant of extraterritoriality in the Treaty of Wanghsia. In 1845 President Tyler had asked Congress for appropriate legislation to set up consular courts, but the matter had quickly lapsed for "want of time and the pressure of other important business." Under prodding by Secretary of State Buchanan, however, Congress finally passed the necessary bill in 1848. This act gave the commissioner and consuls in China complete power to hear charges against and to try all citizens of the United States accused of crimes, both civil and criminal, committed in China. On 29 November 1849 Buchanan issued *The Regulations for the Consular Courts of the United States of America in China*. Due to Washington's neglect, however, years were to pass before these consular courts became effective in the performance of their duties.

After Davis's resignation in May 1850 the U.S. legation in China was left without a commissioner for nearly three years. Peter Parker was appointed chargé d'affaires, and he managed Sino-American relations until the arrival of Humphrey Marshall in March 1853. This three-year interval witnessed the outbreak of the Taiping Rebellion, a gigantic upheaval that was to last until 1864 and shake the Chinese empire to its very foundations. Like John Bowring, the British consul at Shanghai, Parker felt that the rebellion gave the Western nations a good opportunity to extend their treaty privileges. Consequently, Parker wrote to Secretary of State Daniel Webster on 22 April 1851, calling for the reversal of Everett's plan of joint action to restrain Britain. Parker proposed instead "an important modification of . . . [Everett's] dispatch," namely inviting "the Government of Great Britain . . . to cooperate *with* those of Russia, France, Spain and the United States, and not the latter to combine *against* her."[36] When he heard that Commodore Matthew Perry was to go to Japan, Parker immediately requested that the East Indies Squadron be used in China to enforce American claims. Webster took no action on either proposal, however, and there the matter rested until the arrival of Marshall.

Like his predecessors, Colonel Humphrey Marshall received no specific instructions as to U.S. policy toward China. While Marshall agreed with Parker that the time was opportune to extend Western privileges in China, he did not favor cooperation with the British in an aggressive move. Rather, he maintained that the Western powers should pursue a policy of "absolute neutrality in good faith" until such time as joint Western intervention should bring the civil war to an end. But the British had decided to fish in troubled waters, for they had come to the conclusion that more concessions could be gained from the rebels than from the imperial government.[37]

Marshall soon came to the same conclusion, but increasing British secret activity on the Yangtze River, combined with a decided British coolness toward Marshall himself, led the American commissioner to fear that Britain was seeking "an opportunity of assuming the *protectorate of the young* [Taiping] *power* . . ." and that such a move might lead ultimately to the dismemberment of the Chinese empire.[38] Disillusionment with the Taipings and suspicion of British (and French) intentions led Marshall to the conclusion that "the highest interests of the United States are involved in sustaining China . . . rather than to see China become the theatre of widespread anarchy, and ultimately the prey of European ambition."[39] Marshall did not completely write off the possibility of dealing with the Taipings, but he advised Secretary of State William L. Marcy that emphasis should be placed on maintaining and even extending relations with the imperial government.

As far as treaty revision was concerned, both the British and the Americans in China were agreed that definite action should be taken. But whereas Parker advocated close American cooperation with Britain in a move against China, Marshall felt that the United States should play an independent role in formulating a new treaty. Consequently, in 1853 the British Foreign Office went over Marshall's head by making direct overtures to Washington, where they succeeded in convincing the Department of State that Great Britain was interested in gaining greater access to China "not exclusively for its own subjects but for all nations." Consequently, on 7 June 1853 Marcy wrote Marshall that "the end proposed [by the British] commends itself to the approval of the President and he directs you to do what you can within your proper sphere of action, towards its accomplishment." However, Marcy cautioned Marshall not to join the British in any aggressive action, but to keep "only cordial relations and free conference with them" and to use his "own judgment to accomplish the desired object."[40] Although these instructions were the first explicit statement of U.S. policy toward China since the Treaty of Wanghsia, Marshall chose to use his "own judgment" by ignoring Marcy's directive altogether and going his own way.

Indeed, Marshall's relations with the British had deteriorated to such an extent by the fall of 1853 that any kind of cooperation on his part was virtually impossible. The American commissioner was suspicious of British intentions in China, disliked the means they employed to achieve their ends, and was quite outspoken in his opinions. But Marshall was running into difficulties from even his own colleagues in China. In the summer of 1853, for instance, Marshall had a serious quarrel with Peter Parker over the extent of the commissioner's authority over the secretary of the legation, namely, Parker himself.[41] Edward Cunningham, the vice consul at Shanghai, openly defied Marshall's instructions concerning the payment of customs duties to the Chinese and informed the American merchants that they were free to disregard the commissioner's orders. This was a serious case of insubordination on the part of Cunningham, but he was supported by the merchants, and so on 4 January 1854 Marshall was forced to concede the issue and accordingly reversed his position.

Marshall's authority as commissioner was being challenged from another branch of his own government—the navy. When Commodore Matthew Perry arrived to take command of the East Indies Squadron, he worked on the assumption that he could control the squadron regardless of the commissioner's wishes. After much acrimony over the use of the ships, Marshall wrote Marcy on 20 May 1853 that Perry's behavior "amounts to the assumption of a right to supervise the action of the Commissioner and to render the cooperation of the naval force of the country solely dependent upon the approval of the course of the Commissioner by the naval commander." Finally, on 30 October of the same year, Marshall wrote Marcy that "the government at home should establish some absolute regulation defining the 'prerogative' of the naval commanders . . . [for if] the view of the commodore obtains, there will be no sphere of action for civil officers, except as assistants to the *naval diplomatists*."[42] Marcy sympathized with Marshall's point of view, but it was not until the appointment of Robert M. McLane as Marshall's successor that the State Department took firm steps to resolve the issue.

Emergence of a Policy

Robert M. McLane, who arrived in China in March 1854, was the first United States commissioner to receive comparatively specific instructions concerning policy toward China. Secretary of State Marcy wrote McLane on 8 May 1854 that he was to attempt to negotiate a new treaty with the imperial government, recognize and deal with whatever government or governments in China were able to maintain stability, and cooperate with Great Britain "in a proper way to get liberal concessions of commerce. . . ."[43] Marcy also took steps to bring the various agencies of the government under the control of the commissioner. On 16 November 1853 he wrote McLane that all correspondence between the secretary of the legation (i.e., Parker) and the State Department should be transmitted through the commissioner. In the same letter, Marcy informed McLane that henceforth the consular service was to be subject to the supervision of the commissioner and that consuls were not to act independently of the commissioner's wishes.[44]

Perhaps the most important step Marcy took was to clear up

the question of jurisdiction over the naval squadron in the Far East. He obviously won the cooperation of the Department of the Navy, for on 28 October 1853 the secretary of the navy wrote Perry that "the President trusts it will not seriously incommode your operations in regard to Japan to co-operate with our Commissioner [to China]. . . . you will on receipt of this communication, immediately dispatch one of the war steamers of your squadron to Macao, to meet the Hon. R. M. McLane, our Commissioner to China, to be subject to his control until other orders reach you." Perry was furious, but accepted the new orders. "I have no alternative," he wrote the secretary of the navy on 14 January 1854, "though I cannot but express the deep disappointment and mortification to which I am subjected."[45]

With this new authority in the diplomatic, consular, and naval spheres, McLane was in a much better position than his predecessors to carry out a positive policy toward China. Shortly after his arrival in China, he came to the conclusion (as had Marshall) that nothing much could be expected of the Taiping rebels and U.S. interests would best be served by negotiating directly with the imperial government. The two outstanding issues were treaty revision—which included free navigation by Americans of the Yangtze River, free movement by Americans anywhere in the empire, and permanent residence at Peking for a U.S. ambassador—and the settlement of "local problems" at Shanghai, which included the issues of customs administration and municipal government.[46]

Strictly speaking, the issues at Shanghai were Anglo-Chinese problems, but Charles Bowring, the British consul at Shanghai, had persuaded McLane to support the British position. In the ensuing negotiations the Chinese authorities gave in to the British demands. As a result, the Chinese ultimately lost control of their own customs service and witnessed the spectacle of autonomous foreign enclaves growing up on the coast of China. These were serious infringements on China's sovereignty, but McLane supported the British in the hope of improving the United States' trading position in China if and when Britain should force further concessions from the Chinese.

Having settled the Shanghai problems to their satisfaction, McLane and Bowring entered into a "cordial co-operation" in order to press for treaty revision. The two envoys thereupon carried out a joint sea expedition to northern China, hoping to put pressure on the imperial court at Peking, but this "unprecedented peak" in Anglo-American cooperation produced no results. The

Chinese had no intention of revising the treaties along the lines the foreigners desired and so maintained their policy of virtual nonintercourse. Discouraged in his efforts at treaty revision, McLane wrote Marcy on 19 November 1854 that the United States had three possible alternatives: to maintain neutrality in the civil war and patiently await the return of normalcy, to enter upon a "new line of policy" by militarily enforcing existing rights and then extending them, or to respond to the imperial government's desire for assistance in suppressing the Taiping Rebellion. Should the Chinese persist in their opposition to treaty revision, McLane expressed his preference to adopt alternative number two and launch a program of "*quasi* hostility." "I would recommend in such a contingency, that the [major rivers of China] . . . be placed under blockade by the united forces of the three treaty powers— Great Britain, France, and the United States . . ." until the Chinese agree to an acceptable treaty revision.[47]

In actual fact, however, McLane's proposals were impractical for two reasons. As far as Britain and France were concerned, the Crimean War was raging and this effectively handicapped their efforts in the Fast East. As for the United States, squatter sovereignty, the Kansas-Nebraska issue, and the worsening problem of slavery absorbed the country's attention. The nation was bitterly divided and in no mood to consider a war in far-off China. In his reply to McLane's proposals (26 February 1855), Marcy noted that both he and President Franklin Pierce were sympathetic to McLane's general point of view as to treaty revision. "I think however," Marcy wrote, "I can anticipate that he [Pierce] will have serious objections to uniting with Great Britain and France in what you call the aggressive policy. . . . Such an association would not at all suit the present feelings of this country."[48] And so McLane's proposals for an "aggressive policy" were rejected by Washington. But McLane had no intention of carrying out this policy himself, for within a week after formulating it he decided to return to the United States.

The man chosen to replace McLane was none other than Peter Parker, the missionary doctor who had served as secretary of the legation ever since the days of Caleb Cushing. He had a wealth of experience of both China and the diplomatic service in China, for his combined service as chargé d'affaires and commissioner was longer than all the terms of the different commissioners put together. In spite of these obvious qualifications, his missionary zeal, aggressive attitude toward China, and ignorance of American-European diplomacy combined to render him ill-equipped to formulate a China policy appropriate to the interests of his country. Indeed, Parker's policy of virtual "adventurism" in dealing with China forced Washington, which had been rather passive in its concern with China up to that time, to take policy formulation out of the hands of the resident commissioners. In fact, Parker's term as commissioner marked the turning point in the formulation of U.S. policy toward China.[49]

Secretary of State Marcy gave Parker essentially the same instructions as McLane had received: to work for treaty revision and to cooperate with the other Western powers within certain limits. With the blessing of the State Department, Parker stopped off at London and Paris on his way to China to consult with foreign ministers Lord Clarendon and Count Walewski on the possibilities of joint action. Parker was favorably received at both capitals and continued on to China confident that a joint project was feasible. Indeed, during the interview at London, Clarendon had expressed the firm conviction that "not only do our consciences approve, but the whole world must commend our policy."[50] After arriving in China in late December, 1855, however, Parker found the British and French envoys surprisingly cool to his proposals for joint action against the Chinese. But Parker's plans received new encouragement from the British attack on Canton in October 1856, which resulted from a heated quarrel over the status of a Chinese merchant vessel flying the Union Jack. The so-called Arrow War that resulted led to the British occupation of Canton and a sudden revival in Bowring's interest in the possibilities of American and French cooperation against the Chinese. Accordingly, Parker wrote Marcy on 12 December 1856 proposing a definite course of action: a joint expedition by Britain, the United States, and France to north China to force the Chinese to concede to treaty revision. If the expedition were to prove unsuccessful, the British should occupy Chusan, the French Korea, and the Americans Formosa (Taiwan) until such time as favorable terms were had from the Chinese. In language that is particularly quaint, Parker proposed a "concurrent policy with England and France in China, not an alliance, but independent and distinct action, yet similar, harmonious, and simultaneous."[51]

Parker's proposal that the United Staes should occupy the island of Formosa, an integral part of China, was much more than a mere tactical move to bring about treaty revision. In 1854 Commodore Perry had sent a fact-finding expedition to Formosa and at the same time had spoken of the necessity of extending the "territorial jurisdiction" of the United States to Formosa. Parker, who shared Perry's interest in the fate of the island, was greatly influenced by the opinions of Gideon Nye, Jr., and W. M. Robinet, two American merchant-adventurers who were active in Formosa. On 10 February 1857 Nye wrote to Parker suggesing the desirability of some kind of American protectorate over all or part of the island. Parker agreed, and forwarded Nye's letter to the State Department, expressing the hope that "the government of the United States may not *shrink* from the action." On 2 March of the same year Robinet also wrote Parker, suggesting that if outright annexation were impossible, "it would advance the cause of humanity, religion, and civilization" if the U.S. government would give protection to Americans who should erect an independent government on Formosa. Much enthused by the whole idea, Parker wrote the secretary of state on 10 March 1857 pointing out that in his opinion Formosa "may not long remain a portion of the empire of China . . . and in the event of its being severed from the empire politically, as it is geographically, that the United States should possess it is obvious, particularly as respects the great principle of balance of power."[52]

By the fall of 1856 and the spring of 1857, therefore, events in China were on the point of getting out of hand, and Washington was called upon to take some decisive steps concerning relations with China. As William B. Reed, Parker's successor, was later to inform the secretary of state, the archives of the legation showed that Parker, "to a certain point, encouraged Sir John Bowring (and others) in the most extravant expectations of cooperation on our part, to the extent even of acquisition of territory."[53] And although Parker's specific proposals for the annexation of Formosa did not reach Washington until the summer of 1857, the authorities there had been aware for some time of Perry's and Parker's interest in the island. But the issue was given immediate urgency by press reports that alleged that both the United States consular service and the naval squadron in the area had directly participated in the British assault on Canton. An immediate investigation was ordered, which clearly established, at the very least, that the sympathies of the American colony were plainly with their British kinsmen.[54]

On top of all this, the authorities in Washington were being pressed by various interest groups to take a firm stand in China. The British and French representatives in the capital were urging American participation in a joint effort, and the China merchants in the United States (whose attitude toward China had been gradually shifting) came out in favor of such cooperation. On 2 April 1857 Gerald Hallock, the editor of a commercial paper, wrote Marcy that "if any one of the three nations were to undertake the negotiation alone, John Chinaman might be tempted to resist."[55] As far as the missionaries were concerned, their general attitude was well reflected in the aggressive opinions of Peter Parker himself. In spite of these multiple pressures urging war, however, President Pierce and Secretary of State Marcy refused to be drawn along. In the first place, they did not believe that the United States' relations with China, while far from satisfactory, warranted war. In the second place, they fully realized that the threat of civil war in America itself precluded any possibility that Congress would approve involvement in a conflict in distant China.

Accordingly, Marcy wrote Parker on 27 February 1857, rejecting the letter's advocacy of aggressive action as a "last resort." "The 'last resort' means war," Marcy declared, "and the Executive branch of this government is not the war-making power." Having decided against close cooperation with Britain and France in a move against China, Pierce and Marcy took pains to ensure that their successors would pursue the same policy. Their efforts were successful, for on 5 April 1857, after leaving office, Pierce wrote Marcy: "I was glad to receive your note of the 3rd inst., and to learn that our policy in regard to affairs in China is not to be departed from."[56] This concern on the part of Pierce and Marcy is of some importance, for it is the only instance to date of a former president's concern over the continuation of his China policy by his successor.

Unlike most of his predecessors, President James Buchanan had served a term as Secretary of State and was relatively well informed as to the situation in China. As a result, Buchanan took control of foreign policy and was not inclined to seek out the opinions of the merchants and missionaries as to the correct policy toward China, as his predecessors had done. Being in general agreement with the policy of Pierce and Marcy, Buchanan on 10 April 1857 formally rejected the British and French overtures seeking American support in a joint venture in China. And shortly thereafter, on 22 April William B. Reed was appointed to replace Parker as United States Commissioner to China. For the first time since Cushing's tenure, the Commissioner was also invested with the powers of Envoy Extraordinary and Minister Plenipotentiary, and was thus in a position to sign a new treaty should the opportunity arise.

Indeed, on the desirability of negotiating a new treaty with

China, Buchanan was in complete agreement with Peter Parker. Unlike Parker, however, Buchanan did not feel that the situation warranted aggressive action against the Chinese. In the "most detailed instructions since Cushing," Buchanan and Secretary of State Lewis Cass spelled out three main areas of policy that were to be Reed's primary concerns: relations with the Chinese, both the Ch'ing dynasty and the Taiping rebels; policy toward the various European powers active in China; and the readjustment of the U.S. diplomatic and consular services in China. Cass acknowledged to Reed that "your position is a delicate one and will require the exercise of your best discretion,"[57] but he made it quite clear to the new commissioner that his efforts in China "must be confined to firm representations, appealing to the justice and policy of the Chinese authorities, and leaving to your own Government to determine upon the course to be adopted, should your representations be fruitless."[58]

With respect to policy toward the Chinese, Cass told Reed that it mattered little as to which side won the civil war then in progress, for both sides were equally bound to existing obligations vis-à-vis the United States. In the meantime, with no prospects in sight of *de facto* recognition of the Taipings, diplomatic relations with the imperial government should be continued and extended if possible. Finally, American claims against the Chinese according to the terms of the Treaty of Wanghsia should be pressed and the treaty itself should be revised. As far as relations with the European powers were concerned, Cass felt that since U.S. interests in China were similar to those of Britain and France, Washington should offer them "peaceful cooperation." But he reminded Reed that the United States was not at war with China, and, contrary to Parker's point of view, had no desire for territorial aggrandizement or political influence in China. Accordingly, the American commissioner was not to join with Britain and France in any military actions against China. Concerning the branches of the U.S. government active in China, Cass informed the consular service (as had Marcy before him) that they were to carry the commissioner's wishes into effect. Finally, the Navy Department agreed on a plan to put the U.S. squadron in the China seas under the control of the Commissioner as far as was practicable.[59]

It should be pointed out that Buchanan's and Cass's refusal to employ force to bring about treaty revisions was by no means absolute. While they were willing to appeal "to the justice and policy" of the Chinese authorities on outstanding issues between the United States and China, there were limits to their patience. In a dispatch to Reed concerning the use of force against China, Cass acknowledged that "it is possible that this alternative may yet be forced upon us by the continued refusal of China to do justice to our citizens, or in the possible but improbable contingency to which you allude that the Chinese authorities should decline to admit the United States to an equal participation in such privileges as may be granted to the belligerents at the close of the present contest."[60]

Thus Cass made it quite clear that the United States was prepared to respect Chinese sovereignty, and to refrain from aggressive action against China, only on condition that the United States shared in the concessions China might be forced to yield to Britain and France. As it turned out, this is exactly what happened. Decisively beaten in 1858 and 1860, China was forced to concede extensive privileges to Britain and France, and United States Commissioners Reed and John E. Ward immediately stepped from the wings to claim the fruits of China's defeat. During the Anglo-French assault on the Chinese forts at Taku, the U.S. naval squadron on the scene displayed a studied neutrality, but an unexpected disaster revealed the true feelings of the Americans present. Immediately after British Admiral Sir James Hope fell wounded, U.S. Commodore Josiah Tattnall ordered some of his vessels to Britain's assistance. Justifying his aid to the British, Tattnall simply exclaimed: "I must either help Hope or return to the *Powhaten* [Tattnall's flag ship]. I can't stand here and see them shot to pieces. . . . Blood is thicker than water."[61] Apparently Washington agreed, for the secretary of the navy, on being informed of the incident, decided to consider Tattnall's action as entirely appropriate and not a violation of American neutrality.[62]

An Ambiguous Legacy

Before concluding my account, it might be interesting to discuss briefly the Chinese view of the United States and the individual Americans who came to China during this period. In general, most educated Chinese felt that America was "maritime, uncultivated, and primitive," In a memorial to the emperor, Imperial Commissioner Ch'i-ying reported: "The location of the United States is in the Far West. Of all the countries it is the most uncivilized and remote. . . . the said country is in an isolated place outside the pale, solitary and ignorant." Although the Chinese generally regarded all "foreign barbarians" as "inscrutable," they believed in the early stages that they might be able to play off the Americans against the British and French. Americans were thought to "resent the English barbarians and revere China," but on one occasion at least an official concluded that "the Americans ordinarily speak respectfully but are taking advantage of the present situation to make demands. . . . absolutely no faith can be placed in them." Finally, in comparing the British and the Americans, one perceptive commentator observed that "the English barbarians' craftiness is manifold, their proud tyranny is uncontrollable; Americans do nothing but follow their direction."[63]

This is, essentially, the general conclusion which I have arrived at in the course of this essay. Up to the time of the Opium War, United States contacts were mostly of a commercial nature, although the missionaries were fast becoming a new force on the scene. In the face of government apathy, the American merchants were forced to formulate their own policy toward China in the interests of trade. The three key elements in their policy were maintenance of equality of trade, respect for Chinese sovereignty, and disassociation from Great Britain. After the Treaty of Nanking was signed in 1842, Washington was called upon by the American merchants to negotiate a treaty with China granting privileges similar to those given the British. It is not surprising, then, that in his instructions to Caleb Cushing, Secretary of State Daniel Webster took the China policy of the American merchants to be the official China policy of the United States government.

The decision of President John Tyler in 1843 to inaugurate diplomatic relations with China opened a new phase in Sino-American relations. But the decision to sign a treaty with China had been encouraged by the pressure of external factors, and so Washington entered upon this new venture with little forethought or preparation. Almost immediately, the inadequacies of the diplomatic machinery set up to deal with China became readily apparent. After much trial and error, in the early 1850s Washington began to take steps to rein in and control the various branches of the United States government active in China. The State Department partially liberated itself from the opinions of interest groups such as the merchants and missionaries, the commissioners were given less "discretionary powers," the consular service was brought under more effective control, and the relationship between the commissioner in China and the commander of the East Indies Squadron was more clearly defined.

In the years after the Treaty of Wanghsia, a profound change

occurred in U.S. policy toward China. The principle of equality
of trade in China was firmly adhered to, as both merchants and
statesmen agreed that America's commercial interests in China
were of paramount importance. It was the U.S. attitude toward
Chinese sovereignty, however, that contained the horns of a dilemma. As long as the Americans thought that Great Britain intended to dominate China and exclude the United States from
its share of the trade, it was in their interest to restrain Britain
and "sustain" China. If, however, the Americans became convinced that Britain did not intend to exclude the United States
from the China trade, and that respect for Chinese sovereignty
only helped China exclude *all* Western nations from more extensive privileges, then U.S. policy would have to be reassessed.
American interests in China were almost purely commercial and
they could best be served by forcing China to open wide her
"door" to foreign penetration of the economy. This desire happily
coincided with the hopes of the rapidly growing missionary element in China, who equally desired the "opening" of China to
the blessings of Western religion and civilization.

And so it was that the Americans began to reconsider their
attitude toward Great Britain, a nation which they had been accustomed to regarding with mixed emotions of respect and suspicion.
The Americans realized that the British were determined to
"open" China by means fair or foul, so they had to make a choice
between helping China, cooperating with Britain, or maintaining
neutrality. Frankly realizing that their interests in China were essentially the same as those of the British, and assured that the
British did not intend to exclude them from China, the Americans
decided on a policy of cooperation. But this was to be "peaceful
cooperation" only, for the U.S. government felt that America's
interests in China were not sufficiently important to warrant war.
Besides, the clouds of civil war were gathering over their own
skies and the nation was in no mood to consider military adventures in distant lands. So, while Daniel Webster instructed Caleb
Cushing in 1843 to impress upon the Chinese the essential difference between Great Britain and the United States, in 1857 Lewis
Cass told William B. Reed to cooperate with the British in the
furtherance of common aims. The policy formulated by Buchanan
and Cass in 1857 marked the watershed between two historical
periods in the evolution of United States policy toward China,
for it ushered in the "era of cooperation" in Western relations
with China.

The ambiguity in United States policy toward China was not

lost on acute American observers as it worked itself out during the following generation. In an article in the *Atlantic Monthly* in May 1887, for example, A. A. Hayes observed that U.S. policy toward China has been to crawl behind the British guns, and come forward at the end of war with our bills for missing dressing gowns, slippers, pipes, and even "loss of peace of mind."[64] This of course is an exaggeration but like most exaggerations, it contains an important kernel of truth.

Notes

1. See, for example, Tong Te-kong, *United States Diplomacy in China, 1844–1860* (Seattle: University of Washington Press, 1964).

2. Ibid., 73. For an interesting account of early American attitudes toward China, see William J. Brinker, "Commerce, Culture, and Horticulture: The Beginnings of Sino-American Cultural Relations," in Thomas H. Etzold, ed., *Aspects of Sino-American Relations Since 1784* (New York: Franklin Watts, 1978), 3–24.

3. Tyler Dennett, *Americans in Eastern Asia* (New York: Barnes and Noble, 1922), 76–77, 89.

4. Ibid., 70.

5. Ibid., 83.

6. Ibid., 105.

7. Tong, *Diplomacy,* 72.

8. S. F. Bemis, *A Diplomatic History of the United States,* 4th ed. rev. (New York: Holt, Rinehart, and Winston, 1960), 344.

9. Paul H. Clyde and Burton F. Beers, *The Far East: A History of the Western Impact and the Eastern Response, 1830–1965,* 4th ed. rev. (Englewood Cliffs, N.J.: Prentice-Hall, 1966), 72.

10. J. W. Foster, *American Diplomacy in the Orient* (Boston and New York: Riverside Press and Houghton, Mifflin, 1903), 73.

11. Dennett, *Americans,* 99–104.

12. S. F. Bemis, ed., *The American Secretaries of State and Their Diplomacy* (New York: Pageant Book Co., 1958), 5–6: 61.

13. Tong, *Diplomacy,* 29.

14. Ibid, 28–30.

15. Paul H. Clyde, *United States Policy toward China: Diplomatic and Public Documents 1839–1939* (Durham, N.C.: Duke University Press, 1940), appendix 1, 314–16.

16. Tong, *Diplomacy,* 31.

17. J. M. Callahan, *American Relations in the Pacific and the Far East 1784–1900,* Johns Hopkins University Studies in Historical and Political Science, ser. 19, nos. 1–3 (Baltimore: Johns Hopkins Press, 1901), 167.

18. Tong, *Diplomacy,* 33–34.

19. John K. Fairbank, *Trade and Diplomacy on the China Coast: The Opening of the Treaty Ports, 1842–1854* (Cambridge: Harvard University Press, 1953, 1964), 2:63.

20. Claude M. Fuess, *The Life of Caleb Cushing* (New York: Harcourt, Brace, 1923), 1:246–47.

21. Dan E. Clark, "Manifest Destiny and the Pacific," *Pacific Historical Review* 1, no.1 (1932): 8–9.

22. Dennett, *Americans*, 127.

23. W. C. Costin, *Great Britain and China 1833–1860* (Oxford: Clarendon Press, 1937), 28–29.

24. Earl H. Pritchard, "The Origins of the Most-Favored Nation and the Open Door Policies in China," *Far Eastern Quarterly* 1, no.2 (February 1942): 166.

25. Dennett, *Americans*, 159.

26. Clyde, *Documents*, 9–12.

27. Fairbank, *Trade and Diplomacy*, 1:196.

28. L. H. Battistini, *The United States and Asia* (London: Atlantic Press, 1956), 15.

29. Foster, *American Diplomacy*, 85.

30. Kuo Ping-chia, "Caleb Cushing and the Treaty of Wanghia, 1844," *The Journal of Modern History* 5, no.1 (March 1933): 44–45.

31. Foster, *American Diplomacy*, 87.

32. Costin, *Britain and China*, 120–21.

33. Tong, *Diplomacy*, 88–89.

34. Ibid., 88–90.

35. Ibid., 95.

36. Ibid., 115–16.

37. Costin, *Britain and China*, 161.

38. Tong, *Diplomacy*, 128.

39. Clyde, *Documents*, p. 26.

40. Tong, *Diplomacy*, 133–35.

41. Ibid., 142–43.

42. Chester A. Bain, "Commodore Matthew Perry, Humphrey Marshall, and the Taiping Rebellion," *Far Eastern Quarterly* 10, no. 3 (May 1951): 263–67.

43. Tong, *Diplomacy*, 146–47.

44. Ibid., 35.

45. Bain, "Perry," 269–70.

46. H. B. Morse, *The International Relations of the Chinese Empire* (1910), (Taipei: Literary Star Book Store, 1966): 414–15.

47. Tong, *Diplomacy*, 170–71.

48. Ibid., 172.

49. Parker's career, including both missionary and diplomatic phases, is traced in Edward V. Gulick, *Peter Parker and the Opening of China* (Cambridge: Harvard University Press, 1973).

50. Costin, *Britain and China*, 195.

51. Tong, *Diplomacy*, 195.

52. Ibid., 203–6.

53. Callahan, *Relations*, 98.

54. Foster, *American Diplomacy*, 227–28.

55. Tong, *Diplomacy*, 196.

56. Ibid., 199–200.

57. Bemis, *Diplomatic History*, 375.

58. Clyde, *Documents*, 40.

59. Tong, *Diplomacy*, 211–14; Clyde, *Documents*, 39–42.

60. Bemis, *Diplomatic History*, 370–71.

61. Callahan, *Relations*, 107.

62. F. H. Michael and G. E. Taylor, *The Far East in the Modern World,* rev. ed. (New York: Holt, Rinehart and Winston, 1964), 139.

63. Earl Swisher, *China's Management of the American Barbarians: A Study of Sino-American Relations, 1841–1861, with Documents* (New Haven: Yale University Press, 1953), 39–54.

64. A. A. Hayes, "China and the United States," *The Atlantic Monthly* (Boston and New York: Houghton, Mifflin—The Riverside Press, 1887), 59: 587–88.

American Views of China, 1900–1915 The Unwelcome but Inevitable Awakening

JONATHAN G. UTLEY

At the 1904 St. Louis World Fair, President Theodore Roosevelt sent a telegraphic message that circled the globe in only twelve minutes, dramatic evidence of how small the world had become. Like it or not, the United States had to participate in that world. Steam power had removed the image of security the oceans had provided. Gone were the nineteenth-century days when Americans could concentrate on acquiring and developing a continent. Increasingly, now, foreign questions thrust themselves on the American people. What worried many Americans was that the world of the twentieth century was much less stable than that of the nineteenth century. Everything was changing and changing rapidly. Thus it was with both a sense of exhileration and apprehension that many Americans looked toward the twentieth century.

In this context Americans examined Asia and particularly China. That nation housed one-quarter of humanity. If the world was changing rapidly would not China also change? It seemed inevitable that China would eventually awake. When it did, could it challenge the world order the West had created? Late in the nineteenth century several American writers warned their countrymen of the pending contest between East and West. Josiah Strong termed it "the final competition of races." Brooks Adams warned that the transportation revolution had created a formidable challenge to the United States, for "even now factories can be equipped almost as easily in India, Japan and China as in Lancashire or Massachusetts, and the products of the cheapest labor can be sold more advantageously in European capitals than those of western cities." This warning by a member of the famous Adams family pointed out that an awakening Asia would have to be controlled or it would overwhelm the West. The leading spokesman for a strong navy, Alfred Thayer Mahan, advised his readers that "civilizations on different planes of material prosperity and progress with different spiritual ideas, and with very different political capacities, are closing together." Few Americans doubted who would ultimately triumph in this struggle for world dominance, for they assumed that the white race was more fit to rule than the yellow race. Nevertheless, it was a challenge that had to be met.[1]

China emerged from its slumber with a vengeance in 1900 as a militant antiforeign group called the Boxers sought to cleanse China of external influence by killing the foreigners. Although the uprising ultimately failed, it succeeded in killing many foreign nationals, destroying much of their property, and riveting Western attention on China for two months as the Boxers laid siege to the foreign legations in Beijing (Peking), a siege that was lifted only after 55 days. In rapid succession the American people despised, feared, laughed at, and pitied the Chinese.

The Boxer Uprising proved to Americans what they had already believed, that the Chinese were not a trustworthy people, that they valued duplicity and deceit rather than honesty. Bret Harte fixed this idea in the American mind when he published his popular poem commonly called "The Heathen Chinee." Harte's character, Ah Sin, is a Chinese who claims not to understand how to play cards, a claim he made "with a smile that was childlike and bland." But one could not trust the Chinese. According to Harte:

> In the scene that ensued
>   I did not take a hand,
> But the floor it was strewed
>   Like the leaves on the strand
> With the cards that Ah Sin had been hiding,
>   In the game "he did not understand."
>
> In his sleeves, which were long,
>   He had twenty-four packs,
> which was coming it strong,
>   Yet I state but the facts;
> And we found on his nails, which were taper,
>   What is frequent in tapers, —that's wax.
>
> Which is why I remark,
>   And my language is plain,

that for ways that are dark
And for tricks that are vain,
That heathen Chinee is peculiar,
Which the same I am free to maintain.

Harte published this poem in 1870 and it proved so popular that it was reprinted, sometimes illustrated, and continued to appear as late as 1900.[2] The Boxer Uprising only reinforced this image of the duplicitous Chinese, for the Chinese government had spoken of its friendship and pledged protection of foreigners while it failed to restrain the Boxers. Thus it was understandable how a cartoonist could depict China as the Jekyll and Hyde of nations, which stood erect offering solemn pledges of safety for the members of the foreign legations yet simultaneously crouched with evil countenance holding an assassin's knife and arsonist's torch. Betrayal and deception were presented as Chinese national characteristics.

In addition to anger for China's duplicity, Americans feared the power unleashed by the Boxer rebellion. Americans had stereotyped the Chinese as a violent people who loved to inflict pain, and this image flourished during the violent days of the rebellion. American cartoonists drew Boxers as giants breaking from their chains or awakening from their sleep. These frightening creatures chased westerners through the streets ready to kill them with long knives. But no sooner were the Boxers silenced than this image was replaced by another image long supported by popular stereotypes. Though most Americans considered the Chinese violent and vicious, they also considered them cowardly and undisciplined. So cowardly were they that the common term for cowardice was "yellow." So incapable of military discipline were they that a smaller number of well-trained troops could disperse the Boxers and restore peace to China. No longer did cartoonists draw hulking, threatening Chinese. Now the Boxer was dwarfed by the powers. It was the large military foot that brought the Boxer to "the end of his rope" in one cartoon when the foot stood on the queue (the long pigtail) of the Boxer who cries out in pain and drops his knife. The ultimate humiliation of the defeated Chinese is shown in a cartoon where the powers use his queue as a clothesline on which they hung their flags.[3] (See illustrated section.)

It was not long before Americans began to look upon the Chinese not simply as defeated but as a frail people facing the unreasonably harsh demands of the powers. As the powers made those demands the American attitude toward the Chinese became almost sympathetic. The Chinese were no longer characterized as disarmed Boxers but rather as weak children or frail old men. The real Boxers, one cartoonist noted, were the powers who were nailing China into a coffin preparatory to partitioning it. Obviously, China needed a friend if it was going to survive, and it found that friend in United States Secretary of State John Hay. In this moment of peril Hay informed the powers that the United States preferred a solution to the China problem that would avoid any lessening of China's political or territorial integrity. Hay was calling for the Open Door in China. It was the mutual suspicion among the powers, rather than Hay's diplomatic efforts, that forestalled the partition of China and preserved the Open Door. Nevertheless the American people were pleased that their nation had come to China's defense. It made no difference to them that China was the object of American diplomacy, a pawn to be acted upon, rather than a participant in determining its own fate. It was not important that Hay held little respect for the Chinese and spoke of the "Chinks." This was not the age of equality, and Americans could agree that the Chinese were an inferior people whose fate was to be decided by the ruling nations of the world, of which the United States was clearly one.[4]

Thus 1900 witnessed an expression of all the popular views Americans held of the Chinese. Unleashed they were to be feared while peaceful they were not to be trusted. Though dangerous because of their numbers, they were hardly a match for the industrial nations of the world. Underlying all of this was an assumption of China's inferiority and backwardness, conditions that justified preventing China from controlling its own affairs.

This unequal relationship was a product of the nineteenth century, when the powers established extraterritoriality (by which China could not prosecute foreign nationals) and maritime customs control (by which China could not control foreign imports). Most Americans understood the necessity for such a system since Chinese ways were barbaric and the all-pervading corruption made justice impossible. Even Americans friendly to China noted how corrupt the legal system was. One dared not stop to give aid to a man lying in the street lest the intervention make the benefator liable to a suit by the family of the afflicted man. Once charged, a local official might extract a substantial bribe to keep the case from coming to trial. Even a fair trial would be impossible, for the Chinese "generally set little or no value upon truth, and this has led to the use of torture in their courts of justice; for it is argued that where the value of an oath is not understood, some

other means must be restored to extract evidence." This view,
put forward in the scholarly eleventh edition of the *Encyclopedia
Britannica,* reveals the dominant views of the time. That corruption characterized the Chinese, was apparent from the encyclopedia's description of the maritime customs as "the one department
of finance in China which is managed with probity and honesty,
and this it owes to the fact that it is worked under foreign control."[5]

Such views dominated the popular American image of China
and the Chinese. In 1904–5, American treatment of the Chinese
in the United States prompted some Chinese retaliation in China.
The issue was Chinese exclusion from the United States. That
Congress would renew the exclusion legislation was a foregone
conclusion. But that it should be expanded to include humiliating
restrictions on the "better sort" of educated Chinese who sought
to continue their education in the United States and the successful
merchants who sought to trade in the United States was too much
for the Chinese, who instituted a somewhat limited boycott of
American goods in China. Though Americans continued to view
the Chinese as inferior, there was considerable sympathy for the
Chinese in this case. Commercial interests recognized that better
treatment of Chinese in America was not only justified on grounds
of justice but benefited American trade. Two leading periodicals
of American commerce, the *Commercial and Financial Chronicle*
and the *Journal of Commerce,* portrayed American restrictions
on Chinese immigration as insulting to China. Outside the commercial circles there was an acceptance of the justness of China's
cause. It was "a rule that works both ways" one cartoonist noted.
If the Americans wanted to give the boot to Chinese, then the
Chinese could give the boot to American goods.[6]

Less apparent to the typical American than the somewhat inef-
fectual boycott, but more far reaching as a symbol of the awakening China, was that nation's attempt to regain control of its own
internal economic development by reasserting control over its
railroad system. The noted correspondent Thomas F. Millard explained this to his American readers. While still too early to say
that China was fully awake, he wrote, "it is certain that she has
opened her eyes and is taking notice of what is going on in the
world about her." Millard believed that the force shaking China
awake was the foreign presence, particularly the foreign concessions. Awakened to the importance of the railroad for the development of China and aware of how foreign powers had used the
railroad concessions to their advantage rather than to China's,
Millard saw that China would insist upon retaining "substantial

control" of the railroads of China. "It is safe to say that hereafter no important commercial or industrial concession will be willingly granted by the Chinese Government in which the government does not reserve the right to take it over under equitable conditions." Beyond that, China was intent upon regaining control of the Canton-Hankow railroad concession from the American-China Development Company. Though the primary stockholder, financier J. P. Morgan was prepared to sell (at a handsome profit), President Roosevelt and the State Department opposed the sale, terming it as a blow to American interests in China. Not only would the consummation of the sale remove the United States from an important railroad line but it would be the removal of the Americans at the insistance of the Chinese. That was not Roosevelt's view of how the world should be governed. This assertion of Chinese independence boded ill for the maintenance of the old system.[7]

Some China watchers sought to alert the American people to China's awakening. Arthur Judson Brown published his warning to the nation in his 1904 book *New Forces in Old China: An Unwelcome but Inevitable Awakening*. Johnson was drawn to his topic as bystanders are drawn to a building on fire. "There is something fascinating and at the same time something appalling in the spectacle of a nation numbering nearly one-third of the human race slowly and majestically rousing itself from the torpor of ages under the influence of new and powerful revolutionary forces." This transformation of old, conservative, and exclusive China was brought by three great forces of the modern world: Western trade, Western politics, and Western religion. Taken with the transportation and communication revolutions, Brown noted that the intrusion of the West into China was bringing about a transformation of Chinese life. As the commercial forces reached into China they created new wants among the Chinese, which stimulated new markets. But this influx of western investment and goods led to an exploitation of China and the subsequent irritation of the Chinese. Brown argued that the Chinese, having been mistreated by the West, struck back in the Boxer Uprising. Defeated by the foreign powers, the victors extracted terms from China that left it humiliated and shook it from its slumber. Brown conceded that for 1904 Japan seemed to have held the primary place in the American perception of the "Yellow Peril" and that China was looked upon as weak and helpless and thus no menace to the West. But what of tomorrow? "It takes a nation of 426,000,000 phlegmatic people longer to get under way than a nation of 43,000,000 nervous people (Japan) but when they do get started, their momentum is proportionately greater." Brown warned that China had plenty of men who could fight if properly led. Nor should the West feel comfortable behind the vast distances that separate it from Asia, for if the West can reach Asia why not Asia the West? Brown yielded to the popular view that the Chinese were incapable of organizing themselves and charged that Japan would provide the leadership. "It certainly needs no argument to prove that if 426,000,000 Chinese are once fairly committed to the skillful leadership of the Japanese, a force will be set in motion which could be withstood only by the united efforts of all the rest of the world." China was already developing, he warned; it was importing guns and training its army. The coming of the Western powers pushed China to change, and would they stop before tossing out the Western powers?

> Yesterday, Chaldea, Egypt, Asyria, Babylon, Persia, Greece, Rome! Today England, Germany, Russia, Japan, the United States! Tomorrow. What? What, indeed, if not some of these now awakening nations! It is by no means impossible that some new Jenghiz Khan or Tamerlane may arise, and with the weapons of modern warfare in his hands, and these uncounted millions at his command, gaze about on the pygmies that we call the powers.[8]

Not all Americans interested in China were comfortable with Brown's apacolyptic tone. Some preferred Millard's more judicious and sophisticated analysis of the situation in China.[9] But Millard's sober-minded analysis came to the same conclusion Brown's rhetorical assertions did. Japan appeared to have sought to direct the awakening of China against the West. These were not simply speculations, Millard claimed, for he had "positive evidence of the existence of a systematic and well-developed plan of Japan to control and manipulate" Chinese public opinion. Part of Millard's evidence was the activities of Chinese language newspapers published in China under Japanese charter. Such newspapers enjoyed the benefits of extraterritoriality and were thus exempt from Chinese censorship. As a result, they carried subtle antiforeign articles that emphasized how badly the westerners treated the Chinese and how much Japan resented this treatment. The only solution, the articles would suggest, was to eliminate the power of the westerner in China.

In addition to the newspapers, according to Millard, literally thousands of Japanese Buddhist missionaries and businessmen lived in China and distributed large numbers of antiforeign posters, cartoons, and circulars. So orchestrated and concerted were these propaganda efforts that they could not have been the result of individual Japanese initiatives but had to be planned and directed from Tokyo. The real menace of such agitation was visible in the more remote areas where Japanese agents circulated propaganda "of an absolutely incendiary character, couched in the same general antiforeign spirit that the Boxer movement took in." The effectiveness of this rabble rousing, Millard believed, could be found in the Chinese boycott of American goods. Under normal circumstances, the boycott would have been, in the words of the United States Minister to China "a flash in the political pan." It was Japanese efforts that made the boycott drag on, Millard believed. Central in this Japanese strategy were the "Japanese students," young Chinese who studied in Japan and returned to China to serve Japan either openly or surreptitiously. Millard worried that they formed "a mobile and intelligent element perfectly adapted to certain political uses in China's present stage of development." These "Japanese students" would pack the meetings of the Chinese commercial guilds and outvote the more reasonable Chinese and shout down the Chinese who, having studied in the United States, wished "to present fairly the American side of the matter and point out the futility" of a boycott. Without this Japanese sponsored anti-foreign agitation the boycott would have been scarcely a ripple.

Brown and Millard both sought to dispel the old popular myths of a helpless China incapable of military discipline, opposed to modernization, and uninterested in political regeneration. Such old views prevented Americans from seeing that China was changing and that it would be guided in that change either by Japan, which was antiwestern, or by the western powers. Neither writer was prepared to argue that the Chinese would accomplish a regeneration of their country without some outside guidance and in this respect both authors reflected the basic perception of the Chinese as inferior. But aside from that, neither sought to denigrate the Chinese. While many of their customs appear strange to us, Brown reminded his American readers, so do many of our customs appear strange to them. Millard admitted to once holding an "adverse disposition" toward the Chinese but the more he became acquainted with them the more he developed "a sincere liking and admiration of the Chinese people." He recognized that one could not easily identify social characteristics with a race, but he considered the Chinese "industrious, reliable, law-abiding, good humored, capable, and tolerant." Brown, in keeping with his missionary background, viewed the Chinese in more religious terms: "back of the almond eyes and under a yellow skin are all the faculties and possibilities of a human soul. The Chinese is not only a man, but our brother man, made like ourselves in the image of God." Brown felt that the Japanese challenge in China had to be met by American missionaries. Millard favored more secular methods that would guide the "good qualities" of the Chinese along the "path of modern progress."

The United States Minister to China, E. H. Conger, expressed the same view in 1898 when he acknowledged that the great powers might preserve China as it stood, but to what end?

> If real progress is to be made mines opened, railways constructed resources developed, markets created, and business established, Orientalism must effectually give way to Occidentalism. In my judgment this is bound to occur. It may and it may not be soon, but the sooner it comes, the better for China, as well as for those who seek her development and the trade which will follow.

Americans were quite sincere when they spoke of the necessity of China's abandoning orientalism for occidentalism. Orientalism was backward and China needed to be cleansed of it. As one cartoonist depicted it, the powers would wield the broom of civilization to sweep out of China not only the Boxers, but every vestige of antiprogress, superstition, war gods, bigotry, violence, and antiforeign feelings. Purged of these negative forces, China could be remade in the image of Western civilization.[10]

Of course, there were those commercially minded Americans who looked upon China as a market and the Chinese as consumers rather than as people. The *Buffalo Express* put it bluntly in 1900 when it declared "there are 400,000,000 active stomachs in China, and each cries for food three times a day." Lest anyone think this was a humanitatian appeal to feed the starving millions of China, the *Express* published a drawing of a Chinese man joyfully devouring a bowl of food and captioned the photograph "a fine opening in China for American Wheat and Corn."[11] Other commercial interests may have been more interested in the number of feet requiring slippers or the number of heads requiring hats or even the number of lanterns requiring kerosene. But in spite of such materialistic views, the development of the China market could not be separated from the spiritual regeneration of the Chinese people and the instilling of western values through education.

Historian Jerry Israel has demonstrated how the values of the Progressive Era at home were reflected in China as well. (See Israel's article in this volume). Just as the social gospel and settlement houses moved people to perfect society at home, so did it move Americans to perfect society in China. Not only must dams be built but such archaic and inhumane practices as foot binding, slavery, torture, and massive corruption had to be stamped out. China would be remade by the combined efforts of Western businessmen, missionaries, and educators.[12]

If the magnitude of such an undertaking did not capture the imagination of all Americans, it proved of interest to many. In the fall of 1911 alone, eight significant books on China were published. It was not difficult for interested Americans to find information on China, which ranged from the more analytical works of University of Wisconsin political scientist Paul Reinsch to several travelogues. Among these books was Edward Alsworth Ross's *The Changing Chinese: The Conflict of Oriental and Western Cultures in China.*[13] In many respects, Ross reflected the view that China was a backward country that was awakening, and when it did it posed a conflict with Western civilization of epic proportions. But unlike many other writers of his day, Ross viewed the Chinese as strong, good natured, polite people who had not achieved the level of intellectual sophistication demonstrated by the West because of an oppressive social structure. If the typical Chinese was inferior to the typical westerner, Ross argued, it was not the result of anything inate but strictly the result of a society which was weighted down by a constant looking back at its ancient heritage and thus opposed to change. Removed from this stultifying environment, he argued, the Chinese would rise to the intellectual equal of the white. Where Chinese had been able to do just that their intellectual growth had been remarkable. Reflecting the popular view that it was the environment rather than inherent characteristics that determined a person's status, Ross argued that one or two score years of western education the Chinese would occupy throughout China the tasks only whites then performed. Ross based his argument on observations during his travels in China. On his journey he asked forty-three white men who had good cause to have the "feel" of the Chinese mind whether they found the intellectual capacity of the yellow race equal to that of the white race. All but five answered yes.

This was a new challenge to the West. For three centuries, Ross asserted, the white race had been expanding and confronted not a single race that could successfully dispute their military superiority, contribute to their civilization, or dispense with their direction in political or industrial organization. Now, after three centuries of such experience, during which the white man has grown accustomed to regarding himself as the undisputed sovereign of the planet, he makes the acquaintance of peoples in Eastern Asia who are, perhaps, as capable as the whites and who threaten to spread into areas he has staked off for himself. In any case, it begins to appear that the future bearers and advancers of civilization will be, not the whites alone, but the white and the yellow races; and the control of the globe will lie in the hands of *two* races instead of *one*.

Here in more intellectual form were the warnings of Mahan that two civilizations were fast closing together and of Strong that a "final competition of races" was approaching. But here too was the ever-present belief that if China was going to ascend to its rightful role in the world, it had to abandon oppressive orientalism for progressive occidentalism. Ross spoke highly of the Chinese and showed no serious apprehension about China's rise to world prominence. But he reflected this basic ethnocentrism when he explained that before China could hope to develop intellectually it had to undergo both massive economic and social reform. On the one hand the Chinese would have to "build railroads, open mines, sink petroleum wells, harness water-power, erect mills, adopt machinery, reforest their mountains, construct irrigation works, introduce better breeds of domestic animals and plants, and apply science to the production of food." But all of this would be to no avail if the population simply increased to absorb the growth in the economy. "It is equally ncessary, therefore, for the Chinese to slacken their multiplication by dropping ancestor worship, dissolving the clan, educating girls, elevating women, postponing marriage, introducing compulsory education, restricting child-labor and otherwise individualizing the members of the family." In short, Ross called for China to abandon its emphasis on familism for an emphasis on individualism that was a more sophisticated expression of E. H. Conger's call for China to abandon orientalism for occidentalism.

No matter how hard they might try, Americans could not bring themselves to accept China as it was. The Chinese could retain their traditional patience but they must change almost everything else. They must adopt the Western concept of progress and accept the liberal values of the West. Unlike the earlier writings of Millard and Brown, Ross did not fear the awakening China. Millard and

Brown feared that what seemed to them an anti-Western Japan would guide the Chinese masses, while Ross argued that the emergent China would be a westernized one thus less threatening to the West. Where Brown worried about a militant China that would attack the West, Ross pictured a developing China that would share in the control of the globe.

A probable reason for the popularity of Ross's work is that it gained a prophetic tone because of its timing. It appeared at the time of the 1911 Chinese revolution that overthrew the Manchu Dynasty. This revolution struck some Americans as the type of progressive step China had to take, a giant stride out of the nineteenth century into the twentieth century, a move from Asian despotism to western republicanism. The contrast was demonstrated by a cartoonist who showed young China in Western dress and driving a sports car forcing off the road the old China with its traditional dress and queue, riding on a dragon.[14]

Though some Americans doubted the Chinese were capable of establishing a republic until they had been educated to intricacies of such a sophisticated form of government, other Americans were products of an optimistic age and were confident that the 1911 revolution heralded a new day. *The Nation* was an exponent of this optimistic position.[15] "Asia has taken center stage," *The Nation* editorialized. "What is now going on in China is bound to transcend in importance all our tariff revision and Presidential speculations, all of Lloyd George's insurance schemes, all Franco-German bickerings and adjustments." In *The Nation*'s view, when historians looked back at this period they would find that, in spite of radium, wireless, and the airplane, the significant change would be the awakening of China. Those who had said that the Oriental mind rejects liberty and demands despotism had been proven wrong. The revolution demonstrated this by showing that the true awakening of China was not in the form of a great standing army as the champions of the "Yellow Peril" predicted. Nor did China's awakening come through the economic regeneration as others insisted it must. Instead, it came through the force of ideas. The education of thousands, not the arming of millions, had transformed China. The Chinese desire for "honest administrators, honest judges, schools, libraries; in other words, Progress" had brought the regeneration of China.

There seemed to be a sense of relief among some China watchers in the United States. For some years they had been waiting for the slumbering giant to awaken, and they had been apprehensive. Now it appeared that the Chinese were taking a peaceful course rather than a militant one. Arthur Judson Brown rushed into print another book on China in which he praised the new China as a far better place and admitted that it was a much better result than he could have hoped for in his 1904 study of the awakening China. As a reviewer of Brown's work reminded his readers, China was undergoing a swift and thorough educational, political, and religious transformation, and the American people had misjudged the character of the Chinese people.[16]

Such euphoric views must be kept in context. If some China watchers and other informed segments of the American public saw the 1911 revolution as a turning point in the conflict between East and West, those people reflected only a small segment of the nation. China watchers were an important part of public opinion because they were likely to articulate their feelings to foreign policymakers. Nevertheless most Americans did not read Ross, Reinsch, or Brown, or even editorials in *The Nation*. Understanding of the popular or mass image of the Chinese requires examination not of informed writings but of the popular literature and the motion pictures of the day. Here the old stereotypical views of the Chinese persisted.

No fictional character personified the "Yellow Peril" and the old prejudices against the Chinese better than Dr. Fu Manchu, the supervillain created by Sax Rohmer (whose real name was Arthur Sarsfield Ward.)

> Imagine a person tall, lean and feline, high shouldered, with a brow like Shakespeare and a face like Satan, close-shaven skull and long magnetic eyes of true cat-green. Invest him with all the cruel cunning of an entire Eastern Race, accumulated in one giant intellect, with all the resources of science past and present, with all the resources of a wealthy government—which, however, has already denied all knowledge of his existence. Imagine that awful being and you have a mental picture of the yellow peril incarnate in one man.

Rohmer, a journalist turned novelist, began publishing his Fu Manchu novels in 1913. They were serialized in the popular magazines of the day, *Collier's, Scribner's,* and *Lippincott's.* They sold in novel form. They proved to be exceedingly popular, standing the test of time. Rohmer continued to write through the 1950s.[17]

Rohmer's plots were fantastic, unreal, not to be believed by anyone. Mystery, intrigue, and murder by the most devious and mysterious methods crowd his pages. Though far fetched, the stories nevertheless seem plausible. The characters in Rohmer's novels bear clear similarities to real characters in public life. While the reader is not likely to believe that the details of the story were true, Rohmer's message had its impact as it was stated again and again. Fu Manchu "is the advance agent of a movement so epoch-making that not one Britisher, and not one American in Fifty-thousand has ever dreamed of it." Do not disbelieve, he warns his readers: "The phantom yellow peril today materializes under the very eyes of the Western world you scoff, sir; and so do others. We take the proffered right hand of friendship nor inquire if the hidden left holds a knife. The peace of the world is at stake." China's friends might claim that the American people had misjudged the Chinese, that they were not the devious and dishonest people that Bret Harte made famous in "The Heathen Chinee," but how convincing could this claim be when confronted by the tales of Sax Rohmer? He fed the prejudices of the American people and reenforced the stereotypes that Americans who thought little about China thought reasonable.

Rohmer's method was to equate evil designs with the Chinese. When confronted by a diabolical plan worked out in great detail and much intricacy, he would comment on how "oriental" it was. When describing a secret door that became invisible to detection upon closing, the workmanship being so intricate, he would note how Chinese it was. In this way it was not necessary to believe the plot of the novel to absorb the stereotypes of the evil Chinese. Lest these messages prove too subtle for his readers, Rohmer was not above stopping his narrative to deliver a clear message. In *The Insidious Dr. Fu Manchu* Rohmer has his hero, secret agent Nayland Smith, tracking down Fu Manchu, who is in the process of killing off all the westerners who might try to alert the West to the Yellow Peril. Fu Manchu has just killed Sir Crichton Davey (an expert on the Chinese threat in Tibet) through the use of a rare and lethal centipede called the Zayat Kiss. At this point Rohmer breaks into the narrative of his novel to inform his readers that no white man appreciates the unemotional cruelty of the Chinese.

Throughout the time that Dr. Fu Manchu remained in England, the press preserved a uniform silence upon the subject of his existence. This was due to Nayland Smith. But as a result, I feel assured that my account of the Chinaman's deeds will, in many quarters, meet with an incredulous reception.

I had been at work, earlier in the evening, upon the opening chapters of this chronicle, and I had realized how difficult it would be for my reader, amid secure and cozy surroundings, to credit any human being with a callous villainy great enough to conceive and put into execution such a death pest as that directed against Sir Crichton Davey.

One would expect God's worst man to shrink from employing— against however vile an enemy—such an instrument as the Zayat Kiss. So thinking, my eye was caught by the following:

EXPRESS CORRESPONDENT

New York

"Secret service men of the United States Government are searching the South Sea Islands for a certain Hawaiian from the island of Maui, who, it is believed, has been selling poisonous scorpions to Chinese in Honolulu anxious to get rid of their children.

"Infanticide, by scorpion and otherwise, among the Chinese, has increased so terribly that the authorities have started a searching inquiry, which has led to the hunt for the scorpion dealer of Maui.

"Practically all the babies that die mysteriously are unwanted girls, and in nearly every case the parents promptly ascribe the death to the bite of a scorpion, and are ready to produce some more or less poisonous insect in support of this statement.

"The authorities have no doubt that infanticide by scorpion bite is a growing practice, and orders have been given to hunt down the scorpion dealer at any cost."

Is it any matter for wonder that such a people had produced a Fu Manchu? I pasted the cutting into a scrapbook, determined that if I lived to publish my account of those days, I would quote it therein as casting a sidelight upon Chinese character.[18]

How many thousands of readers put down the book after reading such a passage understanding that the book was fiction, that Fu Manchu did not exist, but also equally convinced that they had acquired a "sidelight" on the Chinese character? The stereotype that the American people carried with them was much more likely to be Rohmer's than Edward Alsworth Ross's depiction of the Chinese as strong, good natured, and polite.

The influence of the evil Chinese depicted by Sax Rohmer is revealed in the motion picture industry. In the earlier films the Chinese characters are modeled after Bret Harte's Heathen Chinee or portrayed as incompetent inferiors. The 1904 film *Heathen Chinese and the Sunday School Teachers* was inspired by Bret Harte's classic poem, while the 1903 film *The Chinese Rubbernecks* included a lengthy chase of long-queued Chinese laundrymen. Occasionally, as in *That Chink at Gold Gulch* (1910) the Chinese are depicted with some favorable attributes. But the appearance of Rohmer's novels established a Chinese character the American people could understand.[19]

The first Fu Manchu–type character to appear in cinema was called Long Sin and was presented to the motion picture audience clothed in rich oriental costume, "reclining on a divan smoking a strange looking pipe and playing with two pet white rats. Each white rat had a gold band around his leg, to which was connected a gold chain about a foot in length, and the chains ended in rings which were slipped over Long's little fingers. Ordinarily, he carried the pets up the capacious arm of each sleeve." By the middle teens the American film industry had stereotyped the Chinese as lustful, vicious, and immoral. So bad had it become that the Chinese government lodged a protest with the United States government, but to no avail. Rather than abandoning the evil Chinese character, the film industry embraced it. In the popular serial *The Exploits of Elaine,* the evil Chinese called Wu Fang became a standard character. The name Wu Fang not only had the proper sinister tone to be popular but it had a touch of reality as well, for the former Chinese minister to Washington was named Wu T'ing-fang.[20]

In some respects, then, there was a contest between those who would entertain and those who would inform. The entertainers were less concerned about reality than the commercial success of their product. The informers were concerned that the American people understood what was happening in China and would be prepared to guide and support the Chinese as they struggled to raise themselves out of the depressed state they found themselves in. But old stereotypes do not die easily. The writing of Brown, Ross, and their type may have influenced the informed minority of Americans, but it had little impact on the way the masses perceived China and the Chinese. Reenforced by Fu Manchu and other dramatic characters of his type, Americans did not forget the lesson Bret Harte had taught them and their parents in his 1870 poem "The Heathen Chinee." The impact of this image was still apparent in 1916, nearly a half century after Harte's poem first appeared, when *The Literary Digest* summarized an article originally appearing in *The New York Tribune.* Under the title "Movie Ways That are Dark," the *Digest* examined the status of the Chinese motion picture industry. "If nothing else shows that 'the heathen Chinee is peculiar,'" the *Digest* began its story, "his taste in motion-pictures would give it away boldly." The basic problem with Chinese actors, it seems, was that they could not act. If the director wanted the actor to act happy and content he must feed the actor so that he would be content and happy. In one respect, however, the *Tribune* story concluded that the Chinese actors were exemplary. "They never forget their queues."[21]

Such crude attacks reflect the popular perception of the Chinese. On that level the popular perceptions differed dramatically from those of the small number of informed Americans who recognized that the Chinese were children of God just as were the Americans and who reminded their readers that the Chinese were innately good people who warranted understanding help. But like their cruder counterparts in the mass media, these informed individuals looked down upon the Chinese, arguing that they had to give up their Oriental ways for the ways of the West. These friends of China did not talk of the insidious Chinese as did Sax Rohmer nor of the infantile or silly Chinese as did many Americans. But in their minds, progress was measured by how Western China was becoming. Whether crudely stated or sophisticatedly articulated, ethnocentrism was the underlying characteristic of the American perception of the Chinese throughout this period.

Notes

1. The views of Strong, Adams, Mahan, and others are in Walter LaFeber, *The New Empire: An Interpretation of American Expansion, 1860–1898* (Ithaca: Cornell University Press, 1963), chaps. 2, 3.

2. Charles Swain Thomas, ed., *Poems and Stories of Bret Harte* (Cambridge, Mass: Houghton Mifflin Co., 1912), 13–14.

3. Robert McClellan, *The Heathen Chinee: A Study of American Attitudes Toward China, 1890–1905* (Columbus: Ohio State University Press, 1971), passim. For cartoons depicting the Chinese in the Boxer Uprising, see various issues of *The Literary Digest,* vol. 21, particularly 28 July 1900, 94; 11 Aug. 1900, 152; 25 Aug. 1900, 212; 1 Sept. 1900, 242; and 6 Oct. 1900, 394.

4. A sense of the values underlying American foreign policy in this era can be seen in Howard K. Beale, *Theodore Roosevelt and the Rise of America to World Power* (Baltimore: Johns Hopkins Press, 1956), and David H. Burton, *Theodore Roosevelt: Confident Imperialist* (Philadelphia: University of Pennsylvania Press, 1968), passim.

5. Arthur Judson Brown, *New Forces in Old China: An Unwelcome but Inevitable Awakening* (New York: F. H. Revell Company, 1904), 25–33; *Encyclopedia Britannica,* 11th edition (Cambridge and New York: Encyclopedia Britannica "at the University Press"), 6:184–87.

6. For a discussion of the type of treatment the Chinese found offensive, see Ng Poon Chew, *The Treatment of the Exempt Classes of Chinese in the United States* (San Francisco: Chung Sai Yat Po, 1908), passim. A sample of cartoon reaction is in *The Literary Digest* 31 (1 July 1905): 4, and (8 July 1905): 39. The views of the business community are discussed by Paul A. Varg,

The Making of a Myth: The United States and China, 1897–1912 (East Lansing: Michigan State University Press, 1968): passim. See also Delber L. McKee, *Chinese Exclusion versus the Open Door Policy, 1900–1906: Clashes over China Policy in the Roosevelt Era.* (Detroit: Wayne State University Press, 1977), passim.

7. Thomas F. Millard, "The New China," *Scribner's Magazine,* 39 (February 1906): 240–50.

8. Brown, *New Forces,* 310ff.

9. Millard, "The New China."

10. *The Literary Digest* 21 (14 July 1900): 34. For Conger's views and those of like-minded Americans in China, see Michael H. Hunt, *Frontier Defense and the Open Door: Manchuria in Chinese-American Relations, 1895–1911* (New Haven and London: Yale University Press, 1973), chaps. 2–3. To categorize Japan as anti-Western at the turn of the century is perhaps an overstatement. Japan had enjoyed close ties with Bismarck's Germany, had formed an alliance with Britain in 1902, and on the surface was very friendly to the United States, although Akira Iriye has conceded that the seeds for future estrangement were already sown, and Charles New has considered Japan's Western ties to be an uncertain friendship.

11. *The Literary Digest* 21 (29 Dec. 1900): 793.

12. Jerry Israel, *Progressivism and the Open Door: America and China, 1905–1921* (Pittsburgh, Pa.: University of Pittsburgh Press, 1971), passim.

13. Edward Alsworth Ross, *The Changing Chinese: The Conflict of Oriental and Western Cultures in China* (New York: Century Co., 1911), passim. Payson J. Treat's combined book reviews appear in *The Dial* 52 (1 Feb. 1912): 87–90.

14. *The Literary Digest* 43 (28 Oct. 1911): 721; Ross, *Changing Chinese,* passim.

15. "The Changing Orient," *The Nation* 94 (4 Jan. 1912): 7–8.

16. *The Literary Digest* 45 (19 Oct. 1912), 683–84; Arthur Judson Brown, *The Chinese Revolution* (New York: Student Volunteer Movement, 1912), passim.

17. The quotations cited below are taken from Sax Rohmer (pseud.), *The Insidious Dr. Fu Manchu* (New York: McKinley, Stone, and MacKenzie, 1913).

18. Ibid., 120–22.

19. David Manning White and Richard Averson, *The Celluloid Weapon: Social Comment in the American Film* (Boston: Beacon Press, 1972), 31–32; Eugene Franklin Wong, *On Visual Media Racism: Asians in the American Motion Pictures* (New York: Arno Press, 1978), 56–57, 72–73, 76–77.

20. Raymond William Stedman, *The Serials: Suspense and Drama by Installment* (Norman: University of Oklahoma Press, 1971), 38–41.

21. "Movie Ways that are Dark," *The Literary Digest* 53 (30 Dec. 1916): 1757.

The Importance of Being Charlie Chan

SANDRA M. HAWLEY

In searching for the sources of American ideas about China and the Chinese, one of the important places to look is the mystery fiction of Earl Derr Biggers, starring Charlie Chan—detective extraordinaire, Honolulu resident, half-mocked, half-mocking descendant of Confucius.

Charlie Chan's durability and widespread popularity are unrivaled by other fictional Orientals. Although only six books featuring the Hawaiian-based detective were published from 1925 to 1932 (Biggers died in 1933), Charlie Chan's renown equals that of fictional detectives like Hercule Porot and Nero Wolfe. The Charlie Chan books were all serialized in *The Saturday Evening Post,* published in hardcover editions, and reissued in paperback in 1974–75.[1] In addition, Charlie Chan was featured in a comic strip, a radio show, a Broadway play, and some forty-nine full-length films. Students of American popular culture have called him "a national institution" and "very much a part of American folklore."[2] This popularity and longevity indicate that the Chinese detective touched a chord in the American public. Half a century is a good run for any character.

More important than longevity is his effect on images of the Chinese in American fiction. The appearance of Charlie Chan was a turning point in American portraits of and attitudes toward the Chinese people, a perceptible shift in American stereotypes of the Chinese. The older "heathen Chinee" began to yield to a new, more favorable version of the Chinese: a portrait just as stereotyped and racist, but much more human and appealing. Charlie Chan was the key figure in this transformation: he embodied concepts that became widespread and influential.

Images and perceptions of other people and other cultures reach the American public in a variety of ways: scholarly studies, travelogues, news articles, films, fiction, and most recently television. From this flow of information, accurate and otherwise, people tend to select the images that best suit their own needs as well as their own understanding. In many instances—particularly in the case of modern European nations—the amount of information is so vast that enormous selectivity is required, and an image to fit every preconception can be developed. In many ways, the process of image formation follows what might be called a "percolator" process; ideas generated by specialists trickle down into the popular culture, often after being distilled through several filtering layers of high-school and college textbooks and classes.

In the case of China, however, this "percolator" mechanism tended to break down at the upper levels because of a limited flow of information; fictional images became much more important and influential. In American folklore and popular culture, China was long considered "inscrutable"; images of China have been wildly varied, almost schizophrenic in their content, in large part because of the extremely restricted flow of information through formal channels.[3]

Given the lack of information generally available, Americans formed their ideas and images of Asia from any sources they could find, and in large part from the kaleidoscope of images available in fiction and film.[4] The process of creating such images involved considerable feedback. Images too far out of line with what people believed or were willing to accept would not succeed. Thus anyone creating fictional characters had either to adopt prevailing stereotypes or to select a new image that was acceptable even if not widely used.

The popularity of Oriental characters in fiction during this period was probably to some degree the result of this desire for information about the mysterious East. *The Saturday Evening Post,* the most popular and widely read magazine of the period and the site of Charlie Chan's debut, responded to the demand for and appeal of stories with an Asian flavor. From 1920 to 1941 the *Post* published a short story with an Asian cast or setting at the rate of one every other month. The magazine serialized twenty-one novels with Asian characters or locale, approximately one a year. Only the perennial American favorite, the western, appeared with greater frequency and consistency.

In the 1920s, the dominant stereotype of the Chinese was a variation of the traditional "heathen Chinee" theme. Readers apparently still enjoyed a delicious thrill of horror at the idea of the truly diabolical Chinaman. Atrocities, mayhem, torture, and sadism were usually the result of the "warped" Oriental mind and culture and set the tone for these stories. In one *Post,* a

Chinese merchant tried to smuggle a lovely young girl into the country as his bride. When his partner's wife betrayed the girl to immigration authorities, the merchant took his vengeance by pouring molten gold down the woman's throat.[5] In another story, published in 1924, one Chinese family had already strangled three new-born daughters. When the wife of the eldest son gave birth to yet another useless girl, the youth strangled the baby and attempted to kill the wife guilty of bearing a girl.[6] One of the most spectacularly villainous Chinese who appeared in the *Post* was Li Chang. He sought to avenge his father's death in a blaze of filial piety. Discovering that the entire crew of a ship was responsible for his father's death, Li Chang concocted a truly fiery revenge. First, he managed through devious and unscrupulous Oriental methods to infest the crew with lice. Then, playing the innocent and helpful friend, he gave the crew gasoline with which to douse and delouse themselves. When he was sure that ship and crew were thoroughly soaked, Li Chang set fire to them, eliminating lice, ship, and crew in a spectacular blaze.[7]

The most thoroughly diabolical of Charlie Chan's predecessors was Fu Manchu, the brilliant but mad scientist and archvillain. Like Charlie Chan, Fu Manchu appealed to the American imagination: his literary life spanned thirty-five years, from the first Fu Manchu thriller in 1913 to the fortieth and last in 1948. Fu Manchu movies began appearing in 1929 and have been made as recently as 1981, while the Fu Manchu mustache became part of both folklore and football. Paperback reissues of the Fu Manchu novels appeared in 1984.

As a villain in popular fiction, Fu Manchu had no peer in malevolence or malignancy until James Bond began encountering some of his more bizarre foes. The Chinese scientist was tall, gaunt, with cat-green hypnotic eyes. He could read minds and control the aging process to the point that he enjoyed near-immortality. Opium addiction was almost his only human trait. Even his daughter, the irresistibly lovely Fah Lo Suee, was merely an adjunct to his schemes and was eventually consigned to a furnace in which Fu Manchu was casting gold according to an ancient Oriental formula.

However awesome Fu Manchu was in and of himself, he was even more terrifying because of the power he both wielded and represented. He was the leader of the Council of Seven, the dreaded and deadly Si Fan, which sought to rule the world in the name of the yellow race. Death by rare disease, mysterious poison, loathsome insect, or other vile means awaited the luckless soul who attempted to thwart Si Fan. "I hold the key which unlocks the heart of the secret East," exulted Fu Manchu. "Holding that key, I command the obedience of an army greater than any ever controlled by one man. My power rests in the East, but my hand is stretched out to the West. I shall control the lost grandeur of China."[8] In his campaign to vanquish the white race and rule the world for the Orient, Fu Manchu could call upon a spectacular assortment of traditional and exotic creatures of horror. Dacoits and other murder cults of Asia did his bidding, as did African zombies and a menagerie of ferocious and cunning beasts. In many ways, Fu Manchu was the embodiment of a white racist's nightmare.

Despite the dominance of this stereotype, there were some alterations in the image of unalloyed evil and malevolence even before the appearance of Charlie Chan. In 1922, *The Saturday Evening Post* published a short story, "Scout Wong," which presaged the coming shift of images. Young Wong, a resident of Chinatown, sees an American Boy Scout troop drilling and, enthralled by the spectacle, resolves to become a Scout himself. When he approaches the troop, the white Scouts mock him, calling him "Yellow Belly" and assuring him that no such inferior person could ever hope to become a Boy Scout. Undaunted, Wong discovers a discarded copy of the *Boy Scout Handbook* and teaches himself the code and rules. The climax of the story occurs as the Scout troop is dining in the banquet hall of the restaurant in which Wong works. Flames sweep up through an open air duct and threaten to trap the Scouts, but Wong blocks the opening of the duct with his "yellow belly" and permits the troop to escape. He thus becomes simultaneously a hero and a Boy Scout.[9] The tone of "Scout Wong" is patronizing, but Wong does save the white Scouts. Most of his predecessors would rather have shoved them down the air duct directly into the flames.

The American reading public was thus somewhat prepared for the debut of Charlie Chan in *The House Without a Key*, serialized in the *Post* and then published in book form in 1925. Earl Derr Biggers based his fictional detective on an actual Chinese member of the Honolulu police force, one Chang Apana.[10] Biggers was probably also responding to an American willingness to tolerate a more sympathetic portrayal of the Chinese. The Charlie Chan films were in fact deliberately designed to refute or at least challenge the Fu Manchu image, according to their original producer.[11]

Physically Charlie Chan was a great deal less prepossessing than Fu-Manchu, and probably therefore a great deal easier to accept as a nonvillain. "He was very fat indeed, yet he walked with the light dainty step of a woman. His cheeks were as chubby as a baby's, his skin ivory-tinted, his black hair close-cropped, his amber eyes slanting."[12] Not only unprepossessing, but downright disarming, Charlie Chan was "an undistinguished figure in his Western clothes." The expression in his eyes was "a look of keen brightness that made the pupils gleam like black buttons in the yellow light."[13] Size and the suggestion of softness were important in the description of Charlie Chan. Earl Derr Biggers deliberately eschewed the traditional lean and hungry look for detectives to present his Oriental hero as a portly if graceful figure. The heavy-set individual is by tradition kindly, jolly, friendly, neither a threat nor a menace. Chan's size also enables the author to emphasize other characteristics commonly attributed to Asians, especially impassivity and stoicism. After all, who ever heard of a *fat* detective with the bursting nervous energy of a Holmes? In addition, his size also made Chan the ideal candidate for comparison with the Buddha, a relatively harmless touch of Orientalia. At various times Charlie Chan is described as a plain Buddha, an impassive Buddha, a serene Buddha, as immobile as a stone Buddha, and, with magnificent disregard for historical accuracy a grim and relentless Buddha.

The pleasingly plump detective's English is rather peculiar, a mixture of adroitly-used polysyllables and mangled syntax, several steps above pidgin but still exotic. A typical statement might be: "That are wrong attitude completely. Detective business made up of insignificant trifles."[14] One verb is missing completely, the other the wrong number and person, yet the vocabulary is accurate! In Chan's dialect there is an element of condescension as well as the need to portray Charlie Chan as unusual and Oriental. Biggers carefully points out that Charlie Chan's English is different from and better than that of most other Chinese, just as Chan himself is superior to many of the Chinese portrayed in the novels. When Charlie Chan must play the role of a servant to solve a crime, he reluctantly but ostentatiously adopts a vulgar pidgin: "Maybe you wantee catch 'um moah fish, boss?" He bemoans the necessity of doing this: "All my life I study to speak fine English words. Now must strangle all such in my throat, lest suspicion rouse up. Not a happy situation for me."[15] To sharpen the language distinctions, Chan's wife speaks broken pidgin, while his children show off their Western-style slang, often to his disgust. However, the gum-chewing, wise-cracking Number One and Number Two Sons of the movies do not appear in any of the novels.

Biographical information on Charlie Chan is scant. He is almost totally a creature of the Hawaiian and American present, with little of the Chinese past about him. He was born in China, apparently in a small village, and lived in a "thatched hut by side of muddy river."[16] At an unspecified age he migrated from China to Hawaii, where he worked as a house-boy for a rich white family before joining the Honolulu police force.[17] Of his personal life we know equally little; he has a wife, whose name is never mentioned, and by the midpoint of the third book eleven children, eight of them sons. "Good luck dogs me in such matters," he modestly says; "of eleven opportunities, I am disappointed but three times."[18] Beyond this, there is no attempt to show family life in the novels, no portrait of Charlie Chan as the Chinese patriarch. The family provides a convenient prop, an occasional reminder of Charlie Chan's Chineseness, and a touch of humanity. The number of children seems less a sign of any particular sexual prowess than a shadow of the idea of the prolific Chinese hordes and perhaps even the fear prevalent in the United States in the twenties that Orientals would take over the world simply through outbreeding the whites.

There is little of China itself in any of the books. Other than casual discussions in which his early life history unfolds, Chan mentions China only twice. At one point, trying to persuade an aged servant to give evidence so that he can "see again the village where you were born—walk again the soil where your bones are to rest," he speaks fondly but briefly of China.[19] At another point, recalling the peaceful land of his youth (which would make him over a hundred years old if Biggers adhered strictly to Chinese history), Charlie Chan remarks: "China is sick now. But as some one has so well said, many of those who send sympathy to the sick man die before him. That has happened in China's past—it will happen again."[20] Far removed from China itself, Charlie Chan can be Chinese without being overpoweringly alien.

A somewhat warped element of Chinese culture is present in Charlie Chan's frequent resort to proverbs. Although the "Confucius says" tag of the movies is mercifully absent in the books, and Confucius himself is mentioned only three times in total, counterfeit proverbs abound. "As all those who know me have learned to their distress, Chinese have proverbs to fit every possible situation," Chan rather deprecatingly remarks.[21] There is no attempt to present or explore Confucian philosophy or Chinese culture beyond the counterfeit proverbs. In some ways Charlie Chan's being Chinese seems little more than a convenient if somewhat exotic gimmick. Superficially Charlie Chan may appear Chinese, but he is fundamentally stripped of any genuine Chinese culture.

The reader remains highly conscious, however, of the fact that Charlie Chan is Chinese. There are frequent references to the detective's being typical of what is expected of the Chinese, whether it be psychic powers, inscrutability, or diligence. At several points, Biggers takes care to present Chan in a mild, almost gift-shop Chinese setting. For example, the Chan family home on Punchbowl Hill is furnished with Chinese objects: carved teakwood tables, elegant porcelain vases, crimson and gold Chinese lanterns, silk paintings, and a dwarf tree. In this setting Chan greets his visitor, wearing a long scholar's robe, trousers, and felt slippers; he is "all Oriental now, suave and ingratiating but somewhat remote."[22] However, this is the only time the detective appears in traditional Chinese costume and he is seen in his own home only twice. Otherwise his dress and milieu are Western.

Bits of Chinese and quasi-Chinese philosophy worked into the books are often presented as antithetical to, and better than, Western ideas and values. One consistently recurring theme is the virtue of patience and the idea that the Chinese more than any other race, especially the American race, recognize and esteem the virtue of patience. In a typical situation, an American girl urges Charlie Chan to move quickly to close a case. He demurs: "Patience . . . always brightest plan in these matters. Acting as champion of that lovely virtue, I have fought many fierce battles. American has always the urge to leap too quick. How well it was said, retire a step and you have the advantage."[23] According to Chan, this attitude toward patience springs from a deeper Chinese philosophy about life and man's place in the universe. "Chinese knows he is one minute grain of sand on seashore of eternity. With what result? He is calm and quiet and humble. No nerves, like hopping, skipping Caucasian. Life for him not so much ordeal."[24]

Charlie Chan also expresses a complimentary "Chinese" view of life: "Coarse food to eat, water to drink, and the bended arm for a pillow—that is an old defintion of happiness in my country." It is, in fact, a statement made by Yen Hui, Confucius's disciple. The westerner's ambition and impatience have no place in the real scheme of things. "Man—what is he? Merely one link in a great chain binding the past with the future. All times I remember I am link. Unsignificant link joining those ancestors whose bones repose on far distant hillsides with the ten children—it may now be eleven—in my house on Punchbowl Hill."[25]

Biggers tended to use such comments less as statements in their own right or as expositions of Chinese philosophy—to which they are only tenuously related—than as foils for contrast to the usually less worthy Western customs and ideas. Sometimes, Chinese and American culture are directly compared—by Americans—and Chinese culture is usually judged superior. For instance, a very proper lady and former Bostonian comments, with no more than the expected amount of condescension: "The Chinese are my favorite race. The Chinese are the aristocrats of the East. So clever and competent and honest, carrying on among the lazy riff-raff of the Orient. A grand people, Mr. Chan." Biggers doesn't let this opportunity pass. Chan replies: "Appreciation such as yours makes music to my ears. We are not highly valued in the United States, where we are appraised as laundrymen, or maybe villains in the literature of talkative films. You have great country, rich and proud, and sure of itself. About rest of world it knows little, and cares extremely less."[26] This awareness of two different worlds is very much present in all six of the Charlie Chan books and betrays Chan into his only expression of arrogance, personal or cultural, as he greets a young and rather haughty New Englander: "Mere words cannot express my unlimited delight at meeting a representative of the ancient civilization of Boston."[27]

Tied in with but not always directed at Charlie Chan are comments on the basic characteristics of the Chinese people. Some are banal, some condescending and some outright racist. For example, the reader is told that Chinese are night-owls, at their best after the sun sets.[28] Chinese are also assumed to be particularly suited to be detectives. A Scotland Yard man praises Chan for unraveling an especially intricate mystery: "Sergeant, my hearty congratulations. But I know your people, and I am not surprised."[29] In another situation, after Charlie Chan has again solved an enticing mystery, his superior pats him on the back— literally—and remarks, "A great idea, Charlie. . . . The Oriental mind . . . Rather subtle, isn't it?"[30]

Biggers' racially tinged comments are few and mild considering American racist attitudes during the 1920s; he seems deliberately to act as a missionary for a more enlightened view of other races. When open racial prejudice does occur, it is put down immediately, and with such finality that Biggers is obviously using it as a set-piece situation. Furthermore, racial prejudice is generally the property of the more unsavory characters in the books, either the villains or the uncouth and uneducated. For example, a generally boorish Englishman, and a murderer to boot, berates his Chinese cook for exhibiting "all the worst qualities of a heathen race." Charlie responds, "A heathen race that was busy inventing the art of printing when gentlemen in Great Britain were still beating one another over head with spiked clubs."[31] In fact, virtually the only times Charlie Chan expresses anger occur when racial slurs of this sort are expressed. Yet another supercilious Englishman, seeing the Chinese detective arrive to investigate a murder, exclaims, "Good Lord! What kind of place is this? Why don't they send a white man out here?" At this, "a rare light flared suddenly in Charlie's eyes" and he replied "in icy tones" that "the man who is about to cross a stream should not revile the crocodile's mother."[32] Despite the somewhat Delphic quality of the instant proverb, it is clear that neither author nor character regard race as a hinderance to intelligence.

Hawaii, the setting for the first novel and for Chan's permanent home, was simultaneously remote and friendly, exotic and familiar, Asian and Western—an ideal locale for a westernized Chinese detective. The Hawaii of Earl Derr Biggers and Charlie Chan is somehow dangerous to traditional European values, a place in which the white man must work consciously and strenuously to maintain traditional morality. It enjoys the "semi-barbaric beauty of a Pacific island" and is "too lurid to be quite respectable." Hawaii is "too sweet" according to one Bostonian who spent thirty years in the islands, "a little too much like Heaven to be altogether safe."[33]

But this essentially alien, deceptively dangerous quality makes Hawaii the ideal setting for Charlie Chan. Like the islands, he is basically different, alien, perhaps even dangerous, but like the islands he is so pleasant that he cannot be seen as a threat. The islands are the crossroads of the Pacific, where Asian and European races, customs, and cultures meet, compete, and mingle. Charlie Chan is likewise a mixture of cultures, ideas, and values. As Hawaii is neither completely Oriental nor completely American, so too Charlie Chan is caught between the two cultures and tries to find his way through them. He is deeply troubled about becoming too American. The difficulty of remaining Chinese in a non-Chinese and pervasively American setting such as Hawaii is particularly vivid to Chan as he looks at the younger generation of his family, either his younger cousin or his own children. When he uses a particularly reprehensible bit of slang, he apologizes: "Pardon vile slang, which I acquire from my children, now being beautifully educated in American schools."[34] Charlie Chan is both pleased and embarrassed by his cousin Willie Chan who was "attired in the extreme of college-cut clothes [and who] was an American and emphasized the fact." Willie Chan is one of the chief suppliers of slang in Charlie Chan's life and also "captain All Chinese baseball team and demon back-stopper of the Pacific." His customary greeting is a breezy "pleased to meetchu."[35]

There is considerable ambivalence in Charlie Chan's attitude toward the Americanization of younger Chinese. He is pleased that his eleventh child will have American citizenship; "An American citizen, a future boy scout under the American flag, he should have an American name."[36] Charlie Chan's full Chinese name is never mentioned. Yet the Americanization of his older children is a source of perplexity and even annoyance. The oldest are depicted as problems. Henry, smoking cigarettes, wearing college-cut clothes, using slang, "had been Americanized to a rather painful extent." Rose has deviated so far from Chinese tradition that she openly questions her father's judgment. Making the final transition between China and America, she plans to leave Hawaii to attend college stateside. Charlie Chan "had always been proud of the fact that they were all American citizens. But, perhaps because of this very fact, they seemed to be growing away from him. The gulf widened daily. They made no effort to remember the [Confucian] precepts and odes; they spoke the English language in a way that grated on Charlie's sensitive ear." Strongly conscious of his family and his traditions, Chan tries to envision his mother's reaction to these Americanized children. "His mother would not have approved, Charlie knew. She would have mourned for the old ways, the old customs. He mourned for them himself—but there was nothing he could do about it."[37]

Part of Charlie Chan's ambivalence toward the Americanization of his children derives from the fact that he himself is part of the process of Americanization. He constantly tests himself to see how much he has become American and how much that has changed him. This kind of probing makes him more acceptable to American readers for two reasons. First, it implies that the American culture is innately so good and so all-pervasive that it can envelop even a tradition-minded Chinese. Second, Charlie Chan with his partially alien children and his own sense of changing values and identity was also a figure with whom Americans could sympathize, especially during the pervasive identity crisis brought on by the changing styles and values of the twenties.

Charlie Chan is keenly aware of what he considers dangerous signs of this Americanization in himself. "I will confess my shame. It seems I have circulated too long with mainland Americans. I have now, by contagion, acquired one of their worst faults. I too suffer curiosity."[38] Interestingly, Charlie Chan views as faults characteristics that Americans tend to value such as curiosity and ambition. If not tragic flaws, they are at least devastatingly non-Chinese characteristics. Trying to explain his inability to interrogate an elderly Chinese servant, Chan admits that "a gulf like the heaving Pacific lies between us. Because he, although among Caucasions for many more years than I, still remains Chinese. As Chinese today as in the first moon of his existence. While I—I bear the brand—the label—Americanized." Chan is suddenly, accutely aware of his own dilemma, and of its cause. "I traveled with the current. I was ambitious. I sought success. For what I have won, I have paid the price. Am I an American? No. Am I then a Chinese? Not in the eyes of Ah Sing."[39] At one point, discontent because of inaction, the Chinese detective muses to himself, "Can it be that Oriental character is slipping from me owing to fact I live so many years among restless Americans?" He concludes that "cool, calm Oriental gets too much like mainland Americans from circling in such towering society."[40] In fact, it appears that even some of his eating habits have become Americanized. Charlie Chan orders tea with "three lumps of sugar and the breath of the lemon in passing"! These American characteristics are not necessarily happy ones for Charlie Chan, or for anyone else in his opinion. Impatience is particularly insidious in its effects upon the American. "His temples throb. His heart pounds. The fibers of his body vibrate. With what result? A year subtracted from his life."[41]

In the last Charlie Chan novel, *Keeper of the Keys*, Biggers sets up a deliberate contrast between the Americanized detective and an old Chinese servant who has resisted Americanization and who clings to his old ways and pidgin English. In comparison to Ah Sing, Charlie Chan appears more American than the stereotyped servant. However, Charlie Chan is rarely seen with other Chinese. They are either servants in the stereotype of Ah Sing or else residents of Chinatown. Even more rarely does Charlie Chan speak Chinese. In the first of the six novels, he speaks his native language only once. Despite Biggers's references to such "Chinese characteristics" as imperturbability and psychic powers, Charlie Chan is not really very Chinese.

Unlike Fu Manchu, a mysterious and exotic Oriental, Charlie Chan is purely American in his work. He is a detective who could as easily be a resident of New York or Cleveland as of Honolulu. Hercule Poirot, Nero Wolfe, and Gideon Fell (a Belgian, a Montenegran, and an Englishman) are detectives in the same style as Charlie Chan. All employ classical methods of reasoning and logic to solve crimes. As Russell Nye points out in his discussion of American popular culture, Charlie Chan and these other detectives lived and worked in "an essentially rational world in which crime could be solved by the man of logic."[42] As a detective—and it is important to remember that the Charlie Chan books are primarily detective fiction, not social tracts—Charlie Chan operates in a Western world of reason. He does not resort to Chinese jiggery-pokery or sleight of hand; he does not have to. Nye also points out that Charlie Chan is the first fictional detective who is in fact a professional policeman rather than a talented amateur. Disguises and amazing feats of physical prowess have almost no place in the world of Detective Sergeant Charlie Chan. Chan does go undercover once to gather evidence—he is masquerading as a Chinese cook—and resorts to an occasional wristlock on a subject, but his methods are generally nonviolent and almost totally intellectual. Furthermore, the crimes in which he becomes involved are not mysterious murders in the depths of Chinatown. They are murders in the midst of quite respectable white society.

This question of Chinese identity is one to which Biggers returns again and again, worrying it this way and that. In one novel he transports Charlie Chan from Hawaii to the mainland, but then continually sends him into Chinatown on the mainland. It is as if the author does not want to forget, and does not want his readers to forget, that Charlie Chan is Chinese—but that he also does not want this to get in the way of telling the story. Interestingly, the other major Oriental character in the series, a Japanese assistant detective named Kashimo, is the butt of racial and slapstick humor as none of the Chinese characters ever is. Kashimo's specialties seem to be hissing, fouling up evidence, and generally making life difficult for Charlie Chan and the Honolulu Police Department. The Chinese detective is even permitted an occasional jab at the Japanese. At one point, Charlie Chan observes that "cooking business begins to get tiresome like the company of a Japanese" and at another states that a twist of the wrist to disarm a suspect is "one thing I am ever able to learn from Japanese."[43]

Charlie Chan is thus an intelligent and likeable individual who is superficially Chinese but could just as easily be American in many of his most basic traits. Sometimes the Chinese veneer is little more than a facade to create an exotic atmosphere, while at other times it is used to convey information or pseudo-information about Chinese attitudes and to contrast them to American ideas, usually to the detriment of the American ways. There is thus a tremendous paradox in the Charlie Chan books. Charlie Chan himself is Chinese, but his methods and his milieu are American. The Chinese characteristics make him more interesting, but they are not the dominant factor in the life or being of Charlie Chan. They are more than window dressing but considerably less than the whole person. There are enough Chinese characteristics to provide color, but not so many that they overwhelm the reader or remove Charlie Chan from the reader's experience or comprehension. When American and Chinese characteristics are compared, it is usually the American rush against the Chinese calm, American ambition against Chinese acceptance and serenity. These comparisons made Charlie Chan and his culture more appealing to the individual reading the novels for relaxation and enjoyment. Earl Derr Biggers was a careful and cautious craftsman. The Charlie Chan books are vehicles for Biggers's messages, but they are small messages much more concerned with the American condition than with the Chinese. Proper Bostonians, improper Bostonians, and Englishmen of several degrees of propriety mingle with Americans in Charlie Chan's life, but there is not a single rapacious warlord or treacherous spy or even lovely sloe-eyed, boundfoot femme fatale in this essentially Western world.

Charlie Chan's outstanding characteristics—intelligence, good humor, diligence, loyalty—are valued in both Chinese and American cultures. He is Chinese only to the point to which it begins to hinder the plot or force the reader to stretch his mind, and then he becomes very much Americanized. The qualms about Americanization are interesting and express a valid point of view widely shared by the older generation of Chinese in America, but the main point seems to be that Americanization is impossible for the oldest generation of Chinese, incomplete for the generation of Charlie Chan, and inevitable for the youngest generation—not only inevitable, but also eagerly and profitably seized by the children themselves. In many ways Charlie Chan, as he realizes, is himself American.

Stereotyping and unconscious assumptions about race unquestionably appear in the Charlie Chan books. Many of the ideas about Chinese culture are skewed more or less violently, and even the admiration expressed for certain "Chinese" characteristics is often tinged with a patronizing or condescending attitude. One could argue endlessly whether a somewhat favorable stereotype is in the long run more or less harmful than a totally negative stereotype, but the argument is pointless. Both stereotypes are dangerous because they distract from reality, substitute slogans of understanding, furnish a comfortable illusion of knowledge when ignorance is the case, and mitigate against efforts at genuine understanding.

Nonetheless, stereotyped or not, the introduction of Charlie Chan marks a very real change in American images of the Chinese. Neither so villainous as Fu Manchu nor so condescendingly drawn as Scout Wong, Charlie Chan is a human being, with a family of whom he is proud (even if they occasionally dismay him), two cultures which he cannot completely reconcile within himself, a job that he performs superbly, and a set of problems and dilemmas that make him an appealing and sympathetic figure. It is only a few years from the publication of the first Charlie Chan serial to the publication of Pearl Buck's intensely sympathetic and astonishingly successful *The Good Earth*. *The Good Earth*, with its heroes gallantly struggling and ultimately succeeding against overwhelming odds, might not have been readily accepted by a reading public whose primary image of the Chinese to that time had been the barbarous though fascinating Fu Manchu. Chan was the necessary bridge.

In many ways, the portraits of China and the Chinese in American fiction resemble a stratified cross section of the earth; layer rests upon layer, image succeeds image. But in a strange way, just as the archeologist or geologist can view many strata simultaneously, so the student of images of China can see the overlapping and sometimes interwined stereotypes, one dominating a particular period but none totally erased, neither the malignancy of Fu Manchu nor the dauntless and occasionally tiresome patience of Pearl Buck's peasants. Charlie Chan occupies a vital place in this layering of images. He himself is a transitional figure, but there is a very clear demarcation between the image he presents and the images before and after him.[44]

Charlie Chan is the most significant Chinese character in American fiction of the twenties. His success ultimately came less from his Chinese nature than from his essentially American attributes. Ironically, the most sympathetic Chinese of the period—and one of the most successful ever created—is sympathetic and successful largely because he is no longer very Chinese.

Notes

1. The six original novels are *The House Without a Key* (1925), *The Chinese Parrot* (1926), *Behind That Curtain* (1928), *The Black Camel* (1929), *Charlie Chan Carries On* (1930), and *Keeper of the Keys* (1932). Specific editions cited appear in subsequent notes.

2. Russell Nye, *The Unembarrassed Muse: The Popular Arts in America* (New York: Dial Press, 1970), 229, 250, 401; Harold R. Isaacs, *Images of Asia: American Views of China and India* (New York: Harper & Row, 1972), 119. The work originally appeared as *Scratches on Our Minds* (Cambridge: MIT Press, 1958).

3. Isaacs, *Images of Asia,* passim.

4. Isaacs' study, *Images of Asia,* seems to bear out this assumption.

5. High Wiley, "Jade," *The Saturday Evening Post,* 27 March 1920, passim.

6. Harold Mcgrath, "The Pagan Madonna," *The Saturday Evening Post,* 2 Oct. 1924, passim.

7. Frederic F. Van De Water, "Yellow Cargo," *The Saturday Evening Post,* 26 April 1924, passim.

8. Sax Rohmer, *Island of Fu Manchu* (New York: Doubleday, Doran & Co., 1941), 68.

9. Richard Cornell, "Scout Wong," *The Saturday Evening Post,* 18 March 1922, passim.

10. Nye, *Unembarrassed Muse,* 250.

11. Isaacs, *Images of Asia,* 119–20.

12. Earl Derr Biggers, *The House Without a Key* (New York: Bantam, 1974), 60.

13. Earl Derr Biggers, *The Chinese Parrot* (New York: Bantam, 1974), 17.

14. Biggers, *The House Without a Key,* p. 163.

15. Biggers, *The Chinese Parrot,* 53, 55.

16. Ibid., 119.

17. Ibid., 11.

18. Earl Derr Biggers, *Behind That Curtain* (New York: Bantam, 1975), 58.

19. Earl Derr Biggers, *Keeper of the Keys* (New York: Bantam, 1975), 171.

20. Earl Derr Biggers, *Charlie Chan Carries On* (New York: Bantam, 1975), 134.

21. Biggers, *Keeper of the Keys,* p. 200.

22. Biggers, *Charlie Chan Carries On,* 134; *The House Without a Key,* 192–93.

23. Biggers, *Behind That Curtain,* 117.

24. Biggers, *The Chinese Parrot,* 180.

25. Biggers, *Behind That Curtain,* 17.

26. Biggers, *Charlie Chan Carries On,* 132–33.

27. Biggers, *The House Without a Key,* 74.

28. Earl Derr Biggers, *The Black Camel* (New York: Bantam, 1975), 84; Biggers, *Behind That Curtain,* 96–97.

29. Biggers, *Behind That Curtain,* 242.

30. Biggers, *The House Without a Key,* 243.

31. Biggers, *The Black Camel,* 53.

32. Ibid., 67; cf. Biggers, *Keeper of the Keys,* 128.

33. Biggers, *The House Without a Key,* 1, 4, 35.

34. Biggers, *Keeper of the Keys,* 155–56.

35. Biggers, *The House Without a Key,* 156.

36. Biggers, *Behind That Curtain,* 55.

37. Biggers, *The Black Camel,* 111–14.

38. Biggers, *Behind That Curtain,* 68.

39. Biggers, *Keeper of the Keys,* 87.

40. Biggers, *Charlie Chan Carries On,* 4; Biggers, *Behind That Curtain,* 107.

41. Biggers, *Behind That Curtain,* 125.

42. Nye, *Unembarrassed Muse,* 257, 250.

43. Biggers, *Charlie Chan Carries On,* 120; Biggers, *The Black Camel,* 52, 58–59; Biggers, *The Chinese Parrot,* 171, 235.

44. For a general discussion of the formation of images of China, cf. Isaacs, *Images of Asia,* and also Raymond Dawson, *The Chinese Chameleon* (New York: Oxford University Press, 1967).

Carl Crow, Edgar Snow, and Shifting American Journalistic Perceptions of China

JERRY ISRAEL

In a 1924 profile, Herbert Croly suggested that the diplomat-banker-publisher Willard Straight, had he lived, would have found fulfillment at the helm of a chain of influential news magazines.[1] Straight, who died of pneumonia at age thirty-eight in 1918, had already made progress in that direction as founder of Croly's *The New Republic* and figured largely in the economic and reform aspects of America's Open Door policy in Asia. In the next several decades he might have occupied a place usually associated with the American publisher-king Henry Luce. Some twenty years younger than Straight, Luce, the China-born missionary's son, had a chronological headstart in perceiving and reporting American images and interests found in China.[2] Approximately when Croly was eulogizing Straight, Luce and Briton Hadden were creating the news magazine called *Time*. Like Straight, Luce was more than just a publisher.

Despite Russo-Japanese War service with the Associated Press, Straight came to journalism very near the end of his short life via *The New Republic* in 1913.[3] Progressive Era writers like Croly, Walter Lippmann, and Walter Weyl expressed Straight's hopes and frustrations as representative of railroad, banking, and diplomatic interests in China and Manchuria.[4] Commercial-financial ambition and missionary-reform fervor characterized the Open Door policy in action in the period of Straight's career.[5]

Henry Luce, whose roots were deep in the Protestant missionary movement in China, jumped into journalism right out of Yale. When Straight died and Luce chose journalism, the economic component of American China policy was holding firm, but formal missionary enthusiasm was suffering a decline. Having transformed themselves under the banner of a social gospel from evangelical to educational crusaders, missionaries slowed their efforts.

Such a decline resulted from conditions in the church at home and new realities in China. In the United States the Protestant missionary movement was weakened by a "Fundamentalist-Modernist" debate, by confusion over the role of missionary in either of these theological alternatives, and by financial fatigue. In China, Chinese Christians pressed for control of their churches, for the end of paternalism, and for the end of protection of the missionaries under an unequal treaty system. A new pessimism among missionaries was sounded by Methodist secretary Frank Gamewell when he observed: "We cannot evangelize China, we cannot cure China's multiplied diseases, we cannot educate her multiplied millions or feed them. That is to say, there is a limit no matter how far we go to what we can do."[6]

Another interest group emerged to pick up the slack from the legacy of missionary reform activity. It was "secular journalists" who become the new publicists for American images of China and the Chinese. Missionaries—the old publicists—often reported the news for the people back home. Reporters and editors, representing private secular American interests, moved into this critical position. The journalist as press agent performed one of the essential missionary tasks, spreading the good news to Chinese, not now of Jesus but of America. By daily preaching and teaching, mission workers in the field had been concerned with converting individual Chinese to Christianity or at least preparing them for it. Newspapermen continued the commitment to conversion, but this time substituted the consumption of Christian goods as the desired end product. The businessman and banker, rather than weakend by the marked-time of their missionary partner, were reinforced by the even more avid cooperation of secular image makers.

But as there would be two Chinas in the midtwentieth century, so there were two journalistic American images of China. Carl Crow's work serves as a mirror into the China of the Open Door while Edgar Snow's writing moves closer to the China of the Cold War. Crow's China was the treaty-port Shanghai. His Chinese were wise and westernized. Snow's China was the caves of Yenan (Yan'an). His Chinese were red and revolutionary.

Carl Crow, like Snow later, was a product of the "Missouri" school of American journalism. The University of Missouri turned out a large number of image makers. Crow went through the early twentieth-century Progressive Era "muckracking" the cor-

ruption of American cities. He gave *The Saturday Evening Post*
its quota of exposure in such gems as "Cutting Up the Big
Ranches" and "Checkmating the Meat Trust." Crow followed
other Missourians to China in 1911 and worked as a reporter
and then propagandist for George Creel (another Missourian) and
the World War Committee on Public Information. Crow divided
the rest of his life between Shanghai and New York. The first
two decades were spent as China's first press agent. The last
saw him telling Americans about China in a series of humorous
books, the best of which was *400 Million Customers.*[7] The Crow
philosophy and style reflected a commitment to things American.
He dismissed the older Western view of the Chinese as a heathen,
unregenerate, depraved, inscrutable people and converted them
into entrepreneurial, frugal, common-sensical, untiring, and loyal
customers.

Crow's books, published by Eugene Saxton and Cass Canfield
at Harper's between 1937 and 1945, included, in addition to *400
Million Customers,* a study of Confucious called *Master Kung*
and six other Asia books with a political and anti-Japanese tone,
especially *I Speak for the Chinese* (1938) and *China Takes Her
Place* (1944). Many Americans, diplomats, broadcasters, publishers, and advertisers sought out Crow's advice for their images
of China. He was invited to lecture and dine by Dale Carnegie.
He was asked his opinion by such China-hands as "Vinegar Joe"
Stilwell, T. A. Bisson, Walter Judd, and Henry Luce on such
topics as elementary school texts, the Generalissimo and Madame
Chiang (Jiang Jieshi), and China's proposed exhibition at the New
York World's Fair.[8] Crow's advice was sought by advertisers and
journalists on personnel and policy decisions affecting Asia. His
images were transmitted by radio broadcasters such as network
analyst Upton Close; KMOX (St. Louis) sunrise commentator
H. W. Flannery; and newsmen on WLW (Cincinnati) and WTIC
(Hartford) who borrowed from Crow's writings for their China
information.[9]

Two efforts of Crow's early journalistic career foreshadowed
his emergence as a Shanghai press agent. First was his publication
in 1913 (with many subsequent editions to follow) of *A Traveler's
Handbook for China.* This book was designed to "bridge the gap"
for those new to the Chinese scene, like Crow himself.[10] The
other was his work as China coordinator of the war propaganda
efforts of another Missourian, Creel, in spreading American news
throughout the world. While interpreting the two worlds to each
other, or at least to himself and to other newcomers to China,

Crow found a home. Crow thought the work of the Creel Committee a bit tedious and bureaucratic and wanted very much to be a "blood and thunder" war correspondent, a chance he barely missed during the Chinese revolution of 1911 but got finally in the late 1930s. Nevertheless he had found a vocation. At the end of official work he wrote: "I had either to return to America or find something to do in China. I wanted to remain where I was and there appeared to me to be a business which fitted me exactly. The obvious thing for foreign merchants to do in order to sell goods to the Chinese was to advertise in the Chinese newspapers. I became an advertising agent, establishing the first agency in China."[11]

Just how extensive were Crow's contracts as the only American-Chinese press agent? The following only partial list suggests the ingenuity and success of Crow as publicist for American businessmen in a relatively underdeveloped part of the world. Records exist of fairly close relations between Carl Crow, Inc., and the Buick Motor Division of General Motors (later eulogized in the once-muckraker's last completed book, a history of Buick's home town, Flint, Michigan); the Hurley Machine Division of Electric Household Utilities Corporation; the Farmers Union Grain Terminal Association; the Schenley Distillers Corporation, as well as a number of chambers of commerce and trade associations.[12] In addition, Crow was frequently asked to help pioneer new business ventures in such commodities as jade carvings and seed importing.[13] One Philadelphian suggested that Crow publish a book of Chinese recipes and diet suggestions.[14]

Crow, who admired the job done by "America's Globe-Trotting Salesmen," was even more taken with the goods he remembered or had heard about at home.[15] In one of his most reflective statements, Crow observed that the traveling American was early recognized because he was always searching out a familiar face, always sad and baffled. The lonesome American found solace in his native land's material productivity, widely distributed around the globe. Crow wrote: "During the past few years I have visited more than twenty different countries and was never far away from a shop which stocked one or more American products. In a mud-walled village I found a can of Del Monte fruit salad. In a single shop I saw on the shelves Chiclets, Sloan's Liniment and Kodak films and bought an ice cold bottle of Coca-Cola. One may travel all over the world and never get far away from a supply of Gillette blades, Palmolive Soap, Pond's Cold Cream, Kolynos Toothpaste and dozens of other well-known American products."[16]

Some of his writing concerned Japanese aggression and was done for the Writers' War Board or the American Committee for Non-Participation in Japanese Aggression.[17] Much of it was published in *Reader's Digest*. Crow repeatedly utilized themes such as Japanese atrocities and drug traffic after the intensification of Sino-Japanese hostilities in 1937.[18] He shared an animus with an old Shanghai crony, Samuel Blythe, for what the latter referred to as "the machinations of the yellow bastards from Japan." Crow quite clearly allowed a more sympathetic Japan-hand like Julean Arnold to suggest that the reader "would get the impression that you harbor an animus toward the Japanese.[19]

Crow was, in many ways, still the "local" boy, accessible for example to the requests of *Reader's Digest* for a piece critical of "government departments like Nelson Rockefeller's that are responsible for 'administration by press releases' and the prodigal spending of huge sums in an effort to buy goodwill."[20] When Walter Judd or Harry Price of the American Committee for Non-Participation in Japanese Aggression wanted more atrocity stories, or rebuttals of Walter Lippmann's call for negotiations with Japan, Crow produced, sometimes for a fee, usually on schedule.[21] In one such glaring example, Clifton Fadiman, then of the Writer's War Board, suggested to Crow in October 1944 that the possible end of the war in Europe might lead to a call for a "softer" treatment of Japan. "It is the War Board's intention to show up these arguments" announced Fadiman. Crow was assigned the task of producing a document for *American Legion Magazine*. It was to be a thousand to fifteen hundred words, in simple English, a tough, hard-hitting job by a person who knows and who was able to show up the "Grew" line. Grew was a long time advocate of more temporate treatment of Japan in the U.S. Department of State.[22]

Crow had had official experience with such political journalism on the Creel Committee and got a new taste of it with the Office of War Information. From this post he fired off suggestions for stories to magazines and tracked down tips on Japanese industry.[23] But his tenure of "power" was short-lived. Like other prewar journalists he was bypassed by newer men, and mercifully allowed by his chief, the younger Asian scholar, Owen Lattimore, to resign to devote full time to a book on American business habits.[24] Crow could take some pride in "the time when we were fighting the war all by ourselves before MacArthur and Eisenhower got going."[25] But he might have more properly agreed with his Creel colleague Edgar Sisson who noted that "my motion is new men for new wars."[26]

Crow's China had no misery, wretchedness, poverty, or, as already noted, revolution. There was also much that was Shanghai-international in his images. The China Crow observed was that of the treaty-port westerner. The Chinese he knew or reached were servants, clerks, businessmen, rickshaw boys, or those who read newspapers (perhaps 5 percent, or 20 million). Crow thought of himself as a friendly, democratic American, not as a privileged, threatening white. He looked for "Four Hundred Million Customers" but perhaps perceived "Four Hundred Million Number One Boys."

In the chapter "Straights and Flushes," Crow reported on the preparation of Chinese rules for American poker. In response to this, Crow set up in his office an American laboratory and schoolroom of poker-playing to inductively arrive at pragmatic translations appropriate for each situation. He tried to win "so as to give my pupils confidence they were being taught by a master." In time the rules developed proved workable in a real game situation with five previously non–poker playing Chinese.

Crow took great pride in the widespread popularity of poker in China and his "rules" soon surpassed even the Creel Committee translations of Woodrow Wilson's speeches as all-time bestsellers. The international impact was potentially still more significant. One of Crow's friends noted that "the introduction of poker into China and its general adoption as an indoor sport would be a great civilizing influence, would serve to break down the provincialism of the people and provide them with a common interest."

The local American origins also prevailed. "I learned to play poker in Fort Worth," Crow remembered, "and have always played the orthodox game. The Chinese are the only people who play orthodox poker as it was played in Texas thirty years ago."[27]

Crow was a man who created many household images Americans held about the Chinese. Based on twenty-five years' experience, Crow also provided the material that other influential opinion makers used to draw the pictures of China in the American mind during the Second World War.

Edgar Snow's influence as a chronicler of Chinese communism has been widely observed.[28] Other large parts of his career have been ignored through too much subjectivity or too little documentation.[29] Snow, among the first to challenge the Crow–Open Door images of American business and reform in Asia, is often labeled a "propagandist," and surely his own romantic rhetoric supports such charges.[30] But this characterization is one-dimensional. It removes Snow from his place with Crow in the mainstream of American journalists in Asia and makes him symbol, ideologue, or press agent for something strange and foreign. *Red Star Over China* was certainly "the right book, on the right subject, published at the right time."[31] Still, Snow is more than Mao's "Columbus," "Boswell," or "Marco Polo," as he has been described.[32] Such views transmit the impression of Snow as a blank slate, or Rip Van Winkle, waiting to be awakened by his meeting with Chinese communism. According to such reasoning, *Red Star* was his only well-known book, and his singular importance to some scholars was whether he reported the Reds to be "genuine communists," or "agrarian reformers."[33]

Like Crow's, Edgar Snow's work reflected images brought from home and others developed in China before he came in contact with the Communists. As Snow's first wife, Helen Foster Snow, has written, "Ed was directly in line of inheritance as Mr. America of his time."[34] Citing the link to other Missouri journalists, Mrs. Snow, known in her own China days as Nym Wales, has observed that "he was the protege of J. B. Powell, owner of the *China Weekly Review,* who had been the protege of T. F. Millard, who brought JBP [Powell] to be editor." Powell, in turn, "gave Ed a job as editor." Millard had been a supporter of the early stages of the Chinese revolution, and Powell was a strong ally of Chiang Kai-shek and the Guo Min Tang in the late 1920s.

Helen Snow concluded: "Ed took this only a step further and became Mao's Mr. America. We were non-communists," she asserted, "and Ed represented Middle America in person." From his wife's evaluation, Edgar Snow was probably neither a heretic nor a visionary. Considerable stability anchored the Missouri journalistic tradition in China. But the images of Carl Crow made less sense to Edgar Snow than did the changed image of the China of the Cold War.

More than a year before his fateful visit to the caves of the Communists in Northwest China, Edgar Snow told his wife Nym that "now I know why people like W. H. Donald, Punam Weale, Tom Millard and other newspapermen mixed up in China's internal affairs in the past."[35] In less than a decade Snow had fallen heir to the legacy of journalists building images and influencing policy. As James Thomson has noted, "In the thirties Americans traveled to Asia as the private representatives of a multitude of institutions—as the variegated reflection of a pluralistic society."[36] In particular, if the traveler was like Crow or Snow, from Missouri, he arrived in the Pacific with a letter in hand from Walter Williams, dean of the University of Missouri's School of Journalism. Missouri graduates edited publications in Tokyo, Tientsin [Tianjin], Peking [Beijing], and Shanghai, and an ex-student could always pick up a job.

The line of succession began with Millard, Missouri class of 1887, who had worked his way from *The St. Louis Republic* and *The New York Herald* to the Orient. In 1917, Williams dispatched his alumnus and colleague, John B. Powell, class of 1910, to work for Millard. Ten years later, Williams sent Edgar Snow to Powell.[37] Having allotted six weeks to China on his year-long, round-the-world junket, Snow was tempted to stay longer to help edit *The China Weekly Review*. He did not return from Asia until thirteen years later. In that time, Snow assisted Powell; wrote for *The Saturday Evening Post, Fortune, Look, The New York Sun* and *The London Daily Herald;* reported on China's northwest famine, the Formosa massacre, and the Indochina agrarian revolt; married Nym; taught at Yenching University in Peking; had his exclusive first-person scoop of Mao Tse-tung [Mao Zedong] at the post–long march Red Army hideout; witnessed Japan's victories in Asia; and wrote *The Far Eastern Front* and *The Battle for Asia* in addition to *Red Star Over China*.[38]

Snow commented that when his Asian career began, "Powell and Millard doubtless found in me some sentiments latent in many mid-westerners." If not unique, Snow's first twenty-two years had been representative. Born in Kansas City in 1905, Snow had the usual midwesterner's part-time jobs as harvest hand and railway worker before entering Kansas City Junior College and the University of Missouri. Although he did not graduate from Missouri, Snow got additional newspaper training at Columbia University before catching a Japanese ship out of Honolulu en route to East Asia with Williams' letter in his pocket. Indeed, as he was later to comment, "I could have been anyone of my generation of America moving westward."[39] Still his was a new generation. As Nym Wales noted, the days of the "old China hand"—of big investments, missionary-business ties, and gunboat diplomacy—were coming to an end.[40] Gradually, a younger set of "new China hands," many of them born in the twentieth century, was emerging. Though both groups existed side-by-side in the 1930s, the subtle transformation from Crow's world to that of Snow had begun. By analyz-

ing those aspects of Snow's experience that set him apart from
the old China and the old China hands, one sees why what Snow
found in the Yenan caves made sense for him.

Edgar Snow was young and inexperienced in his China days,
exuberant, reckless, and only thirty-two when *Red Star* was published. As he put it, "When I first arrived in Shanghai I was
every youth, full of curiosity and wide open to the world." He
was born the year the Russo-Japanese War ended, only six when
the Republic of China came into being, ten at the time of Japan's
Twenty One Demands, fourteen when nationalist Chinese protested pro-Japanese provisions of the Versailles Treaty on 4 May
1919, and a twenty-year old undergraduate when Sun Yat-sen (Sun
Zhongshan) died. Contrasts with the lives of Crow, Powell, Joseph
Grew, Patrick Hurley, Douglas MacArthur, George Marshall, and
Joseph Stilwell—all born in the early 1880s—are obvious. They
were acting out roles in a drama in which they had a vested
interest. Snow was involved in something new and different, free
from any long-standing obligations.

Other factors fostered a free and easy Snow style. Where most
of those before him had come to China inspired by a missionary
impulse, however secularized, Snow was genuinely "indifferent
to sectarian religion of any kind."[41] His paternal roots went far
back to the antipapist Snows of Kentucky. His own father had
married an Irish-German Catholic with priests on both sides of
the family. Though confirmed in his mother's faith, Edgar, the
family's youngest child, received the full force of his father's growing dissatisfaction with the religious compromises of courtship.
Edgar remembered listening on Sunday afternoons to well-chosen
lines from Robert Ingersoll or others on the Index. He reported
losing his faith when he noticed that communion wafers, baked
in ordinary coal stoves, could be consumed by altar boys without
retribution. Thus he arrived in China, perhaps searching for something to replace his childhood dogma, but without any ties to
formal religion. Indeed he became highly skeptical of the missionary movement. He was not above taking a cheap shot at the
stereotyped tract-carrying missionary with his shiny alpaca coat,
baggy trousers, dusty shoes, gleaming, crossed eyes, and funny
speech pattern. Snow's view of the failure to evangelize China
was unusually frank. "After more than a century of effort," he
measured, "the net result today is but 700,000 communicants
claimed by Protestant Christian crusaders." Even counting rice
Christians "protesting the faith with the hope of snapping up an
occasional square meal," Snow felt the rate of progress was such

that "we may hope to see China a Protestant Christian nation some 500 centuries hence."[42]

Nor did Snow find comfort in the other traditions of western life in China, particularly in the port city. More a "political ulcer" than a "splendid evidence of American influence," Shanghai was to Snow a materialistic, futile place. Selling things to make money, he reported, was the chief American pastime in the city: "The business man goes to market sewing machines, hot water bags or what you will; the missionary goes to sell the Bible. And both use high-powered American merchandising tactics." Snow found Shanghai a caricature of the United States at its most tawdry. "There in the most polyglot city in Asia," he wrote shortly after arriving, "the roving American finds all the comforts of home: Clara Bow and Buddy Rogers, the radio and jazz bands, cocktails and correspondence schools, night clubs and cabarets, neon lights and skyscrapers, chewing-gum and Buicks, wide trousers and long skirts, Methodist evangelists, and the Salvation Army. And there too, he finds such peculiar American institutions as Navy wives, shot-gun weddings, Girl Scouts, Spanish-American war veterans, a board of censors, day-light hold-ups, immaculate barbershops, a Short Story Club, wheat cakes, and a Chamber of Commerce."[43]

In place of Shanghai, the western treaty-port city, Snow came to be at home in China's heartland. He traveled and reported about "the feudal city of Yunnanfu," and took the "grand, 8,000 mile railway tour" from Ningbo to Hankow, from Nanjing to Harbin, and from Peking to the Great Wall and beyond, to Manchuria, and to Korea.[44] Especially in regions of famine and death west of Peking, Snow saw a country in which the real revolution had not yet begun. During the late 1930s, Peking became his home and he found it, unlike Shanghai, to be "incomparably the grandest and most interesting capital in Asia."[45]

He shared this Peking home with Nym Wales, and their marriage added another element to Snow's new and different perception of China.[46] They had met in Asia and never been in the United States together. She was his "frequently tormenting, often stimulating, and always energetically creative and faithful co-worker, consort and critic" during the China years. Her work, including her own follow-up visit to the Communists in 1938, provided competition and stimulation. The marriage itself, tempestuous and romantic, dissolved when both left China in the 1940s. Yet while together, the Snows were independent agents, developing and re-enforcing their new package of China images.

The pattern emerges then that Edgar Snow, within a decade

of his arrival in Asia, was ready to challenge the bases of traditional American views of China rooted in the missionary and treaty-port culture. In their stead, his images would rest on a youthful romance with a less-known China. Snow was prepared, not unlike China, for a bout with communism and revolution that also challenged the long-standing Western views. As early as 1931 Snow had noted that the Communist story would be a good one to tell the world.[47]

Despite his experiences, a good part of the Snow imagery, even in *Red Star,* still was supported by the "middle American" values he had brought with him. Part of Snow remained with the people he knew among "China's tawny hills." "But I was not and could not be one of them," he knew. "A man who gives himself to be the possession of an alien land lives a Yahoo life. I was an American."[48] At the heart of Snow's writing about his different and exciting China stood the belief in what and how America could do for China—a premise that linked Snow to his Missouri predecessors.

Despite his scorn for Shanghai's "neon" version of American material comfort, Edgar Snow did feel that American values had an important place in China. He remarked on the physical similarities between the two nations in terms of continental size and space. He enjoyed the easygoing sense of humor of both societies. In particular, Snow felt America, by extending the doctrines it stood for at home and by spreading the values of its heritage, could take the offensive in China.[49] While starting from an anti-colonial base, Snow's proposals echoed what other Americans had advocated. The United States, for better or worse, was "deep in the power game in the East," and therefore, Snow was sure that there was an "important and progressive role for American aid."[50] In his other two early books from China, *The Far Eastern Front* (1933) and *The Battle for Asia* (1941), which deserve some attention alongside *Red Star over China,* Snow made effective use of the imagery Americans had often used in China. "The door is no longer open but a-jar," he observed, but the role of American trade could not be denied in the "greatest future market on earth."[51]

During World War II, Snow even swelled with pride at the technological "little Americas," which he had scoffed at in Shanghai but now enjoyed. Suddenly, the "razors, meals, movies, pool tables, table tennis, swing bands, radio stations," not to mention, Bob Hope, Jack Benny and Charlie McCarthy were not disturbing anachronisms but homely reassurances. In days when he still could tolerate J. B. Powell's friends in the Kuomintang, Snow wrote that "with so many Harvard men at Nanking, Americans should expand with pride." He noted that it was "China's misfortune that Chiang Kai-shek did not go to Harvard."[52]

The chief obstacle to America's role, and thereby a major determinant of Snow's perceptions, was the menace of Japanese expansionism. Like other Americans, but perhaps more so because he had no memory of Japanese-American harmony, Snow could be alarmist enough throughout his career about Japan's ambitions. Arguing against American withdrawal from the Philippines in 1939, Snow proposed that he couldn't conceive of trading "Uncle Sam's farewell" for the approach of "Master Samurai."[53] All over Asia he saw the same pattern: imposition of Japanese culture, destruction of native industry, removal of all natural resources; and transition to a Japanese market. He wrote fearfully about these moves in pieces such as "Japan Builds a New Colony," "Japan Digs In," and "The Japanese Juggernaut Rolls On."[54] Snow visualized Japan letting "the people survive in a macabre state" and living off "the half-dead body of China like a vampire."[55] In a geographical domino thesis, not unlike that which other Americans would apply later to communism, Snow's imagery ran wild. He foresaw the "enslavement" of Asia to the "new imperialism" of the Japanese "Frankenstein." If China fell, he was sure, the Taiwanese, Koreans, Manchurians, and Mongols would know "permanent subjugation" and "nothing could save the other eastern people." The Filipinos, Indochinese, Malayans, Indonesians, Siamese, Burmese, and Indians all would fall.[56]

While it was common for Amercians to be wildly anti-Japanese, especially in the late 1930s, Snow's Japan phobia should not be underestimated. William Neumann pointed out the very important schism in American postures towards Japan, especially in the 1940s, between hard-line reconstructionists like Snow and others like Joseph Grew and Douglas MacArthur, who argued for a milder form of behavior, a moderate postwar reconstruction.[57] Snow searched about for a reasonable alternative to Japan and found the Chinese Communists. MacArthur, finding Snow's alternative impossible, turned back to a rebuilt and reformed Japan for Asian partnership. Accused by MacArthur of being part of a Russian spy ring in China as early as 1945, Snow attacked the supreme commander as being "soft" on Japan. Snow could not see how those who refused to compromise their fears of Japan could be "traitors" to MacArthur. Did the end of the war "wipe clean the slate of Japan's atrocities in China, or make Pearl Harbor the product of blameless intentions?" Snow asked.[58]

The search for an alternative to Japan colored everything Edgar

Snow did, thought, and felt about Asia. It changed his impression, for example, of the Generalissimo. To Snow, in 1934, Chiang Kai-shek had been "weak China's Strong Man." As late as 1938, even after Snow's visit to Mao, Chiang was still "China's Fighting Generalissimo." At the 1938 writing, Snow found Chiang's leadership secure, dynamic, and progressive; his personal courage great; and the benevolent influence of his wife very strong.[59] By the mid-1940s, as the choice narrowed for postwar Asia to a viable China or a rebuilt Japan, Snow came more and more to detest Chiang, who stood in the way of the former. The new "meglo-maniac" Generalissimo was seen as a tool of the landlords, surrounded by sycophants. Americans who trailed after the Nationalists' cause received equal scorn. Snow took special aim at General Patrick Hurley, that "unfortunate Colonel Blimp in our China tragedy." By the war's end, Snow was denied passage from Manila to China by direct orders of the Nationalist Government in Chung-king [Chongqing].[60]

The perception of the impossibility of a postwar peace led either by Japan or by the Nationalists took Snow further toward accepting Communist victory in Asia. As noted by Tang Tsou and Harold Isaacs, his emergence in 1944 and 1945 as an advocate of a somewhat "softer" image of the Chinese Communists as "agrarian reformers" was tied to Snow's search for a workable and marketable alternative. The more Japan became an option, the more Snow painted a favorable picture of the Red revolutionaries and the more also he came to be able to accept the support of the Soviet Union as an anti-Japanese ally.[61]

As early as 1936 Snow suggested the possibility of Russia as a barrier to Japan's advance in inner Mongolia.[62] Increasingly in *Red Star* (1938), *The Battle for Asia* (1941) and *People On Our Side* (1944), Snow perceived the Chinese question in Asian and global terms. "The position now occupied by Chinese Red Army is strategically the tinderbox of Central Asia," he wrote in 1937, "and around the fate of the Red Army turns the fate of East Asia." By 1941 Snow foresaw that "Japan will meet Europe in the plains of Asia and wrest from her the mastery of the world,"[63] The United States, despite its hold on most of the world's capital and its need for external markets, could not get ready quickly enough. "We have no real continental strategy operating against her," Snow wrote of American military posture towards Japan in 1942, "we have a naval strategy, but no land strategy. We have a pacific front, but no Asiatic front."[64] If Japan was to be confronted, he observed in a rejection of the traditional coastal city—

Open Door approach, it must be on the Asian mainland. Thus the Soviet Union became the key during and after World War II. Snow, in fact, spent most of his war correspondence days in Russia, not China. He glorified Soviet life and sacrifices, and felt the Soviets knew and liked Americans. By 1945, he was confident that the Soviet Union would eventually destroy Japan's present and future ambitions in Asia.[65]

Thus, by war's end, Snow was convinced that the Chinese communism he had first found interesting and attractive in the 1930s, with large doses of postwar Soviet and American support, was the only hope for Asia and perhaps the world. It was neither surprising nor subversive that given this view he attempted to make "the Reds" more palatable to American audiences.[66] In 1938, American support for Japan seemed out of the question and prospects for a coalition among warring Chinese parties was still possible. By 1945, a reformed Japan was suddenly again viable to some Americans, and compromise in China was not. Snow's images underwent no radical nor conspiratorial change, as MacArthur suggested in 1945. Rather, Snow's perceptions continued to fit what were to him the only acceptable alternatives for China and for America.

Edgar Snow did try, even during World War II, to bring about an American-inspired reform movement in China short of a full Communist victory. Perhaps the most ignored and highly illustrative aspect of his career as an American journalist in China was his role in the formation of a united wartime organization called the Chinese Industrial Co-operatives, or Indusco, for short. Along with diplomats, engineers, conservationists, political scientists, social workers, educators, and missionaries, American journalists shared a part in the secular and spiritual effort to "reform" China. Indusco, the brain child of Snow, Nym, and their New Zealander friend Rewi Alley, stood for the long-held reform ambitions of "human rehabilitation, economic progress and democratic education."[67]

In the laboratory of war, the Snows and Alley saw the chance to create a new society. Indusco's drafters felt the Chinese could be made to combine speedy reconstruction with productive refugee relief, the training and mobilization of labor, the building of an economic base for political democracy, and the construction of the means of defending China's outlying regions from Japanese conquest. Instead of concentrating new industries in a few vulnerable Western-based cities, Indusco would work through thousands of small, semi-mobile industrial units built in places inaccessible

to Japanese motorized troops and carefully camouflaged and secured for China's total protracted resistance. Finally, the whole
adventure was to be truly cooperative among workers, consumers,
and the Chinese government.

Blueprints divided the country into three districts. Highly mobile units would operate behind Japanese lines. More substantial
industries would be developed between these lines and rear areas.
Finally, in the safe provinces, mining and production would begin
along with the fostering of other social by-products such as training
schools, co-op hospitals, lunch rooms, printing houses, war veterans' and war orphans' vocational centers, clinics, nursery schools,
and language study schools for illiterate workers. As Snow put
it, where "Lawrence brought to the Arabs the destructive technique
of guerrilla war, Indusco was to bring to China the constructive
technique of guerrilla industry." The idea was to "teach coolies
not only how to manipulate machines but also how to manipulate
ideas in common cause with group ends."

The whole project worked rather well for a while. Under Alley's
driving leadership as China's "blitz-builder," and with a $2-million
loan from Nationalist leader T. V. Soong [Song] to Alley and
Snow, Indusco factories made medical supplies, uniforms, hand
grenades, electrical equipment, wagons, tents, stretchers, and
blankets. In addition, they began such activities as glass making;
coal, iron, and gold mining; leather tanning, sugar and oil refining,
and textile and chemical production. Some felt that Indusco, with
its principle of worker cooperation, was the Nationalists' last
best hope. Nevertheless, elements of the Chungking cabinet, especially Finance Minister H. H. Kung, found Indusco operating
dangerously outside the government's bureaucracy and cut off
its funds. With it died Edgar Snow's vision of American-inspired
reform in China. Indeed it was perhaps one of the best and last
such efforts. The failure of Indusco combined with Snow's earlier
perceptions of China and his consistently anti-Japanese posture
to bring him all the way from Missouri to Shanghai to become
Chinese communism's "Mr. America."

The career of Edgar Snow continued forward from the days
following Communist victory in China in 1949 to his own death
on the eve of the historic visit of Richard Nixon to China in
1972. It is ironic that the man who did most to try to foster
American support for the Chinese Communists would be ostra-
cized and forced to live abroad during the Cold War and only
begin to gain favor and recognition at the time of his death. Snow
maintained his working knowledge of China and Communism and

attempted, even from a political and geographical distance, to make sense of them in the American context. He returned to China in 1960, 1965, and 1970 and was planning to go again to cover the Nixon trip for *Life* magazine. He wrote several books on China and published many articles in *The Nation* after *The Saturday Evening Post* dropped him.

Chairman Mao and Premier Zhou Enlai regarded Snow as their "Mr. America." His reports of the Chinese feeling that the "door is open" and his appearance atop the Gate of Heavenly Peace in October 1970 were signals for a thaw in American-Chinese relations. Yet Snow was increasingly estranged from his homeland. While he won an infrequent award, maintained a few friends and memberships, and did some university work; he hardly participated in Cold War American life. It was a cliché to say at the time of Snow's death that Americans "should have listened to him sooner." His impact on American policy is more realistically assessed when one recalls that Secretary of State Dean Rusk granted Snow only a ten-minute audience upon Snow's return from one China visit.[68] Most of Snow's later years were spent with his second wife Lois Wheeler, his son Christopher, and daughter Sian in a new home in Switzerland.[69] He was a relic, a China-hand grown old, bypassed by some Americans who wondered why he wasn't secluded in Peking with those other strange friends of Chinese communism like Anna Louise Strong, Israel Epstein, or Snow's old crony Rewi Alley.

After the Geneva conference in 1954, Snow observed that "Congressmen convinced themselves they once owned China before Dean Acheson and Owen Lattimore gave it to the Reds." Some felt that Vietnam was now theirs to keep, give away, or perhaps blow up. "It is hardly possible," Snow summarized "to destroy Ho's (Ho Chi Minh's) leadership of the Vietnamese Revolution by the practical means available to General Motors. The war can be enlarged [and] prolonged indefinitely. Ho would not be destroyed." Americans, Snow reminded, had won their independence by revolution and guerilla warfare but forgot the terms of such a war.[71]

Snow put it all together in what he called a "Tru-Deal" for Asia. By this he meant for the United States to recognize the People's Republic in Peking; to refuse to aid colonial powers; to promote United Nations' scholarships; and to revise aid programs in order to make capital, credit, and machinery available to emerging countries. No "native reactionaries" like Chiang or Bao Dai could maintain the status quo no matter how many guns,

planes or hydrogen bombs were used.[72] "Mao's Mr. America"
looked toward a world in which the United States would continue
to play an important, if somewhat redefined, role.

Still, Snow eventually sensed, and so perhaps through him did
Mao, an ultimate truth about himself and his country that none
of his Missouri predecessors such as Carl Crow had been able
to see. The United States had to get back to its own priorities
at home to save itself and its mission in the world. Backward
nations, in a hurry, searched about for their own alternatives while
America's pursuit of Cold War aims abroad left grave questions
piled up at home that aroused little admiration or emulation. "No
foreign policy is greater," Show concluded in his autobiographical
Journey to the Beginning, "than the success of the domestic system
which inspires it.[73]

Thus a part of Edgar Snow's legacy, like his ashes, rest in
the China he loved. The remainder went back "where the Hudson
enters the Atlantic to meet Europe" for it had, after all, been
America which "fostered and nourished me."[74] Or as his friend
Mao had written about the shared experience of Snow's countrymen, "Americans are not Asians and sooner or later must go
home."[75]

Notes

1. Herbert Croly, *Willard Straight* (New York: Macmillan Company, 1942),
354–64.

2. Luce's massive role in American–East Asian relations needs exploration.
See W. A. Swanberg, *Luce* (New York: Scribner's, 1972). I have gained much
from reading Luce's interview in the John Foster Dulles Oral History Project,
Princeton University Library, Princeton, N.J.

3. The Willard Straight Papers at Cornell University are rich and have been
culled by Charles Vevier, *The United States and China, 1905–1913: A Study
of Finance and Diplomacy* (New Brunswick, N.J.: Rutgers University Press,
1955); and Helen Dodson Kahn, "The Great Game of Empire: Willard D. Straight
and American Far Eastern Policy" (thesis, Cornell University, 1968).

4. See Charles Forcey, *The Crossroads of Liberalism: Croly, Weyl, Lippmann
and the Progressive Era, 1900–1925* (New York: Oxford University Press, 1961).

5. See my "For God, for China and for Yale: The Open Door in Action,"
American Historical Review 75 (February 1970): 796–807.

6. On missionaries see Paul Varg, *Missionaries, Chinese and Diplomats:
The American Protestant Missionary Movement in China, 1890–1952* (Princeton:
Princeton University Press, 1958).

7. The Carl Crow Papers are at the Western Historical Manuscripts Collection, University of Missouri Library, Columbia, Missouri. I am indebted to Mrs.

Nancy Prewitt and her excellent staff for assistance in using the Crow collections. In addition, Crow's own writings provide much information. *400 Million Customers* (New York: Harper and Brothers) was published in 1937.

8. In Crow Papers: W. Colston Leigh to Crow, 10 Nov. 1973; Homer Croy to Crow on the Carnegie invitation; Ethel I. Salisburg to Crow, 3 May 1938; Nelson T. Johnson to Crow, 17 May 1938, 27 Aug. 1938; Raymond Moley to Crow, 24 April 1943; Alison Stilwell to Crow, 31 Aug. 1941; Walter H. Judd to Crow 26 Feb. 1940; see T. A. Bisson review of Crow's *China Takes Her Place* in *Book of the Month Club Bulletin,* Crow Papers. Vincent Shehan to Crow, 15 Jan. 1941; Co Tui to Crow, 20 July 1939; Pearl Buck to Crow, 13 Feb. 1942, Crow Papers.

9. Upton Close, "Close-up of the News," 30 Jan. 1944; H. W. Flannery to Harper and Brothers, 4 Jan. 1938; Eldon A. Park to Crow, 24 May 1943; Herbert Moore to Crow, 12 Feb. 1940; important letter of F. B. Warren to Crow, 28 Aug. 1944; George Sokolsky to Crow, 21 May 1944; H. B. Kaltenborn to Crow, 7 Dec. 1937, John A. Brogam to Crow, 5 Sept. 1940, all in Crow Papers.

10. Crow, *The Travelers' Handbook for China* (Shanghai: Hwa-Mei Book Concern, 1913).

11. Crow, "President Wilson's Eyes and Ears," in "Silhouettes," Crow Papers; Crow, "A War Correspondent at Last," Crow Papers.

12. In Crow Papers: Frank Webb to Crow, 6 Nov. 1944; Don Patterson to Crow, 17 May 1944; Gordon Roth to Crow, 5 Feb. 1945; Zena Kaufman to Crow, 20 Feb. 1945; H. F. Seitz to Crow, 8 May 1940; C. H. Dolan to Crow, 27 March 1940; John E. Jouett to Crow, 25 March 1940.

13. Gladys Hoover to Crow, 29 Dec. 1937, Crow Papers.

14. Howard E. Law to Crow, 3 Aug. 1938; J. Hare and Partners to Crow, 12 Aug. 1937, Crow Papers.

15. Crow, "America's Globe-Trotting Salesman," *Harper's* 177 (September 1937), 412–19.

16. Crow, "When the American Travels," Crow Papers.

17. See H. E. Yarnell to Crow, 14 Dec. 1939, Crow Papers. On American Committee see Donald J. Friedman, *The Road from Isolation* (Cambridge: East Asian Research Committee, Harvard University Press, 1968). There is also much material on this group in the papers of the missionary Robert Speer at the Princeton Theological Seminary Library.

18. Crow to H. J. Anslinger, 2 Feb. 1939, Crow Papers.

19. S. A. Blythe to Crow, 27 Nov. 1937; Julean Arnold to Crow, 15 Jan. 1937, Crow Papers.

20. John T. Beaudouin to Crow, 1 Oct. 1941, Crow Papers.

21. Mrs. Harry Price to Crow, 17 Jan. 1940; Crow general letter, 1945, Crow Papers.

22. Clifton Fadiman to Crow, 6 Oct. 1944, 19 Oct. 1944, Crow Papers.

23. Crow to De Witt Wallace, 13 Oct. 1942; Owen Lattimore to Crow, 3 March 1943, 3 April 1943; Crow papers. Also Edward C. Carter to George E. Taylor, 28 March 1946, Institute for Pacific Relations Papers, Columbia University Library, New York, box 208.

24. Owen Lattimore to "The Staff," 26 July 1943, Crow Papers; Lattimore to W. W. Norton, 14 April 1944, W. W. Norton Papers, Columbia University Library; memo Robert E. Sherwood to Lattimore, 24 Jan. 1943, Crow Papers.

25. Crow note, 13 Sept. 1943, Crow Papers.

26. Edgar Sisson to Crow, 1939, Crow Papers.

27. From Crow, *400 Million Customers*, 186–90.

28. See for example Warren I. Cohen's *America's Response to China* (New York: John Wiley and sons, 1971), 142, 170. Also Dick Wilson, *The Long March 1935: The Epic of Chinese Communism's Survival* (New York: Viking Press, 1971).

29. John Fairbank has observed that Snow's writing had a "fairly definite quality" about it and scholars can reconstruct then a fairly accurate account even without substantial personal manuscript availability. See Fairbank's review of Snow's *The Other Side of the River* in *The Atlantic Monthly* 211 (January 1963): 34–36. Fortunately, Snow wrote for publication constantly, and in a highly personal, almost autobiographical, style.

30. See, for example, Anthony Kubek, *How the Far East Was Lost: American Policy and the Creation of Communist China, 1941–1949* (Chicago: Henry Regnery Co., 1963), pp. 371 ff. and *Time* 76 (25 July 1960): 60.

31. Characterization of this kind can be found in the excellent Kenneth E. Shewmaker, *Americans and Chinese Communists, 1927–1945: A Persuading Encounter* (Ithaca: Cornell University Press, 1971).

32. Such images are used by Theordore White, James Thomson, and John Fairbank among others. See *Time* 99 (28 February 1972), 45; Thomson's *While China Faced West: American Reformers in Nationalist China, 1928–1937* (Cambridge: Harvard University Press, 1969), xiii, and Fairbank's review cited above.

33. The significance of this debate, though probably exaggerated by most authors, will be discussed later in the essay. Examples of such discussion can be found in Shewmaker, *Americans and Chinese Communists;* Harold Isaacs, *Scratches On Our Minds: American Views of China and India* (Cambridge: MIT Press, 1958), 162–63, and Tang Tsou, *America's Failure in China, 1941–1950* (Chicago: University of Chicago Press, 1963), 231–33.

34. Helen F. Snow to the author, 25 June 1974. I am grateful to Mrs. Snow for the train of thought upon which this chapter is largely based.

35. Edgar Snow, *Journey to the Beginning* (New York: Random House, 1958), 139.

36. Thomson, *While China Faced West*, xiii.

37. See Lewis Gannett's review of *Journey to the Beginning* in the *Nation* 187 (15 Nov. 1958), 363–64. Also John B. Powell, "Missouri Authors and Journalists in the Orient," *Missouri Historical Review* 61 (October 1946): 45–55, and Snow, *Journey to the Beginning*, 24.

38. See *Current Biography*, 1941, 804–5.

39. Snow, *Journey to the Beginning*, 3.

40. Nym Wales, "Old China Hands," *The New Republic* 96 (1 April 1967): 13–15.

41. See Snow on religion, *Journey to the Beginning*, 12–14.

42. Snow, "The Americans in Shanghai," *American Mercury* 20 (20 Aug. 1930): 438.

43. Ibid., and Snow, *Journey to the Beginning*, chap. 4.

44. Snow, "Gateway to Oldest Asia," *Travel* 66 (November 1935): 11–13; Snow, *Journey to the Beginning*, 4–7.

45. Snow, *Journey to the Beginning*, 119.

46. Ibid., 102, 258, and Nym Wales's introduction to *The Chinese Communists*

(Westport, Conn.: Greenwood Publishing Co., 1972).

47. Snow, "The Strength of Communism in China," *Current History* 33 (January 1931), 521–26.

48. Snow, *Journey to the Beginning,* 238–41.

49. See Snow's review of Pearl Buck's *My Several Worlds* in *The Nation* 179 (13 Nov. 1954): 426, and Snow's "How America Can Take the Offensive," *Fortune* 23 (June 1941): 69.

50. Snow, "Is It Civil War in China," *Asia* 29 (April 1941): 166–70.

51. Snow, *The Far Eastern Front* (New York: Harrison Smith and Robert Haas, 1933).

52. Ibid., 160.

53. Snow, "Should the United States Stay in the Philippines," *Asia* 39 (September 1939): 492–96.

54. These articles were all in *The Saturday Evening Post* 206–8 (1933–36).

55. See Nym Wales' article, "Japan's Vampire Policy," *Reader's Digest* 33 (September 1938): 61–62.

56. Snow, "Chiang's Armies," *Asia* 60 (November 1940): 569–82.

57. William Neumann, *America Encounters Japan: From Perry to MacArthur* (Baltimore: Johns Hopkins University Press, 1963), 295.

58. Snow in *The Nation* 168 (February 1949): 202–3.

59. Snow, "Weak China's Strong Man," *Current History* 39 (January 1934): 402–8, and "China's Fighting Generalissmo," *Foreign Affairs* 16 (July 1938): 612–25.

60. Snow's break with the Kuomintang is traceable through his "What We Could Do about Asia," *The Nation* 170 (28 Jan. 1950): 75–79; his review of Robert C. North's *Moscow and Chinese Communists* in *The Nation* 172 (November 1953): 406–8; *Time* 46 (17 Dec. 1945), 58; *Publishers Weekly* 148 (15 Dec. 1945), 2623; and *New York Times,* 7 Dec. 1945.

61. My thinking in this area has been shaped by Neumann and by James Peck's "America and the Chinese Revolution," in Ernest May and James Thomson's *American-East Asian Relations: A Survey* (Cambridge: Harvard University Press, 1972) and by Wolfgang Franke's *A Century of Chinese Revolution, 1851–1949* (Columbia: University of South Carolina Press, 1970).

62. Snow, "Japan at the Gates of Red Mongolia," *Asia* 36 (January 1936): 9–13.

63. Snow, "Direct from the Chinese Red Area," *Asia* 37 (February 1937): 74–75. Snow, *The Battle for Asia* (Cleveland: World Publishing Company, 1941).

64. Snow, "Must We Beat Japan First?" *The Saturday Evening Post* 215 (24 Oct. 1942), 215.

65. Trace through the *The Saturday Evening Post* 215–17 (1943–45).

66. See Snow, "Soviet Society in Northwest China," *Pacific Affairs* 10 (September 1937), 266–75.

67. On Indusco (which needs a complete study), see Nym Wales, "Can China Re-Mobilize," *Antioch Review* 4 (December 1944), 553–68; Snow, "Showdown in the Pacific," *The Saturday Evening Post* 213 (31 May 1941), 4; Nym Wales, "China's New Line of Industrial Defense," *Pacific Affairs* 12 (September 1939), 285–95; Snow, *Battle for Asia,* chap. 6; *Journey to the Beginning,* 198–203; and *Time* 35 (22 April 1940): 32.

68. See obituaries in *New York Times,* 16 Feb. 1972, and in *The Nation* 204 (28 Feb. 1972), 261. Also see the articles in *Life,* 30 April 1971, 7046–48,

and 30 July 1971, 22–27.

69. Snow's second marriage may have been as important to his career as his first. His relationship with women needs further examination. On Lois, see her writing, *China on Stage: An American Actress in the People's Republic*. (New York: Random House, 1972); "China: Insights into its Vigor, its Enduring Beauty and Women," *Vogue* 158 (December 1971), 36–39, and "The Cultural Revolution is Over, But Mao's Melodies Linger on," *Saturday Review of the Arts* 55 (November 1972): 36–40.

70. Snow, "The New Phase—Undeclared War," *The Nation* 175 (10 March 1951), 220–23.

71. Snow on the Geneva meetings in *The Nation* 178 (24 April 1954), 350–52.

72. Snow, "What We Can Do About Asia," *The Nation* 170 (28 Jan. 1950: 75–79.

73. Snow, *Journey to the Beginning*, 442–23.

74. Lois Wheeler Snow, "The Burial of Edgar Snow," *The New Republic* 170 (26 Jan. 1974): 9–11.

75. Snow, "Mao and the New Mandate," *The New Republic* 160 (10 May 1969): 19.

Part III
Images of Contemporary China

The American View of China, 1957–1982: The Personal Experience of a China-born Sinologist

PAOCHIN CHU

It was a dark and snowy January morning in 1957 when I walked out of the Greyhound Bus Terminal at Twenty-eighth Street in New York City after a two-and-a-half month voyage from Taiwan that began on a World War II liberty cargo ship. Thus ended my only vacation since the Marco Polo Bridge incident in 1937, when at the age of eleven, I began to shoulder the rifle of a guerrilla-student in the war of resistance against Japan. With a few borrowed dollars and without friends or status, I plunged into the sea of job hunters. Hours stretched into days of hard work, the only life I had in New York. The opportunity for making friends was so rare and so exciting that I refused almost no invitation.

One day several young men from Taiwan and I found ourselves in a luxurious car, being taken to a magnificent uptown house. Passing through a large garden and flowering pathway, we entered a formal hall lit by a chandelier. All kinds of traditional banquet foods were on the long table.

We tried our best to enjoy these dishes although we had not yet developed our appreciation of Western foods such as butter, cheese, and olives. Our eating was interrupted by the loud voice of the host. A prestigious Congressman appeared and began to speak. Finally, I figured out with my poor English that this well-known politician was giving a speech attacking Chinese communism. When the show was over, we were rushed back to our headquarters, the Sino-American Amity Center on beautiful Riverside Drive.

Not long after this, I was fortunate to be able to go to Philadelphia to attend the Graduate School of the University of Pennsylvania.

On another chilly evening in Philadelphia, I was informed by my friend Wang that Professor Li was asking students to attend a meeting at his home to hear Felix Greene's talk about his recent trip to mainland China. Mainland China was still mysterious and very much feared by me, and to have anything to do with it made me feel guilty, a feeling not unlike the guilt of stealing office supplies or smoking pot. Nevertheless, my love for China and concern about my relatives drew me to the meeting. I went that night ready to take whatever consequences might follow, including a record with the FBI and Taiwan's security authorities.

The meeting was held at Dr. Li's home. There were around forty folding chairs, and within fifteen minutes they were filled by people from all walks of life, not just Penn students and Chinese youths. We heard Mr. Greene's experiences in mainland China, and I was moved by his pleas that Sino-American friendship should be normalized and commercial and cultural exchanges between these two countries should be restored.

During those years, I attended many other similar meetings (sometimes held in reception rooms of the student dorms) and talked with other speakers, including Mrs. Edgar Snow, who had been with Snow in China during the anti-Japanese war and who published a book on women of the Chinese mainland. Many years have passed since then, but I still have the greatest respect for Dr. Li and those visitors who dared to speak what they saw as the truth at great personal risk.

When I passed my preliminary exams, I began looking for a teaching position, setting up my file at the University Placement Service, sifting through the professional journals, and trying not to miss any interviews at the various academic conventions on the East Coast. In 1967 I was lucky enough to receive an academic appointment in southern California. As soon as friends learned I was heading for the West, they warned me that southern California was the stronghold of the Young Republicans and hence anti-Communist views. They warned me to speak as little as possible. I thanked them for their friendly concern.

After those first busy years of teaching new courses in an American college and completing my Ph.D. theses in 1970 under pressure of the "two years or out rule," I received calls and invitations from many civic groups who wished to hear about China. I tried to appear as often as possible, to discharge my duties of community service, which counted as 20 percent of the credit for my tenure and promotion.

In 1973 I was invited by a Society of Friends (Quaker) meeting to speak on "China Today" in a naval town. When I first appeared I received an overwhelming welcome from a meeting largely made up of naval captains and commanders. In a hall with at least two hundred dignitaries, I became the focal point of attention. They showered me with smiles and inquired of my studies in Taiwan. Many of them had stayed in Taiwan during their tours of duty in the 1950s and 1960s.

After the enthusiastic introductory words of the president, I began to describe the century-long story of China's modernization from the Opium War in the 1840s to the socialist system in the 1970s. At my conclusion, I urged the normalization of relations between these two traditional friendly nations because of the benefits normalization, including strategic, commercial, and cultural advantages to both sides. Even before I completed by speech, I noticed the changed faces of my friends and the presiding leaders. Questions were numerous and heated, and I tried my best to answer in a scholarly and objective manner. When my speech was finally over, I returned to my seat between the president and the vice president. I found long faces without even a gesture of courtesy. As I walked out, I found the warm clouds of affection gone and the hall frozen into a stiff and cold atmosphere. Although saddened, I felt no regret, because I had discharged my duty as a sinologist. I had prepared myself for rejection long before my appearance.

In later years, I gave similar speeches to many groups. I was not surprised at the consequences of my speeches. Fortunately, there had never been loud shouts from the audience to "shut up my mouth" nor threats that they would never send their children "to my school of Pinkos," as some of my colleagues experienced. Nor have I ever received any administrative warnings from the school authorities or from my peers in my department. I think it may be the influence of basic human rights as described by the Constitution and also that the American people are used to political controversies. Or maybe the long friendship with the Chinese people and the common sense of restoring cordial relations with a billion Chinese made some Americans see the wisdom of normalization long before politicians acted.

By the 1970s the Cold War atmosphere seemed to be changing. China was getting more and more attention on campuses and in

society. Our Chinese Students Association began to organize political debates and show movies from mainland China, such as "Red
Detachement of Women" and "The East Is Red." Naturally I,
as their faculty adviser, helped present events like these. The
movies attracted enthusiastic audiences. Nearby campuses also
hosted movies and political debates concerning normalization of
Sino-American relations. Gradually, the conciliatory voice was
no longer a single aberration but rational talk free from intimida-
tion.

The shock of the visit to China and subsequent Shanghai Com-
munique of the anti-Communist President Nixon and National
Security Adviser Kissinger finally broke the ice between these
two peoples in 1972. Formal diplomatic relations were established
in 1979, and China was subsequently granted most-favored-nation
tariff treatment. Chinese-American trade rapidly increased from
several hundred million dollars to $6 billion and included American
Boeing airplanes and Chinese oil. The influx of students from
China suddenly picked up momentum from several dozens sifting
through Hong Kong or unnamed routes during the late 1970s to
eight thousand arriving under government scholarship or private
sponsorship between 1979 and 1982. Official Chinese delegations
came and left the United States regularly. "Closed-door" China
opened more than 122 cities for the more than 7 million tourists.
It even established special institutions to train hotel service personnel. For many Americans a China tour became a symbol of
social status. I know of professors in unrelated disciplines who
began to offer courses about China or the Chinese revolution
after only a two-week tour of China.

After two recent trips to China to visit the homeland where
I was born and had grown up and to see my sisters whom I
had not seen for thirty-two years, I came back finding myself
among the speakers. Again I have been busily hopping from one
campus to another and to numerous civic organizations, giving
speeches and showing my slides on China today. Instead of stiff
faces and frozen civility, I am treated with real enthusiasm and
warmth. Clouds of fear and suspicion have been replaced with
trust and friendship. When I begin to look back, I can hardly
believe that what faced me in the past existed at all. I am still
not sure whether the permanence of Parmenides is the real nature
of things or whether the ongoing change of Heraclitus is. At least
for the time being, I hope permanence is the real nature of things
no matter from what angle—national, economic, academic, or
personal.

ROMANTICIZED IMAGES OF CHINA

Bucolic and romantic decor are images of China and Chinese conveyed to early Americans on this lacquered Chinese-export wooden tea chest. Elongated octagon, about 1815, 14½ inches high, 17⅞ inches long, 13¹⁄₁₆ inches deep. Top of the hinged, flat lid and seven slides are decorated with inlaid mother-of-pearl floray sprays featuring peonies, Hand of Buddha citrons, and peach blossoms. Front decorated with two men carrying fishing poles and fish on either side of a basket. Overhanging tree, water in background.

STEVEN GIRARD COLLECTION, GIRARD COLLEGE, PHILADELPHIA, PA.

Bucolic and romantic themes also characterize this rose medallion Chinese-export porcelain plate commissioned by General Ulysses S. Grant, elected President in 1868. Similar decor also characterized cheaper grades of porcelain viewed by early Americans. Diameter 20.3 cm. The cipher *USG* is surrounded by melon-shaped reserves.

PEABODY MUSEUM OF SALEM.

Hong merchant typical of the "real" as opposed to "idealized" Chinese viewed by early American on artifacts. This "calling card portrait" is attributed to Spoilum, one of the first Chinese painters to work' in the Western style, active from about 1785 to 1820. Oil on canvas, mounted, 26½ × 20 inches.

STEVEN GIRARD COLLECTION, GIRARD COLLEGE, PHILADELPHIA, PA.

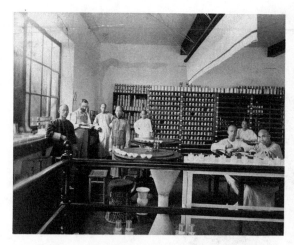

Chinese worked under a foreigner's supervision
in the tea-tasting rooms of George H.Macy and
Company, 1A and 1B Nanking Road, Shanghai,
about 1900. The drape overhead was rigged to
fan the air on hot summer days.

PEABODY MUSEUM OF SALEM.

Two foreign professors pose with a Chinese c
league and their students. "Professors and s
dents of the Peking University, Chin
Stereopticon slide produced by Stereo-Tra
Company, New York City, 1910.

PEABODY MUSEUM OF SALE

SINOPHOBIA

BREAKING THE SPEED LAWS.
—Shiras in the Pittsburg *Gazette Times*.

From *The Literary Digest* 43 (28 October 1911): 721.

COURTESY OF JONATHAN UTLEY.

By the late 1890s, labor-management tensions in the American West and anti-Western violence in China combined to fan the flames of Sinophobia in the United States. While the nineteenth-century American visual image of China as bucolic and/or pro-Western remained in tourist photos and salable artifacts, many blatantly racist anti-Chinese stereotypes circulated in the "pulp" press. *Reminiscences of a Ramble through the Chinese Quarter of New York, 1875–1880.* Frederick Barnard, New York City. Wood engraving, 13¾ × 8⅞ inches. This engraving originally appeared in an unidentified American popular magazine. It was included in a album of popular prints pertaining to China and the Chinese, collected by Thomas F. Hunt.

THE GOVERNOR OF CALIFORNIA.

Illustrated by G. F. Keller in P[ierton] W. Dooner, *Last Days of the Republic* (San Francisco: Alta California Publishing House, 1880).

THE OPEN DOOR THAT CHINA NEEDS.
—*The Brooklyn Eagle.*

From The Literary Digest 21 (14 July 1900): 34.

THE CHINESE QUESTION.—[See Page 147.]

COLUMBIA.—"Hands off, Gentlemen! America means Fair Play for All Men."

Although Sinophobia was widespread and ultimately resulted in the Chinese Exclusion Act of 1882, some Americans denounced that racist tendency. Thomas Nast, artist, cartoonist, and municipal reformer, was a strong advocate of fairness toward Chinese immigrants—a cause that he espoused in several cartoons. The caption of this cartoon quotes the figure of Columbia: "Hands off, Gentlemen! America means Fair Play for All Men." *The Chinese Question, 1871.* Drawn by Thomas Nast (1840–1902). *Harper's Weekly*, 18 February 1871, 149. Wood engraving on paper, $13 \times 9\frac{1}{8}$ inches.

IMAGES OF SINO-AMERICAN FRIENDSHIP IN THE 1930s AND 1940s, AND OF COMMUNIST CHINA

Chiang Kai-shek on the cover of *Time*, 11 December 1933.

COPYRIGHT 1933 TIME INC. REPRINTED BY PERMISSION.

Mao Tse-Tung and Chu Teh congratulate Colonel David D. Barrett on receiving the Legion of Merit. On Mao's right is Brooks Atkinson, for many years the drama critic of *The New York Times*, then (1944) on the staff of the United States Information Service in Yenan.

DAVID BARRETT COLLECTION, SAFE, HOOVER INSTITUTION ARCHIVES,

STANFORD UNIVERSITY.

IMAGES OF SINO-AMERICAN FRIENDSHIP IN THE 1930s AND 1940s, AND OF COMMUNIST CHINA

Editorial cartoon by Paul Conrad in the 11 March 1972 *Chicago Tribune*.

Mao Tse-Tung on the cover of *Time*, **1 December 1958.**

The China Syndrome: Some Thoughts and Impressions after a 1979 Trip

DAVID B. CHAN

The English historian George Macaulay Trevelyan wrote: "History cannot prophesy the future; it cannot supply a set of invariably applicable laws for guidance of politicians; it cannot show by deductions of historical analogy, which side is in the right in any quarrel of our own day. It can do a thing less, and yet greater than all of these. It can mould the mind itself into the capability of understanding great affairs and sympathising with other men."

Twenty-five years ago when I first began my teaching career and introduced the subject of China to the rather naive and innocent students in a small Midwest College, China was perceived as a remote and exotic country that was unfortunately being perverted by a group of Communists who were turning a traditionally peaceable people into a nation of "blue ants" and slaves. This Communist ogre, with orders from Moscow, was the new "yellow peril" as Americans were told constantly by newspapers, journals, and demogogic politicians. And if there were any doubts about this portrait of "Communist China," Secretary of State John Foster Dulles, a rather self-righteous but "principled" man, went on television from time to time, with maps and a pointer in hand, to instruct the American people about the tentacles of Chinese communism reaching into Southeast Asia and threatening the peace of East Asia and the entire world. My students' impression was that China was a friend and ally of the United States just a few years back, and that Harry Truman and all those "communists" in the State Department had abandoned our greatest friend and Christian gentleman Jiang Jieshi (Chiang Kai-shek) in 1949. How difficult it was for a historian to try to change such misconceptions (if not prejudices) and to present to my innocent and misinformed students a historical understanding of the great revolutionary trends in modern Chinese history. And how challenging

it was to counter Henry Luce and the American press in general
that Chiang was neither a true friend nor a Christian gentleman.
China had become a monstrous ogre, an object of suspicion and
hate until 1972.

Unfortunately, since those youthful years in the Midwest, I
feel that our understanding and knowledge of China continue to
be appallingly limited if not perverted into another direction—at
least for the time being. After President Nixon's trip to China
in February 1972, China was no longer the great menace of the
1950s and 1960s, but a friend (and once more a potential ally)
anxious to learn the secrets of American capitalism for the "four
modernizations." In the period after 1972, the press bombarded
Americans with articles about an elightened and pragmatic leadership (*viz.* Deng Xiaoping's visit to the United States in January
1979); the difference between Russian and Chinese communism
(the latter less severe); the Chinese solutions of multitudes of
problems from the miracles of acupuncture to the recycling of
human dung into new energy. The Chinese variety of socialism
was seen as the new panacea for crime, unemployment, prostitution, homosexuality, famines, alcoholism, and the like.

This sudden exuberance is explainable by a most peculiar phenomenon, especially in American circles: the inability to be objective about China, an attitude that is pervasive among laymen as
well as scholars. China either seduces or repells. It is a country
that creates excessive enthusiasm or excessive disillusionment—a
love-hate relationship with the United States that may date back
to the first U.S. voyage to China in 1784. Hence, there are sometimes profound misinterpretations and misunderstandings. China
is either the monstrous "yellow peril" of difficult and inscrutable
people, as interpreted by Dulles and others, or the land of art,
poetry, and porcelain, as interpreted by scores of sinophiles, "old
China hands," and ex-missionaries, who are still nostalgic about
the past. Both are misconceptions, but I suspect that it is the
cultural and exotic interpretation that Americans prefer to es-
pouse, accounting for the disillusionments and misunderstandings
of the past and present.

Such misconceptions have a historical basis and go as far back
as the Middle Ages, when the Roman Catholic Church looked
upon the tolerant Mongol ruler Kublai Khan as perhaps another
John the Baptist, the precursor of Christianity in China. Unquestionably, the Venetian Marco Polo and other medieval travelers
stimulated the imagination of Europeans about the fabulous wealth
to be gained in "Cathay," a dream that has persisted to the present

day. In the seventeenth and eighteenth centuries, the Jesuits who served the Chinese court extolled China in every aspect— political, cultural, economic, and social—as an empire that was more brilliant and admirable than the defunct Roman Empire of antiquity. Such exuberance influenced the thinkers of eighteenth-century Europe and carried over to the founding fathers of the American republic: Franklin, Jefferson, and John Adams.

American enthusiasm can be epitomized in the nineteenth century by President Abraham Lincoln's appointment of Anson Burlingame as Minister to the Chinese Empire. Ignoring Washington's warnings in the first president's farewell address, Burlingame became such a sinophile that he started to represent Chinese interests rather than American interests to such an extent that upon Burlingame's retirement in 1867, the Chinese government appointed him "Imperial Envoy" to the Western world. In the twentieth century, there are several examples, but most interesting was the case of Paul Reinsch, President Wilson's "evangelical Christian" ambassador. Like Burlingame, Reinsch served the interests of China, and when the Chinese students in 1919 protested the Versailles Treaty decision to give the former German concessions in Shantung to Japan, he resigned his ambassadorship and joined the student protest.

In the recent past, especially after 1972, American academics and school teachers, with or without a knowledge of the Chinese language, are particularly vulnerable and gullible in extolling ecstatically the marvels of Chinese socialism, sometimes to the embarrassment of the Chinese themselves. Hence they persist in an exaltant refrain, probably with an unconscious guilt that Americans were overly anti-Chinese prior to 1970. Unconscious or not, it is little wonder that school teachers and academics return to America in an enraptured state: the school teachers, scorned as second-rate citizens, harassed by parents and administrators, reduced to the level of genteel poverty; and the academics, whose positions are at best ambivalent, respected and rejected in a society that worships crass materialism and wealth. As "honored guests" and "foreign friends," they are wined and dined, taken to schools, universities, model communes, and factories; and they are allowed to converse freely (but with carefully selected Chinese who praise the achievements and merits of China under communism). But these "honored guests" are so gullible that they are unable to distinguish public relations and theater from reality. Many appear to be uncritical and euphoric to the point of ridiculousness. In a society that traditionally has respected and worshipped its teachers, many downtrodden American pedagogues seem to feel their worth for the first time, experiencing in China a heady feeling of stature and status that they could never experience back home. Hence, these "foreign friends" return to America with their exaggerated praises.

Now my students are supposedly more sophisticated and cosmopolitan; unfortunately, they are no more knowledgeable of China than my provincial midwestern students of twenty-five years ago. "History of Modern China" attracts a few history majors (history is "unsalable"). The course also enrolls accounting, computer science, and business administration majors who are not only fulfilling upper division general education requirements, but who might learn something from the course to confirm preconceived notions that China is still that exotic land with vast natural resources and riches, not with a mere 400 million customers as Carl Crow wrote some forty years ago, but with a billion potential customers! And even if business ventures are not contemplated, a trip to the People's Republic of China might be interesting, besides being the "in" thing these days.

That our understanding of China has not improved in twenty-five years was illustrated to me during a recent trip to China. Riding the fast train from Hong Kong to Guangzhou (Canton), I was struck once more and impressed with this incredible naivete and ignorance. This love-hate relationship was vividly illustrated by a group of visiting American university students with their mentor, presumably a China "expert" who also boarded the Hong Kong–Guangzhou Express. The male students were smartly dressed, in grey flannel slacks, white shirts and ties, reminding me so much of the clean-cut fraternity boys that I encountered twenty-five years ago in the Midwest. The heat and humidity were merciless, and the boys were sweating profusely, especially before boarding the air-conditioned train. The girls were slim and graceful, attired beautifully in the latest fashions.

As the train passed the border between Hong Kong and Guangzhou, the personnel of the train not only changed, but also the South China landscape. Lush green rice paddies, bamboo, rows and orchards of ripening brownish-red lichees, scraggly pine trees in the hills, villages, fish ponds, and water buffaloes greeted the eye of the tourists, most of whom had settled back to relax for the three hour ride to Canton. But not so our handsome students, who preferred to get up from their seats to take pictures of the Chinese attendants and soldiers. Then the students draped their arms around them as if they were long lost brothers. The students' sweaty underarm odors must have reinforced the Chinese prejudice that "barbarians" do smell horribly. Then, with their smattering of crudely learned classroom Chinese, they chattered incessantly and praised and quoted the late Chairman Mao (now passé)! When not exercising their smattering of Chinese, they burst into songs such as "The East is Red" and "I Love Tian An Men Square," encouraging the Chinese attendants to participate in an orgy of music, still with their sweaty and smelly arms around the Chinese. One willowy and dull looking blond girl spoke and sang in a squeakish falsetto as if she were the lead lady in a Beijing opera. They amused (or perhaps embarrassed) the Chinese whom they tried to befriend in this typically American exuberance to win friends and influence people. They must have convinced themselves that the Chinese like America and Americans and are interested in democracy and the American way of life. An English couple on board was horrified.

This exuberance of youth is innocent and perhaps excusable enough, but the sins of our great pundits (including the students' mentor), the so-called China watchers in our great universities are unpardonable. Having spent long hours reading some very lengthy tomes on Mao Zedong, Maoism, Mao in history, and the like, I have come to the conclusion that most of these "experts" (mostly political scientists) know very little. And with their discussions at professional meetings of the riddles of Maoist ideology, they indicate that they have only a shallow understanding of China. For example, until recently, their analysis of the why and wherefores of the Cultural Revolution, not to mention some of their discussions of Mao Zedong, are tantamount to "bunk," to use a phrase coined by Henry Ford. Some publications will continue to be bunk until our experts cease to be American chauvinists and measure everything Chinese with American norms. Even more important is the use of the historical methods of searching, sifting, analyzing, synthesizing, comparing, and corroborating the multitudes of sources confronting them. But to do so requires a knowledge of the Chinese language—not the standards of an eighteenth-century Chinese scholar to be sure, but certainly a spoken knowledge and at least an elementary reading knowledge. Without these linguistic skills, there can be no understanding of China's history or people. The historical sources are often overwhelming, and the Chinese have developed subtleties of expressions and allusions over the centuries that sometimes imply trenchant criticisms of society and politics. The crux of our understanding is not just language, but an area that is sometimes ignored by scholars of contemporary China, that is, a serious study of Confucianism and the Confucian classics (preferably in Chinese), supposedly swept away during the Cultural Revolution as part of the feudal past. But Confucianism was never dead in a historical-minded society such as China's, a fact that some of our scholars should never have forgotten. The law of the continuity of history operates in China as in other countries.

Rather than touring the cities and major attractions during the recent trip, I decided to stay with peasants in villages in South China. In this age of technology, this seems like an old-fashioned notion that a historian should come into contact with the people and environment that he talks and writes about. But for a person accustomed to the amenities of modern civilization, the experience at first can be disconcerting. The lack of running water, the incredible sticky heat, stench, and thousands of mosquitos at night would have driven an American academic out of his mind—or perhaps make him wonder whether the glories of the Tang dynasty (A.D. 618–907) were anything like this. But such an experience was memorable and insightful, and certainly more valuable than the experience of those who stay at the New Peking Hotel, interviewing only government bureaucrats and ignoring the views and feelings of the people.

I learned that, as a contrast to all the exhaltations and "marvels," the problems that confront China are immense and historic—problems sometimes admitted by the Chinese leadership, but curiously often ignored by Americans, especially academics. These are not the great national problems of the "four modernizations," but the more mundane and age-old problems of corruption in the local bureaucracy and regional differences and antagonisms.

One learns constantly of the avarice, arrogance, and cunning of the local bureaucrats, some of whom are indiscriminately dubbed as "northerners" taking advantage of the relatively richer south. No doubt there is an element of truth in these charges, which makes it all the more disappointing that in the years since "liberation," the so-called correct line of thought has not eradicated or minimized such "bourgeois" practices.

The arrogance of bureaucrats (perhaps ubiquitous throughout the world) was keenly illustrataed to me on one occasion while I waited for a ferry to cross a small river to visit another locality. There was a jeep with a group of these "northerners," most likely lower Chang Jiang (Yangtze) valley Chinese (and hence technically not northerners) standing apart among the crowd, smoking and conversing in what I thought was a thick Jiangsu accent. As is usual at such junctures in China, vendors converge upon the travelers. One was a wrinkled and dark-complexioned old woman, with a bamboo pole on her right shoulder that supported two baskets of lichees, hawking her product in a soft and rather pathetic voice. Suddenly, before the arrival of the ferry, a tall man from the jeep, with a condescending expression approached her and helped himself to two handfuls. He said, "Do you think I am afraid to eat your lichees?" He did not pay for them, and the crowd looked at him impassively and helplessly. I wondered what might have transpired in their thoughts. This type of larceny is more reminiscent of Chiang Kai-shek's China than some of the glowing accounts of Mao's China as described in so many books in our libraries.

The animosity toward these so-called northerners is such that fights and beatings are endemic in buses in the major centers of the south. This pettiness is extended to those southerners who married "northern" girls (or vice versa), for these are considered as renegades who deserve to be victimized when occasions arise. Besides, there were constant complaints that "northerners" have saddled the top bureaucratic jobs in such phases of administration as government, railway, and trade.

This disturbing pugnacity is extended even to language on the local level. Speaking to a small group of elementary school teachers, I used Mandarin Chinese to discuss what little I knew about elementary education from the experiences of my own children. A few minutes into my discussion, a rather hefty young lady with an expression of disdain on her face asked whether I could continue in Cantonese rather than Mandarin. I replied in the affirmative and continued, realizing that it was not ignorance on her part that prompted her to request a dialect change, but tenacious regional feelings. It was somewhat disturbing that after thirty years since "liberation," the problem of language is still with China—for regional dialects encourage the persistence of regional feelings that could hamper China's national unification and meaningful modernization objectives, at least during this century. I could not help but to be reminded of a paper delivered at a professional meeting by a prominent scholar concerning the unity of thought through Maoist-Leninist ideology, and I wondered once again about such impassioned interpretations that were generally accepted in the early and mid-1970s.

In numerous conversations with peasants, I learned of their past and present bitterness and grievances: the rapaciousness of the Guo Min Tang period, the cruelties committed by the Communists after "liberation," and especially during the 1960s. It is not that there is any desire to return to those hoary days of the Guo Min Tang, but there is a desire for a betterment of their lives. Although Mao's revolutionary uniqueness was based upon the peasantry, the peasant is still at the bottom of the social ladder, working the land as his ancestors had done for centuries past. His prospects for self-improvement are bleak; and any chance for the betterment of his children's lot through education beyond the elementary level is almost hopeless now that the population has reached the staggering 1 billion mark. Despite the admonitions of the government, some peasant families continue to have five or six children, contributing to their own burden as well as to the nation's.

Random conversations about the Cultural Revolution revealed lingering bitterness from a period that was probably more responsible for discrediting "ideology" and confidence in political institutions than anything else. Its motivations are being studied, though they are not yet fully comprehensible; and its excesses and damages to China's intellectual leadership are inestimable. On the local level, there were constant charges of indiscriminate killings, of innumerable dead bodies that could be seen floating down the river, of wanton destruction of cultural relics (some of which I saw), and the forceful confiscation of last bits of jewelry and "artistic" items (charged as being from the "feudal past") by local cadres. Although these charges are not new or revealing, I thought of the students on board the Hong Kong–Guangzhou Express when one old peasant woman exploded and said: "I hated those revolutionary songs. They ["Red Guards" presumably] made me stand in front of a portrait of Chairman Mao before each noon meal to sing one of those songs before allowing me to eat. And since I could not read or carry a tune, they taunted me and forced me to stand until I fainted from heat exhaustion." Another older lady in her eighties, holding a staff on her right hand, nodded slightly. In a whispering tone she said: "They say it was the 'Gang of Four'; but it was the 'fat one' that brought about so much misery for us during that period." Some peasants even pushed the beginning of their period of difficulties back to 1958 with the Great Leap Forward movement.

One day I decided to tour the southern countryside on bicycle. With the company of a few companions, I started the somewhat long trip southward from Guangzhou on an unpaved but good two-lane road. We loaded the bikes with lichees, bananas, bread, and sweetish Chinese soda pop for the journey. It was hot and humid; and I was fortunate that my companions urged me to purchase a peasant hat. Sudden rain storms would force us to seek cover in roadside bus stops or even latrines. On one of these occasions, a bus filled with foreigners roared passed us, splashing rainwater all over the wayside shelter. One of my companions looked at the bus, cynically laughed, and said, "They are taking those 'foreign devils' to see that model commune again!"

We ourselves eventually passed that "model" commune, and I expressed a desire to see that particular one. It turned out that this "model" commune was not significantly different from others that I had seen on a previous trip. It was immaculate and tidy—the descriptions of which are described so often in the literature on contemporary China. But what was significant in this instance was my experience in the commune headquarters, a massive rectangular concrete structure that was bereft of any style or artistic merit. We entered the building, but we were coldly received by the youngish cadres until I showed them my calling card, which indicated my position in the United States. Their attitude quickly changed. We were served tea in the sitting room and offered fans to cool ourselves from the sweltering heat. Some of the doors were already warped, and the paint and varnish were either chipped or peeling. On the second floor, there was a large meeting hall, with wicker chairs surrounding a long table, ash trays on the table, and the usual spittoons on the floor. On the north side of the elongated room were portraits of Marx, Engels, Lenin, and Stalin; on the opposite wall was a portrait of the late chairman. One of the cadres went into a long (and rehearsed) speech usually delivered to "foreign friends": the nature of the locality, past inequities, present amenities and statistics that *are* tiring and tortuous to visitors. When the lengthy babble was over, one of my companions looked toward the north wall and said softly, "One of these days we will tear those portraits down." I replied facetiously and said: "Fine. Why not put up portraits of the greatest Chinese who ever lived—Confucious and Lao Tzu?" We looked toward the south wall, and there was silence. There is no doubt that times have changed since 1976, and faded slogans and portraits everywhere become meaningless (if they ever were meaningful to the sophisticated Chinese). And ideology, if mentioned, is either ignored or cursed.

After about a month's stay in China, one wonders about the seemingly insoluable problems that confront this ancient land: population growth, lack of capital, lack of managerial and organizational skills, and bureaucratic bungling. Then there is the question uppermost in the concerns of the people: the fate of China after Deng's death. Moreover, modernization, if pursued somewhat along Japanese patterns, means a certain amount of westernization and the adoption of Western values, all of which would put the political future of China in flux and uncertainty.

Above all, it should be remembered that the peculiar pendulum in United States–China relations could swing toward the direction of hatred or contempt once again very easily—especially when chauvinistic Americans come to the realization that the Chinese don't really want to be like Americans, or when American merchants discover that China is not "the Great Cathay of towns of silver walls and golden doors" extolled by William of Rubruck, a medieval traveler. Or the leadership in China, which is still flexible, could change. Then we might witness again some American press, politicians, and toadying academics conjuring another "yellow peril." Hence, the present euphoria should be tempered with an understanding of China on its own terms and not in accordance with narrow American standards. To gain this understanding, it is best to take the historical approach, in the Trevelyan sense, in studying this great civilization and people.

Democracy Spring: Firsthand Impressions of China, 1979

FRANCE H. CONROY

Preface, 1989

With the addition of an Afterword, I have left this essay "as is," a memoir of a trip to China at the height of the democracy movement in the spring of 1979. Since its interest is primarily as a time piece, it would be foolish to retouch it to fit later developments. The persona who narrates it—wide-eyed, small-town American suddenly a guest among Communists—is actually quite true. No matter how much we who were China sympathizers in the 1970s may have already promoted the ideas of Mao in our activism and writings, for each of us the first trip to the PRC was always a watershed event; the anticipation of it brought as much anxiety as thrill. We wondered if we would really like a communist country, or if the long-awaited, first-hand experience would, ironically, put a damper on our enthusiasm. I, in particular, was struck by the precariousness of my situation: hosted by the Chinese Communist Party (CCP) in a traveling group led by the American Maoist party newspaper. As our CAAC jet from Zurich passed over the Sinkiang desert and I heard our leaders discussing the possibility of making a special request to visit the "war zone" where People's Liberation Army troops were battling the Vietnamese "invader," I wondered how I had gotten into such an unlikely situation. But as it turned out, our CCP hosts had more wisdom than our adventurous American Maoists; we didn't visit any war zones, but experienced a month of invigorating political discussion and social observation. The following is what I wrote when I returned.

Overall Impressions, 1979

Is democracy budding in Communist China? Do orchids bloom in a desert? Does the sun rise in the west?

Every American fourth grader knows that communism and democracy don't mix. The principle is one of the pillars of a red-white-and-blue education, a truth passed along as self-evident in every class from geography to gym. To dispute it could be cause for an FBI investigation.

Yet the news in 1979 from China set some Americans to wondering. Reports from many sources indicated that citizens in that communist land were engaging in free-wheeling political debates on "big-character posters" plastered to "democracy wall" and other public fences in downtown Beijing. Passers-by on Shanghai streets and students on college campuses were chatting candidly with American journalists about everything from Mark Twain and Charlie Chaplin (whose film *Modern Times* was touring China) to human rights. Chords of Beethoven and Gershwin were floating out of conservatory windows where three years ago only a few "approved revolutionary works" could be heard. On misty Shanghai evenings couples could be spotted kissing on newly claimed lovers' lanes. Whatever happened to "proletarian austerity"? It all seemed quite startling to the typical American boy raised to equate communism in China with 1984, Big Brother, red ants, and smiling robots.

I traveled to China in 1979 as a "young journalist" guest of the sort of Chinese Americans had been taught to fear the most: Communist Party members. I was to spend the most time in China with a particularly sinister-sounding bunch of party members, the "propagandists." This is what the party's leading writers and journalists call themselves.

I approached the trip with mixed expectations. To the "typical American boy" side of me it seemed like a dubious, if not crazy, venture; but to the scholar in me, it came as a kind of culmination. For years (as a doctoral student and young journalist and teacher) I had researched Mao Zedong and the Chinese Communist Party. In my investigations I had been particularly fascinated by a period in the early 1940s when it appeared to a wide variety of American visitors in Mao's "liberated zones" that the "reds" were becoming "democrats." Edgar Snow, the American journalist, wrote in 1941 that even missionaries who formerly saw nothing but evil in the Reds now returned from brief visits singing the praises of the "liberals" of Yenan, who overnight had "abandoned Communism in favor of democracy." A U.S. State Department delegation reached similar conclusions a few years later—and was fired for it upon returning to Washington. Such findings opened my mind at least to the possibility of a strong democratic current within Chinese communism. Yet I retained many doubts, especially concerning this ominous-sounding field called "propaganda."

So when I left for the People's Republic on 28 February aboard a Chinese Boeing 707, I was full of questions, many of which were shared by millions of Americans. Is the democracy movement genuine? Or is "democracy" just being used as a temporary tool in a power struggle between two factions of a Chinese elite? How far does the "new freedom" really go? Could I find freedom of conscience here? What about the Communist Party: Is the democracy movement in opposition to it or is the party itself encouraging democracy? Is it possible to get to know Chinese Communists as individuals, or do they all say the same thing?

I traveled with a delegation of thirteen writers and journalists, all of whom had some background in Chinese affairs. We were granted almost unlimited freedom to conduct interviews and pursue candid, informal discussions with leaders in the party's propaganda field: journalists, critics, novelists, poets, radio and television producers, actors, and actresses. Included were people at the top of their fields, the Chinese equivalents of the Cronkites and Brinkleys, Restons and Buchwalds, Steinbecks and Fondas. Our hosts were the staffs of the *People's Daily,* China's largest newspaper; the China Broadcast Administration Bureau for all-China radio and television; the most prominent literary association; the leading film studio; and the Central Committee Propaganda Department itself, whose function was to "give guidance" in all these fields.

The words "propaganda" and "guidance" scream Orwell. Say them to almost any American creative writer and you will get that reaction. But to close the book already would be premature. What do the Chinese really mean by the word *propaganda*? What does the guidance really consist of? This seemed to be at the heart of the question of the "new democracy." After all, no matter how free-spirited a few wall posters might be, if the basic character of the governing political party is repressive, if "guidance" means "faceless bureaucrats" uttering Orwellian edicts and slinking around spying on people, how deep can the democracy really be?

I will present my impressions in two parts. The first: "Sights and Sounds," from the passing parade of life in the streets; The

second: "The Party." What did we learn about the mysterious
Chinese Communist Party?

Sights and Sounds

China surprises the senses. The eyes and ears and skin are
treated to a cloudburst of the unexpected, a bath of new sensations
and a tempest of contradictions. Have you ever seen hundreds
of shadowy cars swishing along a center city boulevard in the
middle of the night with their headlights out? How about top
national political leaders bustling around forty-degree buildings
in three layers of long underwear? Ever see a rush hour with
10 million people on bicycles? They are all common fare in People's China.

Contradictions: China abounds with them. Here is a country
where you can still get thick 78-rpm records—brand new; where
the automobiles off the assembly lines look like 1947 Studebakers;
where it is cheaper to fix something, almost anything, than buy
a new one. This is a society that is poor and yet has done away
with poverty; that is very old, yet so refreshingly young it makes
American society seem beaten down by comparison. Stirring, like
an April morning, with sprouts of democracy and science, this
China is at the same time still heavy and stagnant with autocracy
and frozen minds. Its people are at ease, lively and candid—but
on the next block they are clammed-up, evasive and speak in
pat, dry clichés.

Such striking contradictions in sights and sounds are the reason
why there is so much disparity in the testimonies of American
visitors returning from China. In a sense the visitor can find evidence of whatever he came looking for. One of my colleagues
who visited China in February wrote pages and pages dwelling
on China's "seediness": the nasty smell of the outhouses, the
dusty alleys where children played, the overcrowded and out-
moded housing, the cold inside homes and workplaces, and the
few modern improvements. News magazines like *Time* have run
photo stories to document the same things. Are they accurate?
Has socialism failed?

Another colleague, a Chinese who supports Taiwan, told me
before I left how Chinese society had been "frozen" for the
last thirty years. He said that the universities, formerly thriving
with cosmopolitan intellectuals (among them his own family), were

now barren and lifeless, cut off from the mainstream of the world's learning; and that the technology of the whole mainland was far behind Taiwan, where "every family has their own TV." He described a Chinese populace pent-up with resentment and who would condemn communism in a minute were they not held mute by fear.

Other friends and colleagues have always returned from China with a totally different picture. Consisting mostly of humanitarian liberals and leftists but occasionally including an idealistic conservative, these people would paint China as a very bright society. They would tell of carts heaped high with cabbages and fish leaping out of ponds; of barefoot doctors who cured all health woes; of liberated, pig-tailed women driving combines and captaining fishing boats; of ruddy-cheeked intellectuals side-by-side with peasants in "open-door" education; of coalminers enjoying evening classes in philosophy; and of earnest leaders in work clothes who "served the people." China in their stories seemed like a socialist paradise.

Before my trip I tended to side with the bright China view. I knew that the American government and press had done a "job" on China in the forties and fifties and suspected they were still doing so, though in less ranting terms. So when I arrived in Beijing, my first surprise was to find myself gazing at many of the negative things that I had not believed.

The poorness: much of the society, thirty years after the revolution, looked like it was still camping out. Most houses were tiny, cold, and without indoor plumbing. The lighting was scanty; the number of furnishings meager.

The backwardness: I couldn't help thinking, "What have they been doing for the last thirty years?" We toured the headquarters for all-China radio and television; the facilities looked like those on an American university campus whose endowment had run out. We toured a Shanghai shipyard; the hard hats the workers wore were made of wicker. We passed through many miles of agricultural lands; never have I seen so many hoes and donkeys.

The barrenness: We spent a day at Shanghai's Fudan University. Immediately I noticed the desolation my pro-Taiwan colleague had talked about. Everything a Western intellectual loves was lacking. The books and periodicals were few and dated; the most advanced science exhibit was on neon lights and looked sophomoric; and there were amazingly few students, considering we were in a country of 900 million people.

The isolation: I could see how a cosmopolitan person could feel depressingly out-of-touch here. The television news was a week late. There were no newspaper stands on the corners. China's equivalent of the Sunday *New York Times* had only six pages.

We asked for explanations of these things wherever we went. Our hosts in each place were open about admitting that conditions were "still quite backward." But their explanations themselves seemed backward. This is when I most noticed the robot-like qualities that some Western observers have ridiculed. It seemed like every problem China had today was attributable to the "treachery of the Gang of Four" (Mao's estranged wife Jiang Qing and three colleagues, arrested in 1977). Their "insidious political line" had made China "lose ten years" during the Cultural Revolution, which everyone now characterized as a period of "feudal autocracy," "anarchy," and "all-around dictatorship." The phrases flowed out identically at each factory, campus, or studio: an odd, unconvincing, programmed jargon. I felt like knocking on the speakers' heads to see if there were real persons inside. Where had *they* been during these ten years? If everything was so cut and dried, why hadn't anybody done anything about it?

The most disturbing aspect was that three years before, while the Cultural Revolution was still in progress, visitors were told that everything good about China had come during the Cultural Revolution and that it was the preceding years that were the source of all evil. From this it was easy to get the impression, as many of China's detractors have, that the Chinese do complete flip-flops in their stories just to suit whatever is the current line that comes down from the top. This would mean that the current flurry of talk about democracy could end in a moment at the wave of a baton.

The dark aspects of China were quite real, and they especially jumped out at someone like me who had been influenced by the glowing stories of the many humanitarian and left-wing people who visited China during the Cultural Revolution. But they were far from the whole story. Where was the bright China that visitors from Shirley MacLaine to Wallace D. Muhammad had found? It was there, too; by turning the kaleidoscope of one's own perspective, everything fell into a different place.

The poverty became almost a positive thing. It is hard to glorify poverty in a north Philadelphia ghetto or a Manila shantytown. The daily reality of dilapidated housing, filth, malnutrition, run-down schools, and the like defies transfiguration. But poverty in China is different. For one thing, it is shared by everyone remarkably equally—from the top party officials on down. We saw evidences of this wherever we went. But even more important, it is a poverty without disease, hunger, and rats; without evictions, boarded-up windows, and turned-off heat; without lay-offs, drugs, "hustles," and muggings. Many houses are old and small, but they are almost universally well-tended, patched, and swept. And new construction, though slowed for the decade 1966–76, is now booming; in some cities we saw scaffolding on almost every block.

Rent is a dollar a month; health care virtually free. Outside of some troublesome smog from the coal furnaces, Beijing is a picture of health. At dawn thousands of people grace the sidewalks with the fluid movements of traditional shadow boxing. Others sweep and scrub the already spotless streets, as if cleaning their own kitchens.

The lack of household furnishings and other goods in a way comes across as a healthy thing, too. With social cooperation and security, the Chinese get along admirably with less, and the lack of gluttony is refreshing. The department store around the corner from the Beijing Hotel is hardly the Cherry Hill (New Jersey) Mall, but who wants it to be? The stocks of peach-colored and lavender mandarin jackets, giant thermoses, fur hats, bulky televisions, and long underwear are adequate. It is pleasant to be able to go somewhere in the world where the goods haven't taken over from the people.

Backwardness? Again it can be looked on in a positive light, both aestetically and ecologically. A society that can get along with bicycles instead of cars? Many Americans would be envious. A technology that operates on preserving rather than replacing? It sounds like an ecologist's dream. The shortage of large cranes and bulldozers? The people make up for it with impressive team-work and enthusiasm. Moreover, the Chinese are in the enviable position of having most of the process of modernization in front of them, with the successes and failures of the advanced nations to learn from; and of having no great urgency, no desperate sectors of the population that might preclude a deliberate pace. China is a very "together" society on the verge of coming into the modern world—at a time when many Americans might like to have much of the last hundred years back, without the Love Canals, Three-mile Islands, and South Bronxes.

In addition, there are the new features of China since 1977.

It would be one-sided to speak any longer only of the sense of desertedness and bleakness at the universities. There are powerful remnants of this. But I also found a renaissance-like inquisitiveness sprouting among the rapidly growing campus population. In 1979 I found that hundreds of new periodicals were being ordered from abroad. And I found that every yuan available was going toward updating science equipment.

It would be one-sided, too, to speak only of hearing stereotyped jargon. I heard my fill of this, but I also found an increasing number of Chinese expressing themselves more forthrightly, especially by writing wall posters. I spent many hours hanging around "democracy wall" and other poster sites, reading posters and talking with the crowds through interpreters. The viewpoints ranged much more widely than I had expected from reports in the American media. There were several criticisms of Mao, but even more expressions of love for him and his close political associate, Zhou Enlai. There were many personal grievances against mistreatment by local governments or party committees, but just as typical was a poster saying, "China is now like spring, the thawing of a frozen society" and calling for "harmony, peace, democracy and love." Another poster advertised a privatedly produced maverick literary journal called *Fertile Land*.

Finally, it would be one-sided to speak of the moon-like sense of isolation in China. I, too, felt it. But from another perspective, this isolation is understandable; for a hundred years before 1949, China's experience with the Western powers was one of being raped by them. A period of antiforeign sentiments was natural. And now there is no longer a deliberate policy to keep out "things foreign," though only a trickle is currently available. To be sure, there were no *Playboys* for us to read or Forty-second Streets to explore, but I could have walked into a Shanghai theater any evening and seen Ali McGraw in *Convoy,* or turned on my television sets and watched an old British spy movie or an English lesson. During the three weeks I viewed a delightful (if sometimes demure) variety of plays, operas, and cultural shows borrowing from many foreign and traditional Chinese styles, all for a few pennies each. The highlight was a joint concert of the Boston Symphony and Peking Central Philharmonic orchestras 19 March, a vivid symbol of the abandonment of the kind of communism that bans Beethoven. The crowd responded with contagious enthusiasm to both Beethoven's Fifth and the playful Chinese revolutionary tune, "Theme from the White-haired Girl."

Yet when added up, what impressions about democracy can

be gathered from the sights and sounds of China? Hardfast conclusions are still oddly elusive. For one thing, the testimonies of
the senses tend to report only on "negative freedom," or "freedom
from." Can the Chinese do as they please? This is one question.
But do they control their own government? This is quite another.
Secondly, the question of genuineness in democracy seems to
have led to an even deeper issue: the genuineness of the People's
Republic altogether. The rote answers about the Cultural Revolution strain credibility. Does China chronically lie to itself, its own
people, and the rest of the world? Is it forced to lie because
its political-economic system has failed, as the poverty and backwardness might indicate? Or is the political-economic system succeeding, as the social cooperation, health, and enthusiasm might
indicate? Can China's leaders *afford* to "go democratic" because
the people on the whole approve of the direction of the country
since 1949, especially now that the grievances of the Cultural
Revolution are being redressed?

Only a deeper look into the Chinese Communist Party itself
could shed light on these questions.

The Party

What are these thirty million people like who flow in and out
of the crowds, the neighborhoods, the factories, and universities
of China as members of the Chinese Communist Party?

Seated in the periphery of the airy conference room, Ma
Sunglin, age fifty, looks motherly in her blue polka-dot tunic, wrinkled at the bottom where it merges into a soft lap. Her hair,
still black and pulled back in casual pigtails, frames a pleasant,
warm face, with slightly pudgy red cheeks and a furrow of atten-
tiveness across her forehead. Her eyes dart back and forth as
she follows every word of the conversation. One of five women
in a Chinese delegation of thirteen, she has raised a family and
now sparkles with independence and intellectual stimulation. At
the break she approaches me and asks about her favorite authors:
Mark Twain and Michael Gold. "Are they read much in the United
States? What *do* people read?" As we chat, I am surprised by
how much she already knows about America and her inquisitiveness to learn more.

Li is seventy. In the 1930s he had studied anthropology at Harvard. Now he is using his knowledge to guide research on minorities at the National Minorities Institute of the Chinese Communist

Party in Beijing. That he is a casual and simple fellow, in rumpled clothes and with a laughing face, hides the thoroughness of his scholarship, which comes through as he relates the years of research he has spent among the Tibetan, Chuan, Uighur, and other minority peoples of China. There is a sea of humanity in this man. With transparent affection he shows us a dance class of teenage Tibetan girls recreating an acrobatic, centuries-old dance. We are sad when it is time to leave.

Chu sits upright and holds her pencil upright, too, in the style of traditional calligraphy. She is a beautiful woman, her soft, blushing features set off by a light blue Mao jacket with braided buttons and a pink scarf around the collar. Unceasingly her pencil flows across the pages; again and again her lips move with animated tones, first in Chinese and then in English. A picture of concentration, she shows no sight of strain from the mental gymnastics of her job. Yet she is more than a translator and a party member. As she guides us through Beijing's Forbidden City one Sunday, we begin to learn about Chu the person, Chu the prototype of the modern, democratic Chinese. As an English student in London during China's Cultural Revolution, she was watched by an Orwellian "Big Sister." The elder party member forbade her to watch British television or go out at night. "In our party we still have some people like that," she adds with a sigh. "What do you call them—stooges? But much fewer now. We are winning the struggle against this kind of mentality."

I could go on with such descriptions. I met many party members, all unique individuals. A few used what westerners might consider to be clichés; but with patience, one could dig beneath these to the person. Of course, how much does this prove? Even a totalitarian regime could have a few charmers speaking for it.

Yet it is important to look for patterns; and the patterns that kept repeating themselves in the party people I met, from Beijing to Yenan, were personality traits like inquisitiveness, scientific-mindedness, humor, openness, modesty, the ability to be self-critical, and the ability to listen. These were strikingly opposite to the traits I had heard attributed to Communists during my upbringing.

Yet such party members were not elected, I determined through persistent questioning. The party was not democratic in this sense, and was not even moving in this direction. The members were chosen more as Americans would select members of an honor society: by recommendations from peers and the final decision from already existing members. Beginning in 1979 state office holders, such as People's Congress representatives, were to be elected by secret ballot. Supervisors on the factory floors are also elected. But party members, no. So although I had come across "democratic personalities," I was still looking for concrete democratic features in the system itself. I first found what I was looking for during a lengthy interview with the editors and staff of the *People's Daily*.

The *People's Daily* did not use to be democratic in any sense of the word. It had a dismal reputation during the Cultural Revolution, a reputation that fit the American stereotype of "Communist propaganda." During this period, the paper was controlled tightly by a small clique led by the Gang of Four. As one staff reporter put it, "We printed only the good news about China—and much of this we made up." Reporters were expected to describe China as a "socialist paradise," and contrary words raised suspicion that one was a "capitalist roader." Also, reporters were expected to double as spies for the Gang. And readers who wrote letters to the editor expressing criticisms found their letters turned over to the Department of Internal Security, the Chinese FBI.

But being a "propaganda organ" today has come to mean something quite different at the *People's Daily*. The atmosphere of pat phrase-slinging and know-nothing rosiness has gone out the window. I found the staff keenly aware, for example, of the built-in problems of being a "party organ," and the stigma that this places on its newspaper for Westerners.

"When I was in the United States last year," a leading editor told us, "the editor-in-chief of a large American newspaper told me that if the Democrats or Republicans put out a newspaper, nobody would read it. People would consider it pure propaganda!" Yet he went on to explain why he didn't think the *Daily* staff was guilty of putting out propaganda in that derogatory sense of the word any longer (they continue to use the word *propaganda* because to them it means only "that which is propagated"); and why he thinks that being "guided" by the party enhances rather than diminishes the paper's democracy.

He argued as follows: The party, now that it is taking up scientific and democratic approaches, is in a better position to represent the people of China than a small elite of journalists and publishers could ever be. Democracy means that the people have control; the party's guidance is how the people control the paper. Only if the party loses touch with the people is there a contradiction.

An example: The party's most recent "guidance" was a recommendation that the *Daily* train its reporters according to the philosophy, "Seek truth from facts." This phrase, first used by Mao in Yenan in 1942, is directed against the practice of a reporter coming into a situation with fixed or dogmatic ideas, such as a rigid party line, and as a result not seeing what is really there. Instead reporters are now being encouraged to "turn over every stone in seeking out an all-sided picture of China, the bad news as well as the good, the dark side as well as the bright."

One member of our delegation asked, "What about the reporter who does 'seek truth from facts' and is fired or arrested by some autocrat still lurking within the party?"

"To prevent this from happening," an editor explained, "to guarantee against the reemergence of a Gang of Four, the party itself must be made subject to the law."

One editor summed up the tricky road to free press and free speech like this: "In the process of bringing China to democracy, some problems will come up. China was feudal for thousands of years. How to exercise our democratic rights but respect the democratic rights of others will take practice. But every citizen of China must be equal before the law. In this way we can prevent a privileged elite from arising. We are not in favor of using arrests to combat wrong ideas—if those ideas do not violate the law, such as blocking traffic."

Our delegation asked for further clarification on the relationship between the party and the paper. A leading editor explained: "Through the reports of correspondents who seek truth from facts, the party can collect the views and practical experiences of people all over the country. Based upon these, it can work out policies scientifically. Through the newspaper it can then propagate these policies. The people can try them out. Then the reporters go back and report on how the policies are working. Do people think they are correct or not? Based on this information, the party can make corrections. The process keeps repeating."

The editor did not define "working out policies scientifically." Nor did he explain which corrections the party made after negative feedback on how policies were working. However, the staff members pointed out some signs that their attempts to make the *People's Daily* a people's paper were succeeding. For one thing, letters to the editor have increased dramatically: over two thousand arrive a day, full of frank and helpful criticisms, now that readers know that the letters won't be turned over to the security police. Also, there are now many columns of print devoted to shortcomings in the first thirty years of socialism in China, even debating provocative questions: "Why did Japan recover so quickly and China's economy develop so slowly? Is socialism maybe not as good as capitalism?"

Debates and audience participation are also blossoming in radio and television. During discussions with the staff of the China Broadcast Administration Bureau, the most striking example I heard concerned the TV broadcast of a Japanese film on prostitution called "Brothel 18." The TV station held a debate on the merits of showing the film after many viewers called in to say that they were shocked. Through the debate, many people were won over to the educational value of the film. Finally it was shown for a second time.

Next our delegation went to the top: the Central Committee itself, to try to determine the type of thinking behind these democratic phenomena. We met for over twelve hours with leaders of the propaganda and other departments. They all said different things, but there were common themes. Here is a summary:

On methods: "Emancipation of the mind" must be achieved through spreading the methods of science and democracy throughout the land. There are still strong remnants of feudal, slavish thinking in our country. Just as Galileo had to break the bonds of medieval dogmas, the party has to lead the Chinese people in ridding themselves of the unscientific ways of thinking that hold back modernization. On the other hand, we need an atmosphere of stability and unity to accomplish this. Democracy does not mean anarchy. So some measures, following proper legal procedures, must be established to prevent a handful from misusing the new freedom to try to undermine our whole system.

On the Cultural Revolution: Among our people there are many different views. Over 700 million people experienced the Cultural Revolution; each has a strong impression of it, since it concerned his or her life for ten years. Each of the "socialist new things," such as "barefoot doctors" or "open-door education," must be evaluated individually. The entire population should take part in that assessment and it should extend not only to the ten years of the Cultural Revolution but to the entire thirty years of experience that the Chinese people have of socialism. Some things have worked well; some have not. Now is a time to "bring it all out." Due to the sudden freedom, our view may not be all-sided enough now. Therefore, our final assessment should be postponed.

On Mao: "Mao's contributions are immeasurable. However, Mao never wanted to be deified, as the Gang of Four tried to do to him, meanwhile wheeling and dealing behind his statues. Unquestionably the shortcomings of the Cultural Revolution were not only the work of the Gang; Mao, too, made some mistakes. We must be careful and prudent in assessing them. We will always hold that Mao's achievements outweigh his faults.

On themselves: We have problems, and we don't have all the answers. We are experimentors; we have been since 1949. There is no blueprint for building a modern socialist country. Give us your suggestions. We want to learn from the best in other societies.

The most heartening to me of all the remarks were the last ones: the modest appraisal by the Central Committee members of their own work. In 1979 no longer were we seeing a China of flip-flops, of the current period always being "all good" and the previous period "all bad."

On our delegation's last day in China we met with eight outstanding novelists, short story writers, and poets. It was a fitting climax to a journey that began in a cloud of doubts about censors and soulless literature, because here I found out that the Chinese Communist writers, even the ones in the official party-"guided" literary association, don't like such things either.

At a point in our discussion when everything was beginning to sound a bit too rosy, a particularly unabashed poet brought the room to silence: "Yes, we now have a fine atmosphere of democracy in literature and art—but not enough yet!" He roared these last words, waving his finger in the air as if to scold any fellow writers who might tend to get complacent.

"The party's guidance? It does not mean censorship," a veteran literary critic jumped in. "The party cannot act as a censorship organ. It can raise suggestions or criticisms, but our editorial board has the final decision." He said this loudly and brazenly, like a freed slave in Mississippi testing his new civil liberties.

Then a young short story writer, Liu Xinwu, took over the stage. Since I am using his name, I will not quote him directly—many of the Chinese requested this, since the winds might always change. But, paraphrased, he told this tale: I experienced the Cultural Revolution as a literature teacher. Many great works and writers were forbidden. It was very miserable for one who loves literature to part with it. In 1975 things turned a little better. Chairman Mao issued an instruction condemning the Gang of Four's censorship of a play called "Pioneers." This was a great inspiration to writers, even amateurs like myself. Under very difficult conditions of repression, Mao played a very good role. At this time I secretly wrote something. But then the criticism of the "right deviationist wind" (led by the Gang) began. Even my drafts still left in my drawers were apt to be targets. I destroyed some of them.

In the thawing atmosphere of 1977, Liu wrote a beautiful love story called "A Place for Love." The title meant that there was a legitimate place for romantic love in the lives of communists. It was the first love story published in China in more than a decade. Broadcast over the radio, it reached millions of people. Surely this story is one of the reasons why young lovers are now kissing in Shanghai and Beijing parks.

To me the story symbolized the change in the character of Chinese communism that I had seen: the rise of something fragile, tender, and new, the budding of democracy.

Afterword: 1985 and 1989

In 1985 I made a return visit to China, not as a guest of the party, but as a private individual touring and doing research, accompanied by my family. What had happened in the six intervening years to the new "buds" of democracy?

First, what had impressed me in 1979—the sense of social connectedness, organization, and uprightness overseen by an all-pervasive wise and caring party—had virtually vanished. The buds of democracy in 1979 under the watchful nurturing of a parternalistic party meritocracy had I thought been the buds of a *new* democracy, a Communist democracy, with a more genuine implementation of party phrases from the past like "people's control," "from the masses, to the masses," and "let 100 flowers bloom." By 1985, the sense that there might be unique Chinese Communist contributions to the world's concept of democracy had given way to a sense that the Chinese might simply be embarking on the same road as others—the democracy of the market, characterized by individualism, free-expression, diversity, and sometimes chaos. Perhaps my view of such a great contrast on the second trip was partly shaped by my no longer being an "insider," whisked by party officials around customs lines, pampered with all arrangements made for me—even on one occasion, when I became ill, hospitalized in the best hospital in Shanghai with no question of any charge. Six years later my family and I fended for ourselves, struggling with avaricious taxi drivers and rude airline clerks and staying in often ill-tended quarters with unhelpful staffs. What previously had been a scrupulously planned society, at least from the foreign guest's standpoint, had now become a Hobbesian battleground. Where was the party that we counted on as the voice of reason and caring to intervene in our behalf as we were victimized by a succession of entrepreneurs and unhelpful bureaucrats?

As a visitor responding on the level of sights and sounds, that is, the perceptual level, I liked the China of 1979 better than the China of 1985. But I have been tempered in my rush to judgment by the reports of my closest Chinese friends from 1979, generally people like Lin, Li, and Ma who shaped my image of the "new Communist person," the post-Hobbesian human being who devoted his life to "serving the people." Invariably, these friends would say that the situation in the mid 1980s was better. While worried about the moral vacuum that had opened up when the Maoist emphasis on putting China before self was shattered, these Chinese friends universally preferred the more lively, open, and free-wheeling atmosphere of the mid 1980s. As one put it: "Yes, in this atmosphere of 'to get rich is glorious' it may be only the 'sucker' who continues to work more selflessly to serve China. But for now, I am content to be that 'sucker.' Later perhaps a new moral ecology can emerge in China."

In early April 1989, before the death of Hu Yaobang and before the memorial service that began the student protests; before the May 4 Movement's seventieth anniversary commerations and before the historic visit of Mikhail Gorbachev; before the martial law declaration and before the turning back of Beijing-district troops by peaceful citizens; and most of all, before the terrible bloodbath of June 3 and 4: before these events that were to change China dramatically, the author made a last visit to Beijing to attend a remarkable gathering, instantly made unrepeatable by the crackdown. This was a people-to-people conference called "Seminar on Economic Cooperation and Development in the Pacific Area," held in an atmosphere of tranquillity and openness at the Friendship Hotel. It was the fruition of years of dreaming and planning by the Interchange for Pacific Scholarship (IPS) of California joined by the Pacific Rim Economic Institute of the People's University of China. The seminar invited scholars, businesspeople, and officials from countries around the Pacific, regardless of ideology, to meet in China to share views on cooperation in the region.

Beijing that week was alive with blooms, commerce, and chatter. Tiananmen Square was bustling with only tourists and passersby. Construction and modernization were visible everywhere. Economics seemed to be on everyone's mind. From television's nightly financial reports, to emerging commercial ties with Taiwan and

South Korea, the talk was of how soon the PRC might be able to follow in the paths of the "Four Little Dragons," South Korea, Taiwan, Hong Kong, and Singapore. The other discussions were about domestic economic problems: inflation, the main problem that brought different sectors together in criticism of government policy; and "profiteering," the cry from many that the Deng Xiaoping's slogan "some will inevitably get rich first" had turned out all too often to mean that those with political influence will get rich, or get privileges, first. This was the only hint of the crisis that was to come. (Another view of this time is available in a remarkable new book, *A Day in the Life of China: April 15, 1989,* edited by David Cohen for Collins Publishers' "Day in the Life" series.)

The events of June 3–4 and after were indeed shocking, for this observer as for others. Several interpretations have already been offered by American scholars, most prominently the old view mentioned at the beginning of this paper: Communism is irredeemable. To such a position the author would submit two observations that may not fit so well: first, that the Tian An Men demonstrators sang the "Internationale" and showed respect to the portrait of Mao; second, that it was Mao himself who warned that Deng represented a new elite within the Party, noting particularly his fear of mass movements. These points would seem to complicate the simple anti-Communist framework for understanding China's latest turn. "What would Mao have thought?" seems an open question.

The View from Mao's Tomb

MARK A. PLUMMER

Chairman Mao Zedong (Mao Tse-tung) died on 9 September 1976. A year of frenzied construction, involving thousands of workers diverted from other projects and tens of thousands of volunteers from schools, offices, and factories, led to the completion of the Chairman Mao Memorial Hall. Constructed in Tian An Men Square, which dwarfs Moscow's Red Square in size, the building is reminiscent of Lenin's tomb. Mao's body is interred there in a crystal coffin draped in the red flag of the Communist Party of China.[1] Upon entering the building, one is confronted by an enormous, white marble figure of Mao, seated as if to survey the present site of the government, the Great Hall of the People, which stands to the west of the tomb and the traditional capital situated to the north beyond the Tian An gate in the Forbidden City of Chinese emperors. Since Mao's death and the arrest of the Gang of Four, there have been significant changes in the leadership, ideology, economy, and social control system in Mao's creation, the People's Republic of China.

As Ross Terrill has observed, Mao is the Marx, the Lenin, and the Stalin of the Chinese revolution.[2] As its Marx, he analyzed the ills of a feudal Chinese society; as its Lenin, he led the revolution that succeeded in creating the People's Republic of China; and as its Stalin, he exhibited obsessive fears, idiosyncrasies, and oppressive behavior. In a remarkable resolution adopted in 1981 by the Central Committee of the Communist Party of China, the party acknowledged Mao's greatness as a thinker and a revolutionary while decrying his role since about 1957. The ill-fated Great Leap Forward (1958–61) and the Great Proletarian Cultural Revolution (1966–76) are officially described as "setbacks." Mao in his later years became conceited, arrogant and smug and his Cultural Revolution was a "gross error," according to the party's official history.[3]

Mao probably launched the Cultural Revolution in 1966 because he feared that the regular party apparatus had lost its revolutionary zeal and he wished to insure that China would continue in his image after his death. He unleashed millions of "born red" (children or grandchildren of workers, peasants, or soldiers) teenagers who traveled around the country, commandeering trains and wrecking everything they perceived to be bourgeois. Buddhist temples and prerevolutionary historic sites were destroyed. Art forms such as the Peking Opera were suppressed. Universities were closed and professors stripped of their possessions and humiliated. Eventually Mao had to rein in the disruptive Red Guards. Apparently the price extracted by Lin Biao was that he would be named Mao's heir-apparent in return for using the People's Liberation Army to quell the disruptions. Lin, however, died mysteriously in a plane crash in Mongolia in 1971 after reportedly planning a coup against Mao.

The leadership struggle that followed saw moderates such as Zhou Enlai (Chou En-lai) and radicals under Jiang Qing, Mao's fourth wife, competing to influence the feeble Chairman Mao. Jiang Qing and the Gang of Four were the usual winners, and they enforced their "red over expert" philosophies. The 1980–81 trial of the Gang of Four convicted them for having "framed and persecuted" 729,511 people and for being responsible for the deaths of 34,800.[4] The suffering was even greater than the indictments indicated. Almost every urban Chinese has a horror story about how he or she was treated during the Cultural Revolution. The greatest crime of this proletarian revolution was to have a bourgeois ancestor or to have had any contact with the West. Seventeen million city youth were sent to the countryside for from one to ten years, and thousands died as a result of the harsh conditions.

Within four weeks after Mao's death in 1976, Deng Xiaoping organized a coalition of leaders who arrested the Gang of Four. As the transitional leader, Chairman Hua Guofeng was pictured with Chairman Mao on large posters that quoted Mao, "With you in charge I am at ease." By 1981, however, the portraits of Hua were gone from Tian An Men Square. All billboard pictures of Mao were removed save the one on Tian An Men where Mao had proclaimed the beginning of the People's Republic.

Before the death of Mao and the arrest of the Gang of Four, the economy was centrally controlled but egalitarian in the extreme. Given a choice between ideology or production (the Red versus expert argument), idealogy usually won. All rank was ostensibly abolished in the army and in the government, and the cadre (government employees) were ordered to learn from the peasants by working in a commune for a year or longer. There were no incentive systems in the factories beyond exhortation. The peasants in the communes continued to plant crops in much the same way they had done for centuries, but they were subject to disruptions when orders came from above that directed extraordinary outputs, often of unsuitable crops.

A rationing system that provides a basic supply of rice, cooking oil, pork, and cotton at low, controlled prices has been a basic apparatus of the government throughout most of its history. Rationing continues sporadically on products in short supply, but the government is moving toward allowing market forces to replace administrative control of the distribution of basic necessities.[5] Individual farmers under the new "responsibility system" may sell their products, beyond a certain amount committed to the government, in "free markets." Some farmers, usually those with fertile plots near the major cities, have become rich. A system of incentives to factory workers has been introduced. A work-point system that results in bonuses for additional production is being used and workers who are lazy are threatened with firing. Few have been fired, however, as the concept of job tenure remains strong. Some workers prefer the security of the "iron ricebowl" to the opportunity to earn more money.

Free markets, street hawkers, and cooperatives (which are really small businesses for profit) have returned to China since the death of Mao. Consumerism is beginning to have an impact on the economy. Although the average annual income is only about $250, controlled prices combined with the new incentive systems leave many Chinese with some disposable income. While television sets were limited to a few hotels and offices in 1978, a decade later there was a forest of antennas in the cities and in the adjacent villages.

Owning a television fulfills one of the "Big Four" aspirations shared by most Chinese. While only 500,000 sets were made in China in 1978, 14.5 milloin were produced in 1986, and in 1987 sales reached 23.3 million. Fourteen million washing machines, 4 million refrigerators, and 16 million cassette-tape recorders were also purchased in 1987.[6] The "Big Four" represent a rapid escalation of aspirations from the "three things that go around" (bicycles, sewing machines, and watches) of the early 1980's. Clothing is becoming more colorful, especially for children, and the basic uniform of white or blue shirts with baggie pants is being supplemented by a variety of more stylish wearing apparel and a smattering of business suits.

The standard of living is rising in China in accordance with the plans of the new leadership that is stressing the production of more consumer goods. However, inflation, so long absent from China, has returned, thus threatening to stifle the new consumerism. It is also questionable whether China's "market socialism" is compatible with the central planning that continues.[7] Consumer aspirations, fueled by legalized advertisements and more knowledge about the standard of living outside China, may outstrip production. If so, the fragile political consensus may be broken, and some of the Maoist economic doctrines may be reinstituted.

The planners of the Four Modernizations (in agriculture, industry, science and technology, and defense) recognize that the fastest way to modernize is by importing foreign technology. To do so, China must obtain vast sums of foreign currency quickly. In their attempts to obtain hard currency, the planners are willing to overlook most Maoist proscriptions, even when the new policies allow foreign "pollution" and create greater inequalities among its citizens.

Under Mao, China's published economic statistics were always hidden behind meaningless percentages and goals. The modernizers, however, have joined the World Bank and the International Monetary Fund. The Chinese government invited the World Bank to investigate its economy, and the bank economists were apparently given access to the essential hard data. The result is a nine-volume report published in 1981, which suggests that China is on the right track to modernization. The report recommends further decentralization, price reform, energy conservation (surprisingly, the bank economists found China short of fuel), and an increased emphasis on light industry. It also recommended that China borrow more money from abroad, a recommendation the Chinese government, both Mao and post-Mao, has been slow to adopt because of its long standing policy of self-sufficiency. The report seems to suggest, however, that the government's goal of reaching a $1,000 annual per capita income by the year 2000 is probably unobtainable, even if China holds its population growth to its 1.2 billion goal.[8]

Although decision making is being decentralized and personal freedoms have increased since the death of Mao and the arrest of the Gang of Four, most of the social control apparatus, much of it adapted from the Russian model, remains in place and a few restraints have been added or reconstituted. Some observations follow concerning the information system, the controls through the work unit, religious freedom, the latitude given to the farmers, the birth control system, and the legal system.

The amount of information the Chinese are allowed to have has vastly increased since Mao's death. It is now acceptable to have a short-wave radio and to listen to foreign broadcasts. Foreign news magazines are allowed in China, and the advent of television news has increased the information available to the Chinese. The Chinese press remains, however, under government control. Movies continue to be selected by cautious censors, although they allow a vastly greater variety than when Madame Mao virtually stopped all film distribution (except in her private viewing room) to the Chinese people. The Democracy Wall, where "big character" protest posters could be plastered in 1979, was replaced by commercial billboards, and the "Big Four" constitutional rights to "speak out freely, air their views fully, hold great debates, and write big-character posters" was deleted in the new constitution. Unauthorized newspapers that were tolerated in 1979 disappeared soon after the arrest of Wei Jingsheng for his critical article in *Tansuo (Explorations)*. In 1982 a Chinese trade journal editor (who was a member of the Communist Party) was given a five-year sentence for having told a foreign journalist the place, date, and agenda of a party meeting. The same year an American graduate student was arrested and deported for having read certain "internal documents" pertaining to agriculture planning. In 1987, Yang Wei, a student who returned from the United States, was convicted for having conducted "demagogical propaganda" by contributing to *China Spring,* a periodical published in America by mainland Chinese who advocate abolishing "The Four Cardinal Principles" in the Chiinese Constitution (adherence to the socialist road; the people's democratic dictatorship; Communist Party leadership; and Marxism, Leninism, and Mao Zedong thought) in favor of Democracy.[9]

Most Chinese are organized through their factory, commune, or office into the *danwei* or work unit system. They are assigned to their work unit after they finish the appropriate schooling and screening and they are unlikely to ever work any other place. The work unit is responsible for issuing housing assignments, travel permits, and health insurance. Without the unit, a Chinese cannot obtain a city residence permit, and without the permit he cannot obtain a ration card. The party secretary in the unit usually determines who is to obtain what accomodations and has the major role in allowing marriage and divorce among the workers. The Chinese say: "The shoe fits very tight," that is, accommodations come very slowly to those who are uncooperative.

Chinese work places and living quarters are usually built behind walls. This is traditional to China, but when going from one office or housing unit to another, people must sign in with a gate keeper who may forward the information to their *danwei*. Chinese who wish to visit foreigners in their hotels or in more permanent quarters are also often required to register, and there is a general reluctance to do so. Although casual contact on the streets and in the parks is allowed, there is a great fear on the part of the regime of "Western Pollutants" (indulgence in material enjoyment, depravity, and crime),[10] and some Chinese newspapers have warned that many foreign tourists and students are spies.

During the Cultural Revolution and Mao's campaign to "Drive out the 'Four Olds': old habits, old ideas, old customs, and old cultures," most of China's churches and mosques were vandalized by the Red Guards and closed by the government. The religious leaders were exiled and most were abused, and many were beaten to death. After Mao's death many of the churches were restored. The reopened churches are well attended by the young adults and old parishioners who are trying to fill the void created by the "lost generation" of the Cultural Revolution. The reopened churches must belong to the Patriotic Associations, which assure the state that no foreign connections will be maintained.[11] The Pope's appointments of bishops are not recognized. The constitution stipulates that Chinese citizens shall "enjoy freedom of religious belief" and shall not be compelled to "believe or disbelieve in religion." Although the official religion of China is atheism, there are about 6 million registered Christians (about equally divided between Protestant and Catholic) and several million more members of the "silent" or "home" churches. Moslems exceed the number of Christians in China, especially in the west. The Chinese government appears to be supportive of the restoration of churches, mosques, and temples. Official publications state that 200,000 bibles have recently been printed in China. No party member, however, is allowed to be religious.[12]

Almost 80 percent of Chinese population is rural. Soon after the founding of the People's Republic, Mao pushed collectivization. Private ownership of land was abolished, often violently. The collectives were organized into Communes (in 1980 there were fifty-two thousand communes with an average of twenty-six hundred households in each),[13] subdivided into production teams (averaging twenty-six households). The production team often corresponds to a village. In general Mao favored placing most of the responsibility for decision making at the commune level. During the Great Leap Forward (1958–61) he tried to turn the communes into self-sustaining entities complete with "backyard furnaces" to produce iron. He also pushed the policy of "everyone sharing the meal in the same big pot," thereby deemphasizing the role of the lower units and the family. He also ordered the transfer of governmental power from the counties to the communes. No private plots were allowed outside the courtyards. In the words of Mao's successors, agriculture was characterized by "unrealistic production commands and absolute egalitarianism which smothered the peasants' zest for farm labor."[14]

Since the death of Mao, there has been a reversal in agricultural policy. The responsibility for decision making has been pushed down to the production team. The party claims that more than 90 percent of the production teams use some form of the responsibility system, which allows contracts to be made with households and even individual laborers.[15] The households are allowed to sell the fruits of their labor, beyond the contracted amount, on the open market. Thus the peasants are encouraged to make their own decisions concerning the crops to be grown and the method of maximizing their profits. The national annual per capita income for the peasants has risen from 135 yuan in 1978 to 424 yuan (U.S. $115) in 1987. The gains may be attributed to the contract system, sideline occupations, and increased food prices.[16]

There is some resistance to these changes by cadre who argue that most projects are better achieved collectively and that certain social concerns are made more difficult to ameliorate by the new individualistic behavior. They are, of course, reluctant to give up their economic power to the individual households and their political power to the revitalized county governments. Some old-line cadre see the new line as a move toward class polarization and capitalism, but the modernizers, in the name of increased production simply turn Marxism on its head. They boldly assert that the widening income gap "is essentially a manifestation of the difference in people's physical ability and labour skills. This difference is unavoidable in a socialist society and need not be feared. It shows the way to become prosperous by one's own sweat."[17]

Although food production has been increased by the new incentives and methods, China continues to be concerned because of Mao's Malthusian mistake. In 1957, Ma Yinchu, a distinguished economist and president of Beijing University proposed a birth-control program. Because Mao believed the masses were China's greatest weapon, Ma was disgraced and dismissed. By the time Ma was rehabilitated by the modernizers in 1978, more than 300 million people had been added to the Chinese population. By the time of Ma's death (at age 100) in 1982, China had 1 billion mouths to feed. By 1987, China's population had increased another 64 million and was growing at an annual rate of 1.24 percent.[18]

The modernizers have embarked upon a stringent, sometimes cruel policy of birth control. Contraceptives and sterilization are made available without cost. Economic incentives (higher pay and bonuses for having only one child, penalties for having more), surveillance (sometimes leading to forced abortions), the new marriage regulations (postponing marriage until age 28 for men and 25 for women) have been introduced. Even if the one family-one child goal can be reached, and there is considerable doubt that it can, the Chinese population will be 1.2 billion in the year 2000. Although the 20 percent of the population that lives in the cities may conform, the 80 percent that live in the rural areas may not. Most peasants continue to believe the old adage, "The greatest filial impiety is failure to produce male offspring." The new production for profit systems also encourages larger families. If the peasants are forced to comply with the new population policy, the party will have to pay a political price for depriving them of children.[19]

On 1 January 1980, a set of codified laws was proclaimed in the People's Republic of China to replace the arbitrary administrative law that had been used by Mao and the Gang of Four to the grief of millions of Chinese during the Cultural Revolution. The modernizers, who had suffered under the system, wanted to assure the nation that the atrocities of the "bad ten years" could not be repeated. Ironically, the first highly publicized trial after the law was proclaimed was for the Gang of Four. The trial and other unrelated events soon made it apparent that the new laws, although they seemed similar to laws in the West, would not be implemented in the same way. When Deng Xiaoping announced in advance of the trial that no one would be executed, when it was revealed that most of the judges had suffered at the hands of the Gang of Four, when the defense attorneys failed to interview their clients or challenge the witnesses, and when the verdict was delayed until the party could make a decision, many people began to doubt that the new laws would be taken seriously. Although the new laws represent a step forward, the

Public Security Ministry continues to have broad discretionary powers to detain anyone. The Chinese *Gulag* has been reduced in size, but it continues to hold thousands of people.[20]

If Mao could be awakened from his crystal coffin in Tian An Men Square, one wonders if he would be shocked. He would see that his old nemesis whom he twice purged, Deng Xiaoping, had "reinterpreted" scientific socialism and placed China back into the "primary state of socialism" rather than the final stage, as Mao once proclaimed. He would see that in 1987 the Thirteenth National Congress of the Communist Party had attacked his partisan's principles for their "dogmatism" and their "ossified economic" theories.[21] He would note that Liu Shaoqui, his one-time second in command, whom he "hounded to death" in 1969, had been posthumously rehabilitated and honored in an anteroom of the tomb. He would learn that his wife was in Qin Cheng prison where so many of his political enemies had once been held. He would observe that the huge portraits of Marx and Engels, and Lenin and Stalin, had been banished, even when the Communist Party held its Thirteenth Congress, an event coincidental to the opening of a large Kentucky Fried Chicken restaurant at the other end of the square.

Mao's tomb was built with great enthusiasm, but the new leadership soon regretted its construction. Yet, once in place, they found it almost impossible to remove without indicting themselves. They temporized by sporadically closing the tomb "for repairs." Similarly, the Chinese accepted Mao's unique brand of revolution and Socialism with great fervor but many came to regret the consequences. Yet, they found Mao's legacy difficult to dismantle so they appear to be temporizing by adopting certain economic expediencies that can be explained as "repairs." It remains to be seen whether the mausoleum and Mao's legacy will be repaired, remodeled, eroded, or replaced.

Notes

1. A brief description of Tiananmen Square may be found in John Summerfield, *Fodor's People's Republic of China* (New York: Urasia Press, 1981), 191–93.

2. Chicago *Tribune*, 5 July 1981.

3. "Resolution on Certain Questions in the History of Our Party Since the Founding of the People's Republic of China," adopted by the Sixth Plenary Session of the Eleventh Central Committee of the Communist Party of China on 27 July 1981, in *Resolution on CPC History 1949–1981* (Beijing: Foreign Languages Press, 1981), 37, 46, 56.

4. The trial combined the Gang of Four (Jiang Qing Clique) and the Lin Biao Clique (charged with the attempted assassination of Mao), but most of those "framed and persecuted" were charged to the Gang of Four. See *A Great Trial in Chinese History: The Trial of the Lin Biao and Jiang Qing Counter-Revolutionary Cliques, Nov. 1980–Jan. 1981* (Beijing: New World Press, 1981), 20–21.

5. *Beijing Review* 30, no. 50 (14–20 December 1987): 11; Robert Delfs, "Piggy in the Muddle," *Far Eastern Economic Review* 138 (17 December 1987): 100–101. Shanghai residents may purchase one kilogram of pork per month at Rmb 3 (U.S. $0.81).

6. Bian Fa, "Reform—China's Second Revolution," *China Reconstructs* 36 (October 1987): 19. *Beijing Review* 31, no. 4 (25–31 January 1988): 30.

7. Lynn Diane Feintech, *China's Four Modernizations and the United States* (New York: Foreign Policy Association, 1981), 58.

8. See Robert Delfs, "A New Kind of Planning," *Far Eastern Economic Review* 113 (14 Aug. 1981): 48–50.

9. Article 45 in the 1978 *Constitution of the People's Republic of China* (Peking: Foreign Languages Press, 1978); "Constitution to Be Revised," *China Reconstructs* 31 (July 1982): 28. Associated Press, 14 June 1982; "U.S. Teacher Ordered to Leave China." *Beijing Review* 25, no. 21 (14 June 1982): 7; *Beijing Review* 30, no. 52 (28 Dec. 1987–3 Jan. 1988): 12–13.

10. *Beijing Review* 24, no. 36 (7 September 1981): 3.

11. John Hersey, "A Reporter at Large (China, part II)," *The New Yorker* 17 May 1982, 50, 60. See also Richard Bernstein, *From the Center of the Earth* (Boston: Little, Brown and Co., 1982), 171–86.

12. "Notes from the Editors: Religious Belief," *Beijing Review* 25, no. 24 (14 June 1982): 3. The 1978 Constitution (Article 46) states: "Citizens enjoy freedom to believe in religion and freedom not to believe in religion and to propagate atheism." No right to propagate religion is included. The draft constitution (1982) statement on religion is Article 35. See *Beijing Review* 25, no. 19 (10 May 1982): 34. *Beijing Review* 30, no. 52 (28 Dec. 1987–Jan. 3, 1988): 18–19; Louise do Rosario, "A Small Concession," in *Far Eastern Economic Review* 139 (21 Jan. 1988): 29.

13. See Jurgen Domes, "New Policies in the Communes: Notes on Rural Societal Structures in China, 1976–1981," *Journal of Asian Studies* 41 (February 1982): 253–67.

14. *Beijing Review* 25, no. 25 (21 June 1982): 3.

15. *Beijing Review* 25, no. 24 (14 June 1982): 21.

16. Bian Fa, "Reform," *China Reconstructs* 36 (October 1987): 17.

17. Statement by Economic Editor Jin Qu in *Beijing Review* 25, no. 25 (21 June 1982): 4.

18. China has only about half as much cultivated land per capita as it did in 1949. Half its population is under age 21 and as it matures the food demands will increase. See *Population and Other Problems* (Beijing: Beijing Review Special Feature Series, 1981), 16–21; *Beijing Review* 30 (23–29 Nov. 1987): 11.

19. There are indications that the peasants are being allowed to have a second child if the first is a daughter. The "little emperor" or spoiled single child has become a widely discussed problem in China as a result of the birth-control policy.

20. See Fox Butterfield, *China Alive in the Bitter Sea,* (New York: Times Books, 1982), 342–69.

21. *Beijing Review* 31 (25–31 Jan. 1988): 18.

How Can We Evaluate the Economic Performance of the People's Republic of China?

RAMON H. MYERS

Suppose one wanted to evaluate the economic development performance of the People's Republic of China (PRC) for the past four decades to make comparisons with other developing countries?[1] What standards should be used? Can scholars agree upon some normative concepts and standards to evaluate the economic performance of societies so different in their stages of economic development and with different policies, cultures, and institutions?

Evaluating Economic Growth

Most experts generally agree that modern economic growth takes place when the annual growth rate of gross domestic product (GDP) per capita begins to accelerate on a sustained basis over long periods of time. At the same time, resources shift from lower to higher value-added activities; economic activity in the sectors of agriculture (A), manufacturing and construction (M), and services (S) begins to dramatically change; population growth accelerates; and the ratio of foreign trade to GDP customarily rises. Structural change occurs in the form of different sectoral contribution to the growth of GDP and employment.

Countries that have experienced modern economic growth experience a transformative period when economic structural change takes place and the annual growth rate of GDP accelerates include England during the period 1760–1860, France and Germany between 1860 and 1914, the Soviet Union between 1928 and 1960, and Japan between 1870 and 1914. Some experts have called this unique turning-point phase the period of trend acceleration or economic transformation. Whichever term one uses, it conveys the characteristics whereby a country's economic growth pattern dramatically and irreversibly alters. This period of transformation will vary from country to country, depending upon complex historical circumstances.

Economists can raise some questions about this unique period in a developing country's history. First, did the rate of economic growth fluctuate, accelerate, and then slow down; or did it accelerate on a sustained basis? The economic growth performance will greatly differ between countries depending on which of these patterns predominated.

Second, what were the sources of GDP growth? In other words, did labor and capital stock productivity accelerate, fluctuate, or rise and then fall? Economists can measure such trends by selecting indices to monitor the factor productivity over time. Another measure of the sources of GDP growth is that of total factor productivity, in which the factor inputs of land, labor, and capital are measured, aggregated, and compared to the growth of GDP. If output per unit of total factors rises over the period in question, one can interpret that to mean resource productivity rose to account for part of the growth of GDP that took place. If total factor productivity had declined, one would interpret that trend to mean the economy was becoming unproductive and only the growth of inputs had really accounted for the growth of GDP, a performance indicating considerable waste of scarce resources.

Third, economists can ask whether the trend of income distribution became more unequal, more equal, or remained unchanged. By ranking households according to income size and share of total incomes, we can derive a measure called the Gini coefficient to determine how income distribution changed.

Fourth, economists can ask how population welfare is improving by measuring the trend of real wages for the three economic sectors, by measuring the change in total household spending for food and drink over time, by estimating the trend for major goods consumed per capita, and by measuring changes in diet, medical care availability, and educational opportunity, for example. All of these measures, when taken together, provide some general indicators with which to judge whether the living standards of the people are improving, remaining the same, or declining.

Finally, economists can ask to what extent destruction of the physical environment has taken place—such things as the smog content of urban air, soil erosion, and pollution of rivers and lakes.

These five standards and their various statistical measures or indices provide quantitative evidence for describing the performance of an economy experiencing trend acceleration or economic transformation. Although there is no single measure that can sum up the five standards, this obstacle should not deter attempts to use these standards to make some general judgments about a developing country's economic performance.

The Case of the People's Republic of China, 1952–1978

Turning now to the example of the People's Republic of China, let me briefly discuss how my first four standards would evaluate the performance of that developing country in the first three decades of its history, namely from 1952 to 1978. I ignore the fifth standard for economic performance because of the difficulty of obtaining reliable information for the entire country. I choose the cutoff year of 1978 because the Chinese Communist Party "line" changed very dramatically after Deng Xiaoping took over the reins of power.

Prior to 1978 the annual growth rate for output per capita first accelerated during 1952–57 and then declined in the subsequent periods, 1957–65 and 1965–78. These rates of growth were 7.3 percent, 5.3 percent, and 5.1 percent, respectively. The same trend was observed for Shanghai, except that during the third period, output per capita, while higher than in the second period, was still lower than during 1952–57. Although these figures show high output per-capita growth rates, the annual fluctuation of GDP was extremely severe during these years. For example, the annual rate of GDP growth was negative in the early and mid-1960s, and it declined sharply in the late 1950s, the late 1960s and the early to mid-1970s. Sharp fluctuation of GDP represents a great loss of output and resources for society.

Typically, the service sector expands its contribution to GDP over time as the economic transformation deepens, but in the case of the PRC, its sectoral share of GDP steadily declined after the 1952–57 period. At the same time, there did not occur any shift of labor from the agricultural sector to the manufacturing and service sectors, a phenomenon that typically occurs because developing countries successfully allocate more labor to urban manufacturing and services. Yet these same developments had occurred in regions like Shanghai before 1937.

Turning to capital and labor productivity, for the years 1949 to 1976 various studies have shown that the productivity of capital declined. In fact, less output was being produced from each new unit of capital in the 1958–62 period than in 1953–57, and this pattern worsened during the years 1966–70 and 1970–75.[2]

Surveys of labor productivity in the stated-owned industrial enterprises of Shanghai, Nanking, Soochow, Nantung, Wuhsi, and Nanchang also revealed that labor productivity had declined between 1971 and 1978. As for total factor productivity, Anthony Tang's estimates for the agricultural sector indicate that productivity growth in the rural sector might very well have been zero during much of the period except for land.

As for income distribution, my measures are fragmentary. But taking these results in their entirety, some experts like Martin King Whyte have concluded that after the early 1950s income distribution remained relatively unchanged, with differences between the urban and rural sectors continuing to exist, especially between social strata.[3] Because of the limited intersectoral flow of resources, consumer goods rationing, and the slow expansion of real income per capita, income distribution probably remained fairly constant between 1953 and 1978.

But how equal had income distribution become after the great land reform of 1949–52, in which rural and urban property rights had been radically redistributed? A recent report shows that the Gini coefficient for urban worker income distribution was 0.185 in 1977 and 0.237 for rural income distribution in 1978.[4] These are among the world's lowest Gini coefficients, but low Gini coefficients characterize Marxist-Leninist regimes because they strongly stress egalitarianism.

What about consumer welfare? Life expectancy increased as public health measures slowly improved, rising from 36 years in 1950 to 64 years in 1979, whereas the average for low-income countries in 1979 was only 51 years and 61 years for middle-income countries. Likewise, the adult literacy rate rose from 20 percent in 1949 to 66 percent in 1979, and primary school enrollment as a percentage of school-age children rose from 25 to 93 percent, although it declined sharply after 1966–67. But perhaps 10 to 15 million people died needlessly during land reform and the socialization of the country during 1949–58, and maybe another 20 million or more died from famine and malnutrition-related disease between 1958 and 1961, when harvests failed because of ill-conceived party-state policies.

Only modest living standard improvement for consumers occurred between 1957 and 1981. Urban worker household real income doubled over this near-twenty-year period at roughly a 3.5 percent annual growth rate, but rural household income rose only 82 percent over the same period. Meanwhile, the income gap between the two sectors had slightly widened by the late 1970s. Because expenditures also kept pace, the savings ratio, already high in the early period, did not rise over the period. Meanwhile, the percentage of household spending for food remained about the same for urban and rural workers. The regime even had to initiate consumer rationing in 1954, and rationing continued throughout the period. In fact, the average per capita consumption of grain and cooking oil declined between 1957 and 1965. Average per-capita consumption of sugar and cloth remained virtually unchanged during 1952–65. To sum up, I observe little substantial improvement in consumer welfare for the Chinese people after the mid-1950s.

The Post-1978 Period

In 1978, the party decided to do something about the economy and try to raise productivity. Party leaders admitted that the previous thirty years had been a period of enormous waste of scarce resources; far too much capital had been produced and inefficiently utilized; consumer welfare had been needlessly sacrificed to produce excess capital, which was merely wasted; worker productivity was low because labor was not properly rewarded; enterprises had little incentive to innovate; the service sector was in disarray.[5] In brief, there had been wasted years, and Mao Zedong's misguided policies were blamed.

After 1978, economic growth picked up and output growth became more stable, with net domestic product growing at an annual rate of 5.8 percent between 1978 and 1982. There were modest indications that labor productivity was slowly rising for the first time since the early 1950s. As for income distribution, a slow tilt toward inequality in the countryside seemed to be taking place, but this was a very modest change: the Gini coefficient had only risen from 0.237 in 1978 to 0.264.

The most impressive improvement occurred in consumer welfare. Urban income increased much more rapidly than in the subsequent period, partly because of higher wage bonuses for urban industry, but mainly because of the spurt in rural income unleashed by the decollectivization policies that had materialized by 1981–82. A great boom in rural housing construction took place in the

1980s. Per-capita consumption of goods and services rose impressively, especially in the cities like Shanghai. All of these developments reflected a sharp break with the pattern of economic development of the previous period.

These changes can be summarized in table 1, listing my four economic standards and denoting the type of standard change that occurred by a plus or minus sign for the two designated periods.

Conclusion

The PRC certainly did not experience long term trend acceleration after 1952, and the economic performance of that huge country was mixed. If economists try to judge that performance by four general economic standards, it is clear that for the first three decades, production greatly fluctuated, productivity remained low or declined, and economic welfare indicators for living standards, as judged by consumption of key goods and services, did not rise impressively. Income distribution did become more equal, but that achievement came as the result of a great land reform in which many landlords and wealthy farmers were dispossessed of their property and even killed. Income distribution did not become more equal as a result of economic growth, as it did in the newly industrializing countries of the Pacific Basin after World War II.

After 1978 the PRC leadership charted a new policy course. The government gave more private property rights to farmers and allowed them to engage in more contracting with each other to rent land and hire labor. The government also encouraged the increase of private service enterprises and even some private manufacturing. But the expansion of the private sector, even after a decade, has been extremely modest. In fact, the regime has publicly claimed that state and collective-owned enterprises will continue to dominate in the economy. Even so, the leadership proposes to relax controls over these socialist enterprises and allow them more freedom to contract with each other and produce only a few commodities under central planning.

The consequences of these new economic reforms have been rather impressive in the short run. Rural income and output rapidly rose, as did the living standards of rural people. But by the late 1980s inflation and scarcity of commodities were becoming widespread, and rapid price increases exceeded the wage gains made by urban workers. Whether labor and capital productivity will continue to grow on a sustained basis still remains a serious question for the new leadership that came to power after the Tienanmen incident of 1989.

An Evaluation of Communist China's Economic Performance:
1952–78 and 1978–83

Four Economic Standards	1952–78 Value change	1978–83 Value change

1. GDP per capita:
  Rises (+)
  Declines (−)
  Fluctuates (0)
	(−) / (0)[a]	(+) / (0)[a]

2. Sources of GDP growth:
  A. Partial productivity change (labor and capital):
    Rises (+)
    Declines (−)
    Remains unchanged (0)
	(−)	(0)?

B. Total productivity change:
    Rises (+)
    Declines (−)
    Remains unchanged (0)
	(−)	(0)?

3. Income distribution:
  More equal (+)
  Less equal (−)
  Remains unchanged (0)
	(+) / (0)[b]	(+) urban
		(+) rural

4. Welfare change:
  A. Engel coefficient:
    Rises (+)
    Declines (−)
    Remains unchanged (0)
	(0) urban
	(+) rural
		(0) urban
		(−) rural

B. Goods and services per capita:
    Rises (+)
    Declines (−)
    Remains unchanged (0)
	(+) / (0)	(+)

[a]First value reflects overall long-term trend; second value indicates serious fluctuations over significant short-term periods.
[b]First value reflects initial change; second value indicates long-term trend.

After 1978 the Communist Party introduced new economic reforms to reverse the economic stagnation that had beset the Chinese economy during the previous decades. Whether those economic reforms will be continued and can reverse that trend and maintain stable, high per-capita output growth rates achieved through rising factor productivity is still the critical problem for the Communist Party to solve in the coming decade.

Notes

1. This essay draws heavily upon my essay "How Can We Evaluate Communist China's Economic Development Performance," *Issues and Studies* 23, no. 2 (February 1987): 122–55. This was a special issue devoted to the theme of Chinese modernization and the methodology of evaluation.

2. Shigeru Ishikawa, "China's Economic Growth Since 1949—An Assessment," *The China Quarterly* 94 (June 1983): 256, table 5, col. 4.

3. Martin King Whyte, "Inequality and Stratification in China," *The China Quarterly* 64 (December 1979): 684–711.

4. Li Chengrui, "Economic Reforms Bring Better Life," *Beijing Review* 28, no. 29 (22 July 1985): 22.

5. Probably the best economic survey undertaken by Chinese economists can be found in Ma Hong and Sun Shangqing, eds., "Studies in the Problems of China's Economic Structure," Foreign Broadcast Information Service, *China Report: Economic Affairs*, JPRS-CEA-84-064: 1–2 (3 Aug. 1984): 1:1–289, 2:299-578.

The Economies of Island and Mainland China: Taiwan as a Systemic Model

JAN S. PRYBYLA

The Economies of Island and Mainland China

THE HISTORICAL RECORD

Under the scrutiny of every major indicator of performance, the economy of Taiwan over the last three decades and a half has been a resounding success, a triumphal march from poverty to prosperity. In real terms, between 1952 and 1985 product growth on Taiwan has been nearly twice that on the mainland (table 1).[1] On a per-capita basis (at current prices) the situation from 1960 through 1987 developed as shown in figure 1.

When other dimensions of growth are taken into account, the comparison is less favorable to the mainland than table 1 and figure 1 suggest.

1. Taiwan growth has been the addition of *useful* output. A sizeable part of mainland growth has been useless because the goods produced were of poor quality, of the wrong assortment, in the wrong locations, or not needed. This is a system-related problem of coordination shared by all centrally planned "Soviet-type" socialist economies without exception. Example: in 1987, despite an acute shortage, 30 million bicycles were in government warehouses because they could not be sold. They could not be sold because they did not work.

2. Despite Taiwan's sensitivity to economic fluctuations beyond

Table 1
Indexes of Gross National Product (GNP) and National Income (IN),
Taiwan and the Mainland[a]

1952 = 100

Year	Taiwan Gross National Product	Mainland National Income[b]
1952	100	100
1985	1,544.2	820.2

Sources: Taiwan: *Taiwan Statistical Data Book 1987*. Mainland: *Statistical Yearbook of China 1986*.

[a]Taiwan: 1981 prices. Mainland: "comparable prices."

[b]National income mainland definition. This consists of the sum of values-added by the "productive" (material) sectors of the economy and is roughly equivalent to net material product.

the island's shores (especially in the United States), Taiwan's growth has been relatively *smooth*. Mainland long-term growth, on the other hand, has been very uneven. This unevenness includes one megasized depression (1959–62), resulting in a population drop of 13½ million in two years (1960 and 1961) according to official figures. The actual drop was probably greater.[2]

3. Taiwan's growth has been *balanced,* with industry, agriculture, transport, communications, commerce and other service trades working in tandem. By contrast, in line with the Soviet-type system's developmental philosophy, growth on the mainland has been highly skewed, resulting in larger inter- and intrasectoral imbalances. Among the more important have been neglect (a) of consumption in favor of accumulation, (b) of agriculture and light (consumer goods) industry compared with heavy industry, and (c) of investment in "nonproductive" construction (e.g., housing) relative to "productive" construction (factories). These imbalances had disincentive effects on the labor force and thus on labor productivity, confirming Milovan Djilas' characterization of the Soviet-type socialist economy as "a non-market, bureaucratic economy . . . where all real values, including the value of work, are lost."

4. Taiwan's growth has been *modernizing* ("going up market") in three senses: (a) the growth has been intensive, that is, attributable mainly to improvements in factor productivity; (b) it has raised the technological level of the economy (from tennis shoes to cus-

Figure 1
Gross National Product/National Income
Per Head*

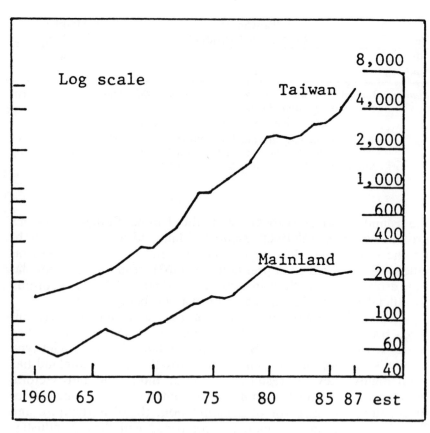

Source: The Economist, March 5, 1988
*Taiwan: gross national product
 Mainland: national income,
 mainland definition.

tomized computer chips) so that today Taiwan is on the verge of joining the select community of the world's high-tech producers; and (c) the growth has restructured the composition of domestic product and employment, away from agriculture, toward industry, commerce, financial, and other services. After 1956 and until 1980, this modernizing process of growth was much less evident on the mainland. Output growth was (a) obtained mainly by extensive means, that is, through addition of factors (especially labor and capital)—in terms of domestic product, there was an annual decline of factor productivity between 1957 and 1982 of 1.1 percent;[3] (b) the technological level of the economy stayed stagnant; and (c) despite industrial advance, both the domestic product and employment of the mainland remained deeply marked by agriculture, while the share of commercial and other services (the tertiary sector) was in retreat (table 2). In 1985 on the mainland, 63 percent of the labor force was employed in agriculture, down from around 80 percent in 1952. In 1985 on Taiwan, 17.5 percent of the labor force was in agriculture, down from 56 percent in 1952.

5. Last, but by no means least, the benefits of growth have been *equitably shared* in Taiwan, increasingly so as the pie grew larger.[4] While the inequality of income distribution on the mainland is low, in fact, one of the lowest in the world,[5] three qualifications should be noted: (a) partly because of the comparatively sluggish product growth over the years, partly because of a low-incomes policy pursued during the Maoist period, the relative equality

Table 2
Sectoral Origin of Net Domestic Product (Taiwan)
and Net Material Product (Mainland)

(Percentage shares)

	Taiwan		Mainland	
	1952	1985	1952	1985
Agriculture	35.7	6.9	57.7	41.4
Industry	13.5	40.2	19.5	41.5
Construction	4.4	5.0	3.6	5.5
Transport[a]	3.8	5.5	4.3	3.5
Commerce	23.9	15.3	14.9	8.1
Other[b]	23.9	27.1	–	–

Sources: As in Table 1.
  [a]Taiwan: Transport and communications.
  [b]Banking, insurance, real estate, government services, other services.

of income on the mainland amounts to poverty equally shared; (b) as with product growth, there have been fluctuations in the degree of inequality in the distribution of income, depending on changes in institutional property relations in agriculture and industry and in policy regarding growth; (c) enormous inequalities between the privileged class of power-holders and everyone else have always existed on the mainland in regard to the distribution of the material "rents" extracted by the privilegentsia of party cadres and state apparatus bureaucrats from the public assets under their control, and the nonmaterial perquisites accruing to them from the political power monopoly of the Communist Party. When dealing with autocratic regimes, especially the really thorough communist autocracies, this "power income" aspect of overall income distribution is of particular significance. After all, at the time of his death, Mao was reportedly earning less than 500 yuan ($250) a month.

Taiwan has become one of the world's leading traders; the twelfth largest trading country in the world in 1987, and the fifth most important trading partner of the United States. Per-capita foreign trade, which was $38 in 1952, came to $3,304 in 1986 (current prices). For a variety of reasons, including bouts of xenophobic self-imposed self-sufficiency, mainland China has been slow to emerge from its cocoon and take advantage of wealth-promoting international specialization (table 3). Taiwan's trade since the mid 1970s has been consistently in surplus, resulting in accumulations of huge foreign exchange reserves—in 1987, at $75 billion, the world's second largest after Japan. Since its emergence as a trader on world markets in the early 1980s, the mainland has had varying trade surpluses and deficits reflected in wide fluctuations of its foreign exchange reserves.

Taiwan's rate of natural population increase fell slowly from 3.3 percent in 1952 to 1 percent in 1986. This decline (like that of Japan earlier) was the spontaneous byproduct of modernizing economic growth, voluntary decisions made by urbanized families to have fewer children. The mainland, after following see-saw policies on the issue, reduced its rate of increase from 2.3 percent in 1953 to 1.4 percent in 1986. The decline was due in large measure to the implementation of Draconian birth-control measures (the one child per family policy), which has earned mainland China criticism from many quarters for violation of basic human rights.

Table 3
Foreign Trade
(US$ billion)

	Taiwan[a]				Mainland[b]			
Year	Total	Exports	Imports	Balance	Total	Exports	Imports	Balance
1952	0.31	0.12	0.19	−0.07	1.94	0.82	1.12	−0.30
1960	0.46	0.16	0.30	−0.14	3.81	1.86	1.95	−0.09
1965	1.01	0.45	0.56	−0.11	4.25	2.23	2.02	0.21
1970	3.00	1.48	1.52	−0.04	4.59	2.26	2.23	0.03
1975	11.26	5.31	5.95	−0.64	14.75	7.26	7.49	−0.23
1980	39.54	19.81	19.73	0.08	37.82	18.27	19.55	−1.28
1985	50.82	30.72	20.10	10.62	69.61	27.36	42.25	−14.89
1986	63.96	39.79	24.17	15.62				

Sources: Taiwan: *Taiwan Statistical Date   Mainland: *Statistical Yearbook of*
                   Book 1987   China 1986.*

[a]Customs statistics.

[b]Figures before 1980 are from Ministry of Foreign Trade. Figures after
1981 are from Customs Statistics, according to the *Statistical Yearbook
of China 1986.*

THE RECORD SINCE 1979

Three years after Mao's death, mainland China began to move
away from the Maoist variant of the Soviet-type economy and,
indeed, perhaps from the Soviet-type centrally planned system
itself (although the jury is still out on that one). This movement
has had three major components: (a) an incentives-related change
of policy regarding the neo-Stalinist priorities (or goals) of the
economy—a movement away from the three imbalances discussed
earlier toward emphasis on consumption, agriculture and light
industry, and "nonproductive" construction; (b) an institutional
reform stressing markets and de facto privatization of property
rights, particularly in agriculture, but since 1984 also in industry
and the urban sector in general (albeit more hesitantly, against
strong opposition), involving attempts to introduce elements of
factor and financial markets; and (c) an opening up to the world
market, including relatively generous provisions for foreign investments on the mainland. Looked at another way, the change since
1979 represents a shift of developmental strategy from near-
autarchy to a combination of import substitution and export promotion with growing emphasis on the last. Perceiving a
not-too-distant threat to its traditional exports from the mainland's

rapidly growing involvement in world trade (and the mainland's comparative advantage in labor costs), Taiwan—which has a long record of correctly and quickly anticipating trends in the international economy—has initiated steps in the early 1980s to upgrade the structure of its economy toward higher value-added, high technology goods and the development of financial services (partly perhaps in anticipation of the likely decline of Hong Kong in the 1990s as one of East Asia's leading financial centers). To blunt the protectionist blow from abroad (especially from the U.S.), Taiwan has also begun to moderate (if not yet give up) its long-standing policy of export promotion-cum-import substitution by taking various measures of import and capital export liberalization.[6] These economic steps were accompanied by political liberalization of genuine democratic content, exceeding quantitatively and qualitatively the political adjustments made by the mainland since the Thirteenth Congress of the Communist Party in 1987. In this way, Taiwan's image as a model not only of materially successful but of politically progressive development is brightened.

The data on GNP/national income per person in Taiwan and on the mainland (figure 1 above) suggest that since 1979 (when mainland economic changes took off) Taiwan has more than held its own. In fact, the gap has grown larger than ever before. Nevertheless the growth performance of the mainland economy since 1979 has been creditable (table 4), approaching the dynamism of the four East Asian tigers (Taiwan, South Korea, Hong Kong, Singapore). Taiwan's precautionary steps appear well founded assuming that the mainland changes will continue in the general direction they have taken so far.

With the adoption of the open door policy, mainland China rapidly increased its foreign trade turnover. Between 1979 and 1986 mainland exports rose 2.3 times and imports 2.7 times. During the same period Taiwan exports rose 2.5 times and imports increased 1.6 times (table 5). This has resulted in the already mentioned massive accumulation of foreign exchange reserves (the bulk of them held in U.S. dollar securities), a "mountain of gold" that is causing Taiwan more trouble than perhaps it is worth by, among other factors, fueling protectionist sentiments in the United States (figure 2). Some academic economists on Taiwan have argued for a reduction of the reserves (through import liberalization, relaxation of restrictions on private investments abroad, and encouragement of domestic consumption), an argument that seems increasingly valid to government policymakers.[7] Neobul-

Table 4
Annual Growth Rates of Real Gross National Product (Taiwan)
and National Income (Mainland)[a]
(Percent)

Year	Taiwan	Mainland
1979	8.46	5.0
1980	7.13	0.4
1981	5.71	2.5
1982	3.30	6.4
1983	7.88	8.3
1984	10.52	11.7
1985	5.08	3.5
1986	11.64	1.4

Sources: Taiwan: *National Conditions of the Republic of China,* Autumn 1986, 1987. Mainland: *Statistical Yearbook of China 1986; Beijing Review* 9 February, 1987, 24; ibid., 2 March 1987, 20.

[a]Taiwan: at 1981 constant prices. Mainland: At current prices adjusted for annual inflation rate; national income defined as in table 1.

lionist sentiments, however, die hard, and the advice to keep the reserves large in case of military emergency remains persuasive to some in positions of influence. The mainland's problem since the late 1970s has been to prevent recurrent massive hemorrhaging of its hard currency reserves (such as occurred in 1978–80 and again in 1984–86. The 1978–80 problem was caused primarily by ignorance. Liberated from Mao's "all-round" self-sufficiency, mainland buyers acted like children in a candy store, necessitating a painful retrenchment and the cancellation of several large import-based investment projects. The 1984–86 seepage was due mainly to the center's loss of control over hard currency imports by local authorities and enterprises, a phenomenon spurred by the system's chronic investment hunger.[8]

As noted earlier, while the long-run (1952–86) quantitative (growth) record of Taiwan is much better than that of the mainland—domestically and in terms of external trade, on an overall as well as a per-capita basis—the more significant difference between the two economies is in the area of qualitative performance, particularly as regards the quality of goods and services produced (the proportion of useful to total output), the attention paid to consumer welfare (which is what economies are supposed to be about), and the modernization of growth (the contribution to growth of improvements in factor productivity through technological invention and innovation). Much of the effort of the mainland's

Figure 2
Foreign Exchange Reserves

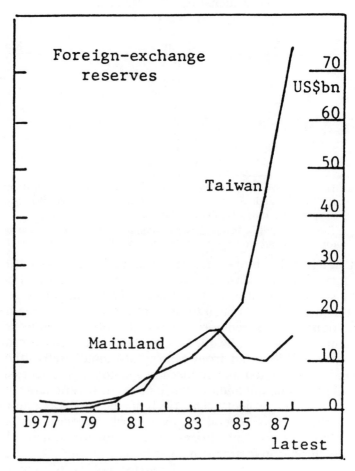

Source: The Economist, March 5, 1988.

Table 5
Foreign Trade
(US$ billion)

Year	Taiwan[a]				Mainland[b]			
	Total	Exports	Imports	Balance	Total	Exports	Imports	Balance
1979	30.87	16.10	14.77	1.33	29.33	13.66	15.67	−2.01
1980	39.54	19.81	19.73	0.08	37.82	18.27	19.55	−1.28
1981	43.81	22.61	21.20	1.41	44.02	22.01	22.01	0
1982	41.09	22.20	18.89	3.31	41.63	22.35	19.28	3.07
1983	45.41	25.12	20.29	4.83	43.62	22.23	21.39	0.84
1984	52.42	30.46	21.96	8.50	53.55	26.14	27.41	−1.27
1985	50.82	30.72	20.10	10.62	69.61	27.36	42.25	−14.89
1986	63.96	39.79	24.17	15.62	73.80	30.90	42.90	−12.00

Sources: Taiwan: *National Conditions of the Republic of China*, Autumn 1986, 1987; *Taiwan Statistical Data Book 1987*. Mainland: *Statistical Yearbook of China 1986; Beijing Review,*2 March 1986, 25.

[a]Customs statistics.

[b]Figures before 1980 are from Ministry of Foreign Trade. Figures after 1981 are from Customs Statistics, according to the *Statistical Yearbook of China 1986*.

economic reformers since 1979 has been directed at reducing this quality difference between mainland and island growth. The success to date has been greater in agriculture than in industry. Spectacular output increases in agriculture have been obtained with a smaller labor force and the use of a smaller farm area than previously. Some 80–100 million farm workers have been made superfluous and most of them have been absorbed by rapidly expanding rural industries. Increases in industrial output, on the other hand, have been obtained in the old way—primarily through additions of capital and labor. Between 1978 and 1983, factor productivity in state sector industry declined. A 28 percent growth of net output was obtained by a 49 percent increase of capital and a 17 percent increase of labor.[9]

The qualitative difference between Taiwan and the mainland is due in critical measure to a difference of systems. Centrally planned socialist economies have in the past exhibited fast rates of domestic product and foreign trade growth, but they were, and remain, inferior to the market system in three qualitative respects: they are enormously wasteful (much useless, substandard, unwanted output—or massive static inefficiency); they neglect demand, treating the consumer as a means rather than the end of economic activity; and they suffer from arthritic technologi-

cal innovation and diffusion which, together with consumer neglect, contribute to low factor productivity (including widespread
labor apathy). These disabilities are traceable to the system's de-
fective institutional arrangements of information, coordination,
motivation, and property.[10] These defects can be overcome by
structural reform, that is, by a change of system. Taiwan provides
a model for such systemic turnaround.

Taiwan as a Systemic Model

It is argued in some quarters that Taiwan cannot serve as a model
of exemplary economic (and political) growth because it is too
small, because it has a peculiar history, because it received generous U.S. aid, or for any number of other reasons that allegedly
make it a "special case." Such argument is erroneous. Of course,
no model can be transferred bodily without some adjustment and
modification. Even on that score it could be contended that Taiwan
and the mainland have a common history, culture, and language,
which should make model transfers easier than in other instances
where these commonalities are lacking.

What matters most, however, are the systemic arrangements,
the economic institutions (legally sanctioned and protected ways
of allocating scarce resources among competing alternative uses)
that deal with information about relative marginal costs and utilities in the system (i.e., scarcity relationships), the coordination
of allocative decisions, the motivation of the system's agents (the
incentive structure), and the nature and distribution of property
rights to goods and services and the products of those goods
and services. These institutional arrangements, through which
economic policy is pursued, are based on an economic philosophy
comprised of positive and normative principles: economic theory
and economic ethics. An economic system is essentially a set
of interrelated, internally consistent ideas about what should be
done, by whom, for whom, and how—ideas embodied in the rule
of law. It is a logical whole. Individual parts cannot be lifted
out of context and grafted onto another, different, perhaps opposite system. If intersystemic transfer is to take place, one system
must be substituted for another. Moreover, such total substitution
necessitates the transfer of the sociopolitical environment within
which the system that is adopted has been conceived and nurtured.
It is impossible, for example, for a centrally planned economy—if
it is to benefit from the market system's superior institutional

arrangements with respect to static and dynamic efficiency and material plenty—to (a) use bits and pieces of the market and some privatization of property, but reject the market as an organic whole; (b) adopt the institutions of the market system, but reject the market philosophy in either its theoretical or ethical form (e.g., adopt the market system, but use a Marxist theory of value to explain it, and "socialist morality" to sustain it); and (c) adopt market institutions and philosophy, but reject the sociopolitical culture (social and political pluralism and freedom, the market-place of ideas) that gave rise to those institutions and philosophy. One has to buy the whole package or nothing. And that is the fundamental reason why voluntary, peaceful intersystemic transfers are so difficult to accomplish.

I would suggest that in the case of island and mainland China, where the superiority of the island system has been so clearly demonstrated over nearly four decades, the transfer of the Taiwan model to the mainland, while certainly not easy, is perhaps relatively easier than the adoption, say, of Western European capitalism by the Soviet Union. That seems to be so not only because of the already mentioned shared history, language, and culture, and the dire straits to which socialist economics (pushed to its extreme by Mao) had brought the mainland, but to the fact that Taiwan's market system has absorbed those elements of the Confucian tradition and Sun Yat-sen's Three Principles of the People that are compatible with and supportive of the dominant free market institutions and free market philosophy.[11] In this sense, Taiwan's market system has truly Chinese characteristics, besides being effective in providing the people with an abundance of goods and facilitating the emergence of an increasingly pluralistic and democratic society and polity. What the mainland has to come to terms with, if it is serious about overcoming its three great disabilities—chronic shortages, static misallocations, dynamic inefficiency—and their many negative derivatives (e.g., apathy, sloth, bureaucratism, corruption) is capitalism with Chinese characteristics, which is what Taiwan has to offer, and as a natural extension of it, political democracy with Chinese characteristics. Such acceptance on the part of the mainland (certainly difficult, but not impossible on the longer view) would produce the only viable solution—not of "one country, two systems," but of one country, one system.

Before looking more closely at the Taiwan model of a market economy with Chinese characteristics, one contributory factor of Taiwan's success must be mentioned. Although U.S. aid and the U.S. military shield were important in that they permitted the system to take root and develop in the early years, more important by far has been the easy access to the huge American market provided by the United States to Taiwan since the beginning and to this day. This liberality, greater than that of any other developed capitalist country or region (e.g., Japan, Western Europe), had made it possible for Taiwan's export promotion policy to succeed and has been a key element in enabling the market system of Taiwan to show what it can do. If reciprocity is secured, there is no reason why this liberal attitude should not continue in a wider context of one China, one (market) system.

Taiwan is a model of a market system with private property as the dominant form of ownership and state intervention in behalf of the market and private property. The underlying philosophy is that of individual economic freedom, voluntary transactions, and competition. Taiwan subscribes with Confucian decorum to Adam Smith's dictum that "consumption is the sole end and purpose of all production; and the interest of the producer ought to be attended to only so far as it may be necessary for promoting that of the consumer." The presence of an interventionist government is sometimes cited to dispute the free market-private property characterization of Taiwan's economic system. This, however, is based on a misunderstanding. Capitalism is what people (perhaps with the exception of the Russians) do when you leave them alone. The essence of laissez-faire is precisely to leave people alone to do their buying and selling and to maximize their satisfactions and their profits as best they see fit on the basis of information supplied by workably supply-demand responsive market prices. Laissez-faire never meant the absence of government from the picture. It meant the limitation of the government's economic functions to certain tasks needed (1) to protect competition and private property rights, including the provision of a legal order (protection of contracts), external defense (critical in the case of Taiwan), money, and public goods; (2) to tackle externalities (through the market mechanism where possible); and (3) to take care of those who cannot take care of themselves.[12] It does not preclude the government from taking steps to initiate and encourage the process of economic growth and development through, for example, land reform that encourages more widespread private ownership of land, research and development expenditures designed to promote an up-market restructuring of the economy, even temporary (but they must be temporary) policies of "sheltered growth" for infant industries, export promotion, support for education (provision of equal opportunity for all at the start), and correction of highly skewed, politically explosive income disparities where these are due to market imperfections. That the government on Taiwan has acted in the promarket, proprivate property spirit is evidenced, among other factors, by the fact that whereas in 1952 the state owned 57 percent of industrial output, by 1962 its share had fallen to 46 percent, 19 percent by 1972, 14 percent by 1982, and 10 percent today.[13] By contrast, the first economic function of government on the mainland has been to severely limit and control when it was not bent on destroying the market and private property, an attitude that has changed only recently but has not been totally reversed. The government of Taiwan encouraged development through its policies of import substitution (1950s), export promotion (1960s, 1970s)—and, more perilously from the U.S. perspective, export promotion-with-import substitution through the mid 1980s. It set an example for others to follow in creating a climate favorable to foreign (export-oriented) investment on the island and lately has begun a process of import liberalization, encouragement of domestic consumption and investment, liberalization of capital exports, and technologically upward restructuring of the economy. In general, the government's policies have been pragmatic, guided by capitalistic financial discipline and the principle of market economics in command of politics.

Taiwan's market institutions and market philosophy dovetail into Sun's key principles of "people's livelihood" (attention to consumption), "land to the tillers" (note Taiwan's exemplary land reform, which provided one of the foundations of the island's industrialization), government intervention to facilitate intersectoral capital transfers from land (traditional use) to modern industrial uses, and the view that international trade and financial relations (the international cash nexus) are not inherently exploitative (rejection of dependency theory; welcome extended to foreign investment and multinationals).

I believe it is by now understood on the mainland, certainly by the brighter academic economists and some economist-officials, that much can be learned from Taiwan. What is not so clearly understood is that to do its work properly in solving the mainland's structural problems, Taiwan's systemic model has to be adopted in its entirety, including the system's economic philosophy and environmental political culture of pluralism and expanding democracy. Even if understood, such a package deal is extremely difficult for a monopoly autocratic party staffed by a multimillion-member privilegentsia to accept. Partial transplants will not do, and whole-sale rejection of the model will mean that the mainland's structural defects will continue to stall the economy, frustrate consumer aspirations, and lead to competitive decadence with other reform-resistant socialist economies. The Chinese characteristics of Taiwan's capitalist model may ease somewhat the painful decisions that mainland leaders have to make on what to do with their obsolete and unworkable centrally planned system with Soviet characteristics. In any event, the Taiwan model is available for the asking: its institutions, its positive theory, and its economic ethics. Who knows, it might yet be adopted by the mainland out of sheer historical necessity, under growing popular pressure.

For Taiwan the first task ahead seems to be to continue on its way toward greater riches. Snooty governments may not diplo-matically recognize but cannot ignore a country with a per-capita GNP of $17,000 or thereabouts, which Taiwan will reach by the year 2000. Taiwan's second task is to maintain social peace and political stability, while modernizing its polity in a democratic direction—a difficult but not impossible assignment. Its third task is to avoid being lured into ever more intimate economic relations with the mainland without concrete evidence, carefully inspected, that each step in the growing intimacy is attended by market-oriented structural changes of the mainland's economic system. Without such common-sense caution, Taiwan, for all its riches and temporal success, could slide into a tragic (for itself), one country–one system situation—the system being socialism with Soviet characteristics.

Notes

1. The validity of Table 1 rests on an enormous act of faith in the veracity and technical competence of the China mainland figures. Given the checkered history of mainland China's statistical services, the belief may well be misplaced. The quality of Taiwan's statistics is equal to that of the most advanced market democracies.

2. State Statistical Bureau, *Statistical Yearbook of China 1986* (Oxford, New York, Tokyo: Oxford University Press, 1986), 71.

3. K. C. Yeh, "Macroeconomic Changes in the Chinese Economy during the Readjustment," *The China Quarterly* 100 (December 1984): table 6, p. 711. The average annual growth of labor productivity in agriculture from 1957 through 1978 has been estimated at 0.2 percent (almost nothing), 2.8 percent in construc-tion, and 1.2 percent for services; ibid., table 4, p. 706.

4. Yuan-li Wu, *Income Distribution in the Process of Economic Growth of the Republic of China* (Baltimore: University of Maryland School of Law,

Occasional Papers/Reprints Series in Contemporary Asian Studies, 2, 1977).

5. Irma Adelman and David Sunding, "Economic Policy and Income Distribution in China," *Journal of Comparative Economics* 11, no. 3 (September 1987): 444–61.

6. Jan S. Prybyla, "United States–Republic of China Economic Relations since the Taiwan Relations Act: An American View," paper presented at a Symposium on ROC-US Relations under the Taiwan Relations Act: Practice and Prospect, Institute of International Relations, Taipei, 5–6 April 1988.

7. S. C. Tsiang, "The ROC's Balance of Trade Problems and Trade Dispute with the U.S.," *Economic Review,* The International Commercial Bank of China, Taipei, no. 241, January–February 1988, 1–4.

8. "If you can wangle an investment project you also become a more important factory with bigger bonuses, even if the production from the new investment is not needed." "One Awful Communist Example," *The Economist,* 2 April 1988, 40. The investment allocation, incidentally, is a free good—a nonreturnable grant from the state.

9. Gene Tidrick, "Productivity Growth and Technological Change in Chinese Industry," *World Bank Staff Working Paper,* no. 761, Washington, D.C., 1986.

10. Jan S. Prybyla, *Market and Plan Under Socialism: The Bird in the Cage* (Stanford, Calif.: Hoover Institution Press, 1987).

11. Like the so-called Protestant ethic, Confucian teachings are supportive of the work ethic required by the market system. Sun Yat-sen's teachings do not constitute a complete economic system, institutionally or philosophically. They can be used as supplements to the existing economic systems of socialism and capitalism—more logically to the latter. A. James Gregor with Maria Hsia Chang and Andrew B. Zimmerman, *Ideology and Development: Sun Yat-sen and the Economic History of Taiwan* (Berkeley: University of California, Institute of East Asian Studies, Center for Chinese Studies, 1981).

12. Adam Smith, *The Wealth of Nations,* book 5; Milton and Rose Friedman, *Free to Choose* (New York: Harcourt Brace Jovanovich, 1980), 29–33; Friedman rejects protection of infant industries as a legitimate function of government in a market system.

13. The 10 percent, however, includes such strategic goods as steel, petroleum, petrochemicals, electric power, and shipbuilding. *The Economist,* 5 March 1988, 13.

From China, with Disdain: New Trends in the Study of China

HARRY HARDING

"It's time to get beyond the American infatuation with the 'new' China."—advertisement for Richard Bernstein, *From the Center of the Earth: The Search for the Truth about China* (Little, Brown), in *New York Times Book Review,* 25 April 1982

Americans always seem to be busy clearing up misconceptions about China. In an attempt to get beyond one set of misunderstandings, however, they often create new ones to take their place. They substitute today's "truth" for yesterday's myth, only to discover that today's "reality" becomes tomorrow's illusion. This is why American attitudes towards China have undergone the regular cycles of romanticism and cynicism, of idealization and disdain, that were so well described twenty-five years ago in Harold Isaacs' classic, *Scratches on Our Minds.*[1]

Over the past ten years, American attitudes towards China have experienced another swing of the perceptual pendulum. The idealistic rhetoric of the Cultural Revolution, together with the dramatic improvement in Sino-American relations, created a period of pronounced fascination with China that lasted through most of the 1970s. The Maoist vision of egalitarianism, populism, and selflessness seemed attractive to many Americans. After twenty years of hostility, the possibility of renewing a friendly relationship with

© 1982 by the regents of the University of California. Reprinted from *Asian Survey,* 22, no. 10 (October 1982): 934–58, by permission of the regents.

This article is a revised version of a paper presented at the Eleventh Sino-American Conference on Mainland China, held in Taipei in June 1982. The author is grateful to the participants in the conference for their constructive suggestions.

a quarter of mankind appealed to still more. A "China fever"—or, as Lucian Pye described it, a kind of "Marco Poloitis"[2]—swept the United States. Its symptoms were not only the enraptured accounts of life in the PRC by the early American visitors, but also the tidal wave of Chinoiserie that deluged everything from art museums to hair salons and from interior design to high couture.

Today, in the early 1980s, China is not the rage that it was a decade ago. American museums now feature exhibitions of Alexander the Great rather than Chin Shi Huang; Americans draw their fashion inspiration from the patterns and colors of their own Southwest rather than from Mao jackets and mandarin collars; and they worry more about crises in the Middle East, Europe, and the South Atlantic than about their relations with China. A lecture by the latest "been-to" no longer draws the crowd it once did, and enrollments in many college courses on China have fallen precipitously.

As Americans recover from their "China fever," their earlier idealization of the PRC is giving way to something more cynical. An advertisement in the *New York Times Book Review* for the memoirs of the first Time-Life correspondent in Beijing offers us "China without illusions." It promises that the book will "get beyond the American infatuation with the 'new' China—past the carefully cultivated images of the Travel Service tours, the spellbound rhapsodies of the returned pilgrims" in its "search for the truth about China."[3] The new image of China that is now emerging is stated most succinctly by the title given to an article in *Harper's* by an American who recently returned from a year teaching English in Zhengzhou: "China Stinks."[4]

This reassessment of China is, on the whole, a welcome phenomenon. Many Americans are indeed beginning to move beyond idealization to gain a more dispassionate and objective understanding of the PRC. And yet there is some reason for concern that the reassessment may yield a revised image of China that is, in its own way, nearly as one-sided, extreme, and distorted as the one it has replaced. Ten years ago American travelers went "to China with love."[5] Now, they return from China with disdain. And this may produce not a healthy realism about China, but rather a debilitating contempt. If so, reevaluation of China may simply set the stage for another round of infatuation and euphoria a decade hence, again in the name of "clearing up misunderstandings" about China.

Changing Images of China

American images of China in the 1970s are to be found in a wide range of literature, from essays in the *New York Times* to articles in *China Quarterly,* and from scholarly volumes published by academic presses to commercial books aimed at much wider audiences. Some of these writings were trip reports, produced by the delegations and individual travelers who visited China in the first years after the "ping-pong diplomacy" of 1971.[6] Others represented the attempts of prominent American and European China specialists to explain the ideals, goals, and policies of the Cultural Revolution to a somewhat skeptical Western audience.[7] Still others were efforts to summarize China's model of socioeconomic modernization and to assess its applicability to other developing countries.[8]

This diverse literature presented no single interpretation of the PRC. Some authors were highly critical of the Cultural Revolution; others were guarded.[9] But the most prevalent view was highly positive—so much so, in fact, that it constituted a virtual celebration of the goals, programs, and accomplishments of China and its people under Communist rule.

The current reappraisal of China is also reflected in a broad spectrum of writings, which began to appear after the death of Mao Zedong and the purge of the Gang of Four in the fall of 1976. There has been a renewed attention to human rights in China, as shown by Peter Moody's scholarly analysis of the suppression of political dissent, the major exposé of political imprisonment in China compiled by Amnesty International, and Susan Shirk's recommendation that U.S. policy towards the PRC take into account Beijing's violation of basic civil and political rights.[10] There have been careful efforts to measure the performance and effectiveness of China's socioeconomic system and to compare them with the record of other Asian developing countries.[11] And, above all, there have been the new first-hand accounts, some by short-term visitors, but mostly by the journalists, scholars, and teachers who were now able to spend a year or two in China.[12]

Once again, these books and articles reached divergent conclusions about contemporary Chinese politics and economics. But the dominant mood has been one of disappointment and disillusionment—a discovery that China did not achieve all that had been claimed for it in the 1970s and a realization that the Chinese social order is seriously flawed. If Americans concluded in the 1970s that Communism had succeeded in China, the most common judgment in the early 1980s is that Communism has failed—and failed rather badly.

The differences between euphoria of the 1970s and the cynicism of the 1980s can, in my judgment, be summarized under five different headings.

First, in the 1970s China was described as an egalitarian society that had provided an adequate standard of living for all its people. Under a Communist system shaped by Maoist values, the Chinese were said to have virtually eliminated the economic differences between leaders and led, between skilled and unskilled workers, and between cities and countryside that marred the record of countries that had followed either the capitalist or Stalinist roads of development. By requiring physical labor and military training for everyone and by encouraging popular participation in politics and administration, the party was ensuring that each citizen— whether cadre or peasant, worker or intellectual—would have an equal role to play in China's socialist society. At the same time, the basic necessities of life—food, medical care, education, shelter—were provided at minimal charge and in adequate amounts to every citizen. There were, according to these accounts, no slums, no beggars, no hunger, no crime, and no flies in the new China.

More recently, however, Americans have rediscovered the fact that some Chinese earn more than others and that virtually every walk of life has been organized around a complex graduated salary scale. They have learned that there is a serious disparity in incomes between rural and urban areas and an even wider gap between the most advanced agricultural regions and the poorest communes.[13] They have seen the arrogance and disdain with which Han officials treat members of China's national minorities.[14] They have begun to write about inflation, unemployment, and inefficiency in the Chinese economy. And, above all, they have come to realize that the Chinese themselves see enormous differences in social and economic status between workers and technicians and between peasants and any type of urban resident.

As a second theme, China was described in the 1970s as a participatory and populist society. In most other modern societies, both capitalist and communist, politics had become enmeshed in bureaucratic routine, and officials had become alienated and detached from the people they led. China was seen as an important exception to this general trend. With the Cultural Revolution, the Chinese Communists were attempting to find ways of reviving direct contact between leaders and led, exercising popular control over the bureaucracy, promoting direct mass involvement in decision making, and thus preventing the formation of the "new class" of bureaucrats that Djilas had identified as one of the major flaws of mature communism.

Few Americans went so far as the Japanese Sinologist Atsuyoshi Niijima, who wrote on a visit to China in 1968: "I could literally hear my heart pounding. Right here, I thought, I was witnessing a commune state—the state withering away."[15] But many Americans did see the May Seventh cadre schools, revolutionary committees, and the "three-in-one combinations" as ways of bridging the gap between elites and masses and of ensuring direct popular participation in politics. Many Americans took seriously the idea that, during the Cultural Revolution, the ordinary people of China were selflessly concerned with ultimate political goals and actively involved in setting state policies. As one political scientist put it, China had created "flexible institutions which are responsive to popular interests, encourage direct mass participation, and are capable of controlling development on the basis of values meaningfully determined by the people.[16]

In their reassessment, in contrast, Americans have begun to emphasize the underlying elitism of the Chinese political system: the enormous gaps in status and power between officials and the public, the chronic use of petty corruption and personal connections to obtain favors from the bureaucracy, the perquisites—better food, housing, resorts, and so on—available to high ranking cadres, and the attempts by officials to pass on their privileged positions to their children.[17] In Fox Butterfield's words, "In purely monetary terms, it is true, the Communists still maintain the appearance of their old egalitarianism. All salaries are limited. But money by itself is not a good measure; the real differences are the hidden privileges, prerogatives, and perquisites that go with political status: the better housing, the chauffeur-driven cars, the special food stores, and the ability to travel. It seemed to me that the Chinese obsession with rank is at least as blatant as the snobbery of New York debutante society."[18]

Moreover, Americans have begun to write not of a flexible administrative structure operating on the basis of direct contact between cadres and "the masses," but rather of an inflexible and cumbersome bureaucracy. James Kenneson, for example, has described it this way: "The leader (of each basic-level unit) is responsible, fiscally and ideologically, to a vast hierarchy of officials towering over him all the way to Peking, each level further removed from the realities at the bottom, each level afraid to take problems to a higher level for fear of being criticized for not solving them themselves, yet also terrified of making a wrong decision. This structure is as unwieldy as a medieval assault tower, and results in a tremendous cost in efficiency and time."[19] Butterfield makes the same point even more succinctly: in China, he writes, "avoiding responsibility has been raised to a national art form."[20]

Third, the accounts of the 1970s often depicted China as a highly committed and virtuous nation, populated by some 800 million new socialist men and women. The Cultural Revolution was described as China's way of preventing the alienation and anomie that characterized other modernizing societies. By requiring regular political study, the Communist Party was said to be building dedication and commitment to a common set of political goals and values. By rejecting the selfish tendency to seek material gain for oneself or one's family, it was promoting service and sacrifice to the society at large.

Thus, American visitors saw in China a sense of harmony and unity, vigor, and dedication, which they contrasted with the elitism, competitiveness, and moral uncertainty of their own society. James Reston of the *New York Times* likened the spirit of China to that of the American frontier in the nineteenth century.[21] The Committee of Concerned Asian Scholars wrote that their most vivid impression was one of "vitality—the enthusiasm, the humor, and the tremendous commitment of her people to this new China."[22] And one of Shirley MacLaine's traveling companions put it this way: "It's just that in China I see all these people working as one person. They're so selfless, and it defies everything I've ever known, personally or in business. It's heavy, you know? . . . If I could stop thinking about myself, I could function better."[23]

The current reappraisal is altering this image of China as a nation of new socialist men and women. Chinese leaders today are described not as committed statesmen, but rather as politicians who are interested only in their own personal power and that of their factions, and in whose hands policy options and matters of state become merely rhetorical symbols that can be manipulated to further those ends.[34] The Chinese people themselves, far from being described as vital and committed, are now depicted as apathetic and cynical. In one account of life in China, physical exercises are done in a "comically desultory fashion," political study is "regarded with almost universal dread," and "getting a soft job and doing as little as possible are the universal ambitions."[25]

Indeed, Fox Butterfield has gone so far as to suggest that "the ubiquity and intensity of the control apparatus have generated tremendous psychological pressures on the Chinese, creating mental strains that few Westerners can imagine." In the old image of China, everyone was happy and at ease; now, Americans are told of a society in which a significant segment of the population suffers from "nervous tension, depression, and anxiety."[26]

Fourth, in the 1970s many Americans used the most glowing terms to describe both Mao Zedong and the Cultural Revolution he led. Mao was depicted as a Chinese philosopher-king: a poet, statesman, strategist, and sage who was grappling with some of the most profound social and moral issues of modern times. Writing a scholarly obituary of Mao in 1976, Michel Oksenberg compared the Chairman to Thomas Jefferson, Winston Churchill, Charles deGaulle, and Franklin Roosevelt. At about the same time, Edward Friedman argued: "By the example of his struggle [Mao] communicates the vigor of hope, the vitality of possibility, the vision of justice. . . . Had he lived longer, he probably would have pioneered yet brighter trails on steeper mountains."[27]

The Cultural Revolution, in turn, was described as the most important and innovative example of Mao's concern with the pursuit of egalitarian, populist, and communitarian ideals in the course of economic modernization. As I have argued elsewhere, through most of the 1970s the prevailing interpretation was that the Cultural Revolution was motivated by Mao's inspiring vision of a fair and just society, that its programs were effective measures for achieving this vision, and that its human and economic costs were both necessary and tolerable.[28] If the Cultural Revolution had a shortcoming, it was merely that it had not completely realized its ambitious goals. One China specialist readily admitted that "Mao's assault did not succeed in totally eliminating privatism, selfinterest, and elitism from Chinese society." But, he immediately asked, "should Mao be condemned for trying?"[29]

Today, in contrast, Mao and the Cultural Revolution are described in very different terms. Writing in the *New York Times Magazine,* A. M. Rosenthal, executive editor of the newspaper, has described the late chairman as a man "possessed of a lunatic destructiveness," and has likened him not to democratic statesmen, but to Stalin, Hitler, and Pol Pot.[30] In the later years of his life, Rosenthal tells us, "Mao destroyed the intellectuals, wiped out the universities and set China back, who knows, perhaps twenty years, perhaps half a century. . . . The simple fact is that Mao's fanaticism—and how painfully often we still underestimate the power of fanaticism, the connection between Stalin and Hitler and Mao and Jonestown—wrecked what there was of China's economy."[31]

The Cultural Revolution, once described as an innovative effort to create a new political order in China, is now portrayed as a period of "chaos and destruction" that produced "one of the worst totalitarian regimes the ancient land had ever seen."[32] One scholar who had earlier praised Mao's intentions during the movement has more recently criticized the "abominations in the 1968 theory and practice of the Chinese Cultural Revolution left, of Maoism," and has concluded that these abominations caused the "red banner" of Chinese communism to be "colored with the spilled blood of so many innocents, heroes, and martyrs."[33] Fox Butterfield has likened the Cultural Revolution to the Holocaust and, in a careful assemblage of official Chinese accounts of the human costs of the movement, has estimated that 100 million people were "affected" and between 400,000 and 850,000 were killed during it.[34]

Finally, in the 1970s China was described as a model of socioeconomic development—not only for other developing countries, but possibly even for the United States itself. Many scholars acknowledged the shortcomings of the PRC, and the difficulty of transferring the Chinese model elsewhere. But the common assumption was that, under Communist rule, China had achieved a record of accomplishment that made it worthy of at least selective emulation abroad. In Michel Oksenberg's phrase, the latter half of the twentieth century had become "the post-Chinese revolutionary era," in which the Chinese revolution would likely have a global impact comparable to that of the French Revolution of the late eighteenth century, or the Russian Revolution of the early twentieth.[35]

More recently, scholars have begun a comparative reassessment of China's social and economic performance, matching available information against stated goals and programs, and comparing Chinese achievements against those of other Asian countries. Nick Eberstadt's series in the *New York Review of Books,* for example, has indicated that China had done a great deal in the promoting of education, literacy, nutrition, life span, equality, and women's rights, but that its record placed it in the middle of the developing countries in Asia, rather than at the very top. The growing awareness of China's actual socioeconomic record, when coupled with the increasing willingness of Chinese leaders to criticize their own economic system, has virtually ended the earlier discussions of the "Chinese model." In Jan Prybyla's words: "When the dust settled in early 1981, people stopped talking about the 'Chinese model' because the model had been largely dismantled. . . . Instead of 'Is the Chinese developmental model transferable to other countries?' the question now became: 'What developmental model can the Chinese borrow to get them out of their bind?'[36]

One of the most striking features of the present reassessment of China is the degree to which the same phenomena are described in very different terms today than they were a decade ago. One obvious example is the treatment of poverty and backwardness in China. In the 1970s many observers acknowledged that China was still a poor, developing country. And yet, as Paul Hollander has pointed out, the prevailing interpretation was that this poverty was spiritually ennobling, since it meant that Chinese were not possessed by the wasteful and acquisitive consumerism of the United States. Indeed, there was a common supposition that, in poverty, the Chinese might still have a higher "quality of life" than in the more industrial—but competitive and polluted— environment of the West. In Hollander's words, China was "undeniably a poor nation, but its poverty was of an elevating, not debilitating, nature."[37] Now, China's poverty is simply debasing. Fox Butterfield has described, in graphic terms, the struggle among beggars over the scraps of food left in a restaurant in Xi'an by a group of foreign tourists.[38] James Kenneson describes daily life in China as "dull," "barren," "sparse," and even "brutal."[39]

Consider a second example. Crossing the Chinese frontier at Lowu, between capitalist Hong Kong and communist Guangdong, has always been a good litmus test of American attitudes towards China. In her survey of the earliest reports by short-term visitors to China, Sheila Johnson noted that a contrast was usually drawn between the "large neat fields of the communes" in the PRC and the "messy villages and fields of Hong Kong's New Territories."[40] The Committee of Concerned Asian Scholars described the "physical shock" they experienced at the transition from "noisy, pushy, and crowded Hong Kong" to "gentle" Guangzhou, where the people were "purposeful but relaxed" and where there were "no raucous horns or street vendors shouting vainly for a sale."[41] Now, the same juxtaposition produces dramatically different reactions. To A. M. Rosenthal, Guangzhou seemed "shabby" while Hong Kong was "shining"; to James Kenneson, the "dull and lusterless eyes" of the people of China were "such a contrast to the eyes of Hong Kong."[42]

Or take the question of sexuality in China. In the mid-1970s,

Joel Fort, a celebrity psychiatrist from San Francisco, could win ardent applause from a student audience at Stanford by proclaiming that there was no rape or premarital sex in China and that this was so because Chinese youth, unlike their American counterparts, sublimated their libidinal energies towards service to the nation. At about the same time, Shirley MacLaine and Norma Djerassi noted in their trip reports that, once arrived in China, they discovered they no longer needed makeup or deodorant, for they had entered a society that, unlike the United States, was not obsessed with sex or personal appearance.

Today, in contrast, China's sexual mores are viewed from a totally different perspective. Now it is Chinese leaders, not Americans, who are said to be neurotic about sex. A. M. Rosenthal, for example, has noted with some dismay that a large proportion of the young women in a Shanghai reformatory had been sent there for "having affairs with boys." He has described Chinese celibacy as the result not of traditional culture or revolutionary values, but rather of a deliberate program of "desensualization" and "neuterization" undertaken by the party itself. He has concluded: "It seems to me that leaders who try to desensualize their people, who try to make them as drab as possible, who find display of sexuality of any kind offensive, have problems of their own."[43]

Finally, Americans now read very different descriptions of the city of Beijing. The Concerned Asian Scholars noted that they "must have seemed dazed, a little distracted" upon arriving in a city that they had been "reading about, talking about, and dreaming of for years" but had never visited. Recovering from their momentary bewilderment, however, they likened the city to one of the most beautiful of the European capitals: "Peking was lush, verdant—Paris, but with still wider boulevards and even more trees."[44]

About nine years later, looking at the same broad boulevards that reminded the Concerned Asian Scholars of Paris, John Fraser of the Toronto *Globe and Mail* came to a very different conclusion: "Chang An Avenue, the main thoroughfare, and Tien An Men Square itself are dismal disappointments. The vast acres of pavement bordered by huge, ugly Stalinist buildings seem designed to reduce human beings to miniscule proportions." And he described the reaction of a Canadian diplomat upon first arriving in the city: "There was no downtown that the diplomat could recognize as such—no sense of the vitality and mystique that marks an exciting city. As his tour came to its harsh conclusion in Tian An

Men Square, he hunched lower and lower in the seat of the car. Finally, he looked around him and surveyed the interminable panorama. 'This city sucks,' he said."[45]

Changing Intellectual Assumptions

It is not only American images and evaluations of China that have changed since the early 1970s. At an even more basic level, there has also been a significant transformation in many of the intellectual assumptions that Americans have brought to a description and analysis of the PRC. Consider three interrelated assumptions, prevalent in the 1970s, which are no longer commonly accepted: first, that Western values and norms were inappropriate to an assessment of China; second, that this was because Chinese had fundamentally different aspirations than did Westerners; and third, that what really mattered about China was the worthy set of goals that its leaders were pursuing.

In the 1970s many Americans assumed that they could correctly understand China only if they suspended their own Western standards of moral and political judgment. In the past, the argument ran, they had misunderstood China largely because they had examined it with their own prejudices and values, and had therefore ignored its achievements and exaggerated its shortcomings. Blind fear of communism—the result of a Cold War mentality—had led them to ignore the fact that Chinese leaders sought to pursue societal goals that were every bit as respectable as those drawn from the liberal Western heritage.

Accordingly, the time had allegedly come for a sympathetic understanding of China, on China's own terms. As Paul Hollander has characterized it, the analytical task of the 1970s was to "dispel misinformation, lay to rest hostile stereotypes, clear up misunderstandings, 'break through the walls of ignorance' and correct misconceptions."[46] And to do so, in the words of an American China specialist, Americans had to begin "by examining [and presumably rejecting] our own assumptions and perspectives."[47] In the place of such Western values as individual liberty, reward according to merit, and consumerism, they should apply the collectivist, egalitarian, and ascetic values drawn from Maoist ideology.

Americans now seem more willing to apply their own values and principles to an assessment of China. In particular, Americans feel justified in asking hard questions about the state of individual liberty and human rights in China, even though the Chinese leadership itself continues to deny the applicability of such "bourgeois" concepts to their own country. Accordingly, much of the new assessment of China has focused on the absence of the right to dissent, the right to individual justice, and the right to privacy. Americans now emphasize the extent to which the state places tight restrictions on the dissemination of information, personal mobility, and political protest.[48] They have started to question a legal and administrative system that distributes both benefits and punishment on the basis of a person's class background or political behavior, rather than on the basis of individual merit.[49] They have begun to pay greater attention to the range of activities that are monitored and controlled by an individual's place of work, and by his residential committee, under a system that "institutionalizes every neighborhood snoop in the country."[50] When subjected to these new standards of evaluation, China has suddenly seemed much less praiseworthy than it did ten years ago, when the only relevant yardsticks were believed to be the Maoist values that China's leaders themselves would find acceptable.

A second, and related, assumption was that the Chinese care about very different things that Americans do. (To a degree, this supposition is embodied in the very title of the China Council's survey of Chinese culture and society, *The China Difference*.)[51] In fact, there were two variants of this argument. The first, more general version was that poor people such as those in China care only about economic values and are not particularly concerned with such things as liberty, or even justice. The more specific version was that Chinese, perhaps more than people in other developing lands, had no tradition of democracy or privacy or liberty or individualism, and therefore that the violations of such values in the PRC were of little consequence. Either way, since the Chinese were seen to be different from Americans, it was easy for American intellectuals to maintain their enthusiasm for a political system in which few would have wanted to live themselves.

Today, in contrast, Americans have begun to ask whether Chinese are really that different from themselves. Susan Shirk, for example, was one of the first to reject the notion that Chinese do not value individual liberty as much as Americans. "Whatever the impact of cultural preferences on contemporary policy choices," she has written, "it is not only presumptuous but also incorrect to assume that the Chinese do not care about individual rights."[52] Addressing the same issue, John Fraser has complained: "I had been warned by all the experts to assimilate the enormous differences and cultural contrasts between ourselves and the Chinese people before attempting to find any common ground. I now know this was exactly wrong, and that the reverse was the correct order: the ties that bind us all together mean more than any barriers."[53]

Third, in the 1970s Americans assumed that China should be evaluated primarily by reference to the worthy goals that its leaders were avowedly pursuing. They often tended to assume that the idealistic policy pronouncements of the Chinese leadership were instantly translated into social and political reality: that if Chinese leaders said that "women hold up half the sky," then Chinese women had achieved full equality with men; or that if they were trying to make officials accountable to the "masses," then they must actually have done so. Moreover, they also allowed those ends to justify the means that were used to pursue them. In looking at the Cultural Revolution, for example, they tended to dismiss the violence and chaos as incidental and unimportant in comparison with the noble values that the movement was designed to achieve. They confused, in other words, policy with performance, and intentions with outcomes, even though they carefully made such distinctions when they criticized their own society.

More recently, Americans tend to discount official policy statements as rhetoric and insist on looking at China's actual social, economic, and political performance before reaching any judgments about the PRC. And they no longer assume that the ends China's leaders have chosen have justified the means they have employed or that the "noble vision" of Mao and his followers warranted virtually any sacrifice demanded in its pursuit. To the contrary, many of the observers currently writing about China have quite clearly concluded that the accomplishments, whatever they were, were not worth the price. As A. M. Rosenthal puts it, "[I]t is neither rational nor compassionate to look at what the Chinese Communist system did accomplish—in health, literacy, life expectancy, cleanliness—and say, yes, this was worth the millions of lives lost, the prison camps, the prison state, the war against China's brain, spirit, and intellect, that it could never have been achieved at a lesser price."[54]

Towards an Explanation of the Reappraisal

Why has there been such a striking reassessment of China over the last several years? The more critical images of China are only partly the result of changes in China itself. Perhaps more important, they are also the consequences of changes in the political and intellectual climate in the United States, changes in the role that China plays in American foreign policy, and changes in the terms under which westerners are able to visit the PRC.

As Merle Goldman has argued, in some ways the earlier American euphoria about China "may have had more to do with American politics than with Chinese politics."[55] It was directly related to America's own "cultural revolution" in the late 1960s and early 1970s—a period of intellectual and political ferment that grew out of the civil rights and antiwar movements. Reflected in everything from popular music to scholarly writing, the principal theme of this period was intense criticism, and often outright rejection, of the American socio-political order and the principles on which it was based, including capitalism, competition, individualism, and material progress. Many Americans came to doubt whether their own society brought a better life, or, if so, at what cost.

The ideological assumptions prevalent in the United States in those years affected American attitudes towards China in a number of ways. For those who rejected the political values underlying the American socio-political order, there was a corresponding predisposition to favor societies, like China, that were organized around the opposite principles—that promoted socialism rather than capitalism, harmony over competition, collectivism over individualism, and egalitarianism over modernization.

For those who questioned, but did not quite reject, Western liberal values, the process was somewhat more subtle. The assumption was that it would be a kind of intellectual imperialism to criticize China for adopting a different set of values than the United States and that China's path was just as morally justified as America's. A society organized around collective principles, in this analysis, was just as good as one based upon individualism. Moreover, such a society might choose to pursue such things as liberty and justice at levels of social analysis other than the individual. Accordingly, when China "stood up" internationally in the early 1950s, it was achieving liberty for the nation if not for every citizen; and when it allocated services and life chances according to a person's family background, it was promoting justice for social classes if not for the individuals of which those classes were composed.

Most generally, the crisis of intellectual confidence in the United States made it difficult to make relative moral judgments. Even if China irrefutably fell short in such areas as individual liberty or individual justice, that was not sufficient grounds for moral criticism. Since the United States was not perfect either, the argument ran, Americans had no right to criticize China's shortcomings until they had eliminated their own. According to this state of mind—what Paul Hollander has called the "who-are-we-to-lecture-others attitude"—a society that violated human rights slightly was no better than one that violated them egregiously.[56]

One important reason for the reassessment of China, then, has been the recent change of intellectual climate in the United States. If the euphoria about China in the 1970s was closely related to the criticism or rejection of liberal Western values by many American intellectuals, today's disillusionment with the People's Republic has been reinforced by the relegitimation of those same social and political values. Whether one looks at the liberals' promotion of human rights or the neo-conservatives' criticism of totalitarianism, it seems clear that, across the political spectrum, American intellectuals have renewed their faith in such "bourgeois" values as individual liberty, privacy, and justice. Moreover, it is now considered appropriate, as was not the case ten years ago, to apply these values to an appraisal of China. In the 1970s, Americans were reluctant to criticize a collectivist society for its neglect of individual liberty. Today, in contrast, A. M. Rosenthal has concluded that what is wrong with China is its disregard of precisely this value: "There simply is nothing more important [about any political system] than how people are governed and whether under freedom, and whether freedom counts. . . ."[57]

The international political context has also affected American attitudes towards China. As several scholars have already noted, much of the American idealization of China in the 1970s was related to the opposition to the war in Vietnam and to the euphoria surrounding the Sino-American rapprochement. To a large degree, it is important to recall, the official American rationale for U.S. involvement in the Vietnam conflict was to turn back a tide of "people's wars" and "national liberation movements" sponsored by Beijing. If the war was wrong, as so many Americans came to believe, then that rationale had to be discredited. And one way of doing so was to show that China was no enemy of the United States, but rather a peaceful country, understandably resentful of American attempts at isolation, preoccupied with its own internal affairs, and trying to build a just and fair society. Calls for a new understanding of China, in other words, were integrally linked to a criticism of American conduct in the Vietnam war.[58]

Moreover, once the Nixon initiatives toward Beijing began to bear fruit—through ping-pong diplomacy, the secret Kissinger trip of July 1971, and then the president's own visit in February 1972—the usual logic of detente began to apply: if the United States and China could find common ground on international issues, then the Chinese must not be adversaries. And if they were not adversaries, then their socio-political system must not be so bad either. Indeed, the logic ran, China and the United States (and Vietnam and the United States, for that matter) had become enemies only because, out of fear and ignorance, Americans condemned anything that called itself communist, without realizing that the Chinese were as eager for peace, modernization, and social justice as Americans were.

Now that Americans have withdrawn from Vietnam, played their "China card" against the Soviet Union, and normalized their relations with Beijing, the anti-war rationale and the logic of detente have lost their force as determinants of attitudes toward the PRC. Today, in fact, Americans are discovering the limits on their relationship with Beijing in a variety of areas: the limits on forging further security ties with China, the limits of Beijing's flexibility on the Taiwan issue, the limits to Sino-American trade, the limits on scholarly exchanges with the PRC, and the limits of China's alignment with the United States on a variety of other international issues. And having discovered these international limits, Americans now feel freer to address the limits, so to speak, of Beijing's domestic performance: the limits on individual rights, on bureaucratic efficiency, on economic modernization, and so forth. If, as I believe to be the case, American attitudes towards another society are closely correlated with the state of our official relations with the government of that society, then the emergent tensions in Sino-American relations over the past two years can help explain the second look that we are taking at Chinese domestic affairs.

Third, Americans must also remember the sources and experiences that shaped their reassessment of China in the late 1960s and early 1970s. At the height of the Cultural Revolution, China was closed to most foreigners and virtually all Americans. Information about the movement came almost exclusively from the official press and from Red Guard newspapers and wallposters, all of which stressed the noble aims and lofty accomplishments of the Cultural Revolution. The tenets of Maoist doctrine—self-reliance, selflessness, egalitarianism, populism, and so forth—were expressed with an enthusiasm and self-confidence that discouraged skepticism and encouraged uncritical acceptance. In contrast, refugee accounts that exposed the darker side of China's society and politics were often rejected as biased and unrepresentative.[59]

Once the Cultural Revolution began to subside, China opened its doors to the outside world—but only part way. Travel was restricted to short-term escorted visits, under a program of what can be described as "revolutionary tourism." Visitors to China were organized not into tour groups but into "delegations"; they were not allowed to wander freely around the country but were confined to a fixed itinerary; and they were taken not only to cultural monuments such as the Great Wall and the Ming Tombs, but also to a wide range of grass-roots Chinese institutions for "briefings" on contemporary Chinese society.

In his *Political Pilgrims,* Paul Hollander has written an extremely useful summary of the "techniques of hospitality" employed by the Chinese (and the Russians before them) as part of revolutionary tourism.[60] Occasionally, these techniques included outright misrepresentation and distortion. More commonly, however, travelers to China were simply flattered by being introduced to leading Chinese officials; given opportunities to meet and talk with "ordinary" Chinese workers, peasants, and students; ministered to by warm and friendly guides who showed a genuine concern for their comfort and well-being; treated to the best hotels and meals that China had to offer; asked for their understanding of China's shortcomings and their suggestions as how China might overcome them; insulated from any evidence of the worst poverty in the country; and kept busy from dawn to dusk with a program that was both interesting and varied. Such techniques were able to hide many of China's defects—bureaucratic inefficiency, lack of personal liberty, lack of privacy, and the like—while displaying the country's accomplishments to greatest advantage.

"Revolutionary tourism" had two additional advantages. Because visitors were treated as guests, rather than simply as commercial tourists—indeed, because their travel expenses were frequently paid for or subsidized by the Chinese—they often felt it would be rude if they returned home with too harsh an account of what they had seen. As Merle Goldman has put it, "Since we were guests of the Chinese, we would be considered impolite if we were critical."[61] Second, it was widely believed that the Chinese were likely to deny visas to foreigners who said "unfriendly" things about the country. To preserve their welcome in China, some visitors were noticeably more reticent about China's shortcomings in public than they were in private conversation.

Today, in contrast, the ways in which Americans can visit China are also undergoing a major change. Like other foreigners, they now go to China to conduct some kind of business—be it teaching, research, journalism, diplomacy, or commerce—and stay there for longer periods of time. They are becoming long-term residents, rather than revolutionary tourists. And, as such, they re beginning to see features of China that revolutionary tourism usually obscured.

At first, the long-term visitor may react to China with much the same, romantic attachment as the short-term visitor of the early 1970s. John Fraser, for example, admits that he "succumbed to Sinophilia" for about a year before becoming disillusioned with the PRC. "I confused love of the people with love of the system, accepting all the frustrations imposed to divide foreigners and Chinese people with equilibrium, while studiously ignoring certain troubling little details that emerged every now and then."[62] Gradually, however, the "techniques of hospitality" begin to break down, and China begins to present a much less favorable face to the long-term foreign resident.

To begin with, the visitors gradually became aware of the impossibility of informal conversation and friendship with Chinese. This difficulty was not readily apparent under the program of "revolutionary tourism," which uniformly provided an abundance of opportunity for contact with "ordinary" Chinese in visits to factories, universities, and communes. Although these exchanges were obviously quite formal occasions, the visitors' inability to move beyond them to strike up more personal and informal relations could readily be attributed simply to shortages of time. Moreover, the Travel Service or Friendship Association guides made a special effort to have informal conversations with each visitor, thus producing a sense of intimacy that suggested that true friendships were possible.

The longer-term visitor, however, is neither scheduled so tightly nor enveloped so completely by his hosts. With more free time available, he wants to have contacts with a wider range of Chinese and pursue deeper friendships with the Chinese with whom he works. And here, the restrictions on contacts between Chinese and foreigners begin to grate: the isolation in a "foreign ghetto," the obstacles to inviting Chinese to his home for a family meal, the difficulties in being invited by Chinese to their homes for an informal conversation. During more liberal periods, such as late 1978 and early 1979, these restraints were loosened and friendships between foreigners and Chinese did form. Even so, as Fraser puts it, "each consummated friendship was an act of conspicuous courage"—and became an act of foolhardiness once the regime decided to discourage such friendships a few months later.[63]

What is more, the foreigner with business to conduct—and a protracted period of time in which to pursue it—becomes more frustrated with bureaucratic delay and inefficiency than the short-term visitor. Under revolutionary tourism, or even its more recent commercial variant, the visitor is essentially following the Travel Service's agenda, which is usually implemented with efficiency and dispatch. Few tourists request major changes in the itinerary, but if they do, the Travel Service's failure to comply can again be attributed to the short notice given. The longer-term teacher, businessman, or journalist, in contrast, has his own goals and priorities in China and becomes indignant when the Chinese do not accommodate him readily. It is not surprising, therefore, that longer-term visitors of the late 1970s and early 1980s have commented on bureaucratic inefficiency much more frequently than did the short-term tourists of a decade ago.

The problems with long-term stays in China are exacerbated when visitors come with unrealistic expectations to begin with. James Kenneson, for example, acknowledges that he went to China ready to be impressed: "We went to China half wanting to find a place to live till we died. We went with hoping minds, not just open ones. . . ." Kenneson's faith in humanity, it would seem, had come to rest entirely on the quality of life in China. And when reality began to shatter these naive expectations, its impact was devastating: "Whatever we had of faith in human nature or of hope for a humane future is far, far dimmer now. Our lives have been ripped raggedly in half."[64]

Finally, of course, Americans must consider whether their changing evaluation has been caused by a changing China. It certainly has—but in a rather paradoxical way. If anything, China has actually changed for the better since the purging of the Gang of Four. There is somewhat more liberty, more justice, more dissent, more stability, and slightly higher standards of living. And yet, despite these improvements, the American image of China has, by and large, changed for the worse.

This paradox can quite easily be explained by the rise of dissent and self-criticism in China since the death of Mao Zedong. To begin with, Chinese leaders themselves are now criticizing the irrationalities, inefficiencies, and injustices of their own system. Indeed, in few other countries—except perhaps the United States in the 1960s—have political leaders moved so quickly and so completely from self-admiration to self-flagellation as in post-Mao China. China's new leaders have criticized virtually all the "newborn things" that Western observers praised during the Cultural Revolution decade: the idea that a new elite could emerge within the party, the need for rustification of cadres and intellectuals, the denigration of individual incentives, the establishment of rural small-scale industry and cellular economic systems, and so forth. Even while continuing to call for party leadership and the dictatorship of the proletariat, they have criticized the absence of democracy, legality, and cultural creativity in their own country. And they have begun to acknowledge the rigidities and waste of their own centrally planned economy.

Even more, as controls on political expression have been relaxed, protest and dissent have emerged as significant and visible features of Chinese political life. The April Fifth movement of 1976, Democracy Wall of late 1978, and the "Beijing Spring" of 1979—all these have had a dramatic impact on American images of China. For one thing, they provided irrefutable evidence that the Chinese people—contrary to the conventional wisdom of the early and mid-1970s—do in fact value such things as individual liberty and political freedom. They also suggested that some Chinese see liberal democracy, as practiced in the United States, as an appropriate institutional model for China. Most important of all, the ultimate suppression of all three movements underscored the severe limits on sustained dissent in China and the inability or unwillingness of Chinese leaders to undertake any fundamental liberalization. To a large degree, these movements created a kind of "revolution of rising expectations" among Western observers— the hope that China might finally be moving in the direction of greater political freedom for its people. The suppression of the April Fifth movement shattered those expectations and produced a profound disenchantment in the West with the Chinese political system.[65]

China's own self-criticism—by party leaders and young dissidents alike—has had a searing impact on the West. It has made it much easier for Americans to write unflattering accounts of China and, conversely, more difficult to write favorable ones. Paul Hollander has noted the similarities between the reassessment of China in the 1980s and a comparable reappraisal of the Soviet Union in the 1950s: "As in the Soviet Union, the self-delegitimation of the regime—its admission that many of its earlier policies were incorrect, and many of its earlier leaders were vicious and incompetent—changed the climate of opinion in the West. As Adam Ulam noted with reference to the Soviet Union, once the facade of total self-assurance and uncritical self-adulation began to crumble, the receptivity of Western intellectuals diminished."[66]

What is more, the economic, political, and intellectual liberalization that have occurred in China since 1976 have made the PRC resemble an authoritarian regime more than a totalitarian one. And, as a general principle, American intellectuals tend to admire totalitarian systems much more than they do authoritarian ones.[67] In totalitarian systems, injustices are more completely hidden and dissent is more thoroughly suppressed, thus making it appear that there are more widespread violations of human rights in authoritarian systems than in totalitarian ones. In totalitarian systems, moreover, those violations of human rights are justified by an all-embracing ideology, which purports to explain why individual liberty and economic welfare must be sacrificed to higher ends. Authoritarian systems, in contrast, lack such consummatory political values and thus the self-assurance of totalitarian regimes. As a result, many intellectuals often see less merit in the bureaucratic stability of the authoritarian system than in the revolutionary mobilization of the totalitarian regime.

Towards an Assessment of the Reassessment

What is one to make of the reassessment of China that is now occurring in the United States? On balance, it is a welcome and long overdue phenomenon: a process that is stripping away much self-delusion about the PRC and enabling Americans, as Donald Zagoria urged seven years ago, to see "China by daylight."[68] Americans are beginning to distinguish goals from achievements, rhetoric from reality, and programs from outcomes. They are also beginning to regain confidence that some of their own values can, when sensitively applied, serve as fair and appropriate yardsticks for evaluating the performance of the PRC. Indeed, perhaps the most appropriate criticism of this reevaluation of China is that it did not take place much sooner.

At its best, this reassessment is producing works that measure China's accomplishments and shortcomings accurately and place them in a comparative perspective. Nick Eberstadt's work on economic and social welfare in China, for example, is a careful and persuasive attempt to assess the levels of nutrition, education, literacy, and equality achieved by the Chinese, and to compare them with the levels attained elsewhere in the Third World. China's performance, by these standards, is respectable, but not extraordinary. It does not, Eberstadt concludes, warrant the adulation that it received in the mid-1970s.[69]

Some of the journalistic accounts are also extremely valuable. Fox Butterfield's recent book on China combines anecdotes of daily life in China with the author's own analysis of Chinese politics, society, and economics. Butterfield interlaces his description of China with comparisons to Taiwan and the United States. And, while generally critical of the performance of the Communist Party, he offers a relatively balanced assessment of China's successes and failures.[70]

But when the reassessment is performed by less skillful, and less objective, hands than Eberstadt's or Butterfield's, there is the danger that the American public may replace one set of illusions with another that, while less pernicious, is only slightly more accurate. For, to a disturbing degree, there are similarities between the current reappraisal of China and the original romanticization of the PRC in the 1970s.

First, there remains a persistent tendency to make sweeping moral judgments about China. In the 1970s Americans looked at smiling faces and clean streets and pronounced China wonderful; today they discover poverty, inefficiency, and political constraints and conclude that "China stinks." In neither period have they been content merely to describe China; there is something about the country that compels them to evaluate it as well. And when they do so, they are prone to reach absolute and simplistic conclusions. They appear unable to see China as a complex society, in which some features are worthy of approval and others demand criticism.

To a large degree, in fact, China is being used as a scapegoat for American misconceptions. James Kenneson, for example, has concluded that China was a vile and brutal place largely because he had gone there laboring under the assumption that it was the last, best hope for mankind. Fox Butterfield begins his book on China by pointing out that he had to "unlearn" some of the myths about the country that he carried with him to Beijing: the myths that China is an egalitarian society, that Mao was able to create a new socialist man, and that the party has destroyed tradition and revolutionized Chinese society. What is being reassessed and discredited in these accounts is less China itself than the delusions that we brought to China in the first place.[71]

Second, there remains a conviction that the only way to remedy misunderstanding is to turn it on its head. In the 1970s, Americans believed that they had to present an image of an idealized China—a China without flaw or blemish—in order to clear up the unfavorable conceptions they had held about China in the past. As a result, they exaggerated Beijing's accomplishments, while either rationalizing, ignoring, or explaining away China's shortcomings. As Merle Goldman has described the failure of American intellectuals to respond to the persecution of their Chinese counterparts during the Cultural Revolution, "We knew, but we didn't want to believe."[72]

Today, many Americans also believe that they must argue that China has totally failed in order to correct the naiveté and euphoria of the Cultural Revolution decade. Where Cold War images were set right through idealization, idealization is being remedied through denigration. As a result, Americans now discount many of the achievements of the PRC since 1949, including a reasonable rate of economic growth, a respectable record of providing basic human services to the largest population on earth, and an impressive degree of economic equality.

Nor have they gotten over their perpetual romanticism about China. In both their euphoric and their pessimistic moods, they repeatedly express their admiration and affection for the Chinese people. References to a writer's "expansive love affair" with the Chinese; to their "natural ease" and "wisdom"; or to the "beauty and radiance that comes from good health, confidence, and pride" are just as likely to be found in writings of the early 1980s as in the early 1970s.[73]

But when Americans pass beyond these sweeping characterizations of China and look more carefully at particular segments of the Chinese population, they tend to be more fickle. In the euphoria of a decade ago, as in similar periods in the past, they idealized the hard-working and honest common folk who toiled in the factories and tilled the fields: the "masses" of ordinary Chinese whose exploits and sacrifice filled the pages of *People's Daily* and *Beijing Review*. The persecution of intellectuals, if not denied altogether, was described in the most euphemistic language, as in the Committee of Concerned Asian Scholars' description of physical labor and thought reform in May Seventh Cadre Schools as opportunities for a "revolutionary sabbatical."[74]

In today's more cynical climate, Americans have idealized not the worker or peasant, but the oppressed intellectual and the dissident of Democracy Wall. Many of the recent journalists' accounts of China are, quite explicitly, written from the viewpoint of the young Xidan protester. In contrast, the ordinary peasant, who constitutes some 80 percent of China's population, plays little role in the recent reassessment of China. According to the index, for example, the word "peasant" appears exactly once in Simon Leys' *Chinese Shadows*—and that one reference literally represents a casual aside within a parenthetical insertion.[75]

Fourth, Americans still seem to be convinced that seeing is believing. In the 1970s, when the door to China opened a bit, they assumed that the understanding acquired by the short-term delegations was more accurate than that obtained through more painstaking but less direct research. One's credentials for analyzing China rested, to a large degree, on how many times one had been there, for it was somehow better to have heard the party line directly from a cadre at the Hangchow tea brigade than to have read it in *Beijing Review*. (I remember vividly the ease with which a young graduate student humiliated a senior Sinologist in the early 1970s simply by announcing that he had spent twenty-four hours in the North China city that the professor had spent half a career studying but had never visited.) As a result, the favorable images produced by "revolutionary tourism" immediately became more credible than the less favorable ones produced by scholarship at a distance.

Just as the short-term visitors of the early 1970s appeared unaware of how little they could learn about China in two weeks, so too do the longer-term sojourners of today seem unaware of obstacles that they face in their attempts to understand the People's Republic. Even a twelve-month stay in China can introduce a foreigner to only a fraction of the country and its people. What is more, the constraints on the long-term visitor may produce a view of China that is as biased in its own way as were the favorable images of the country generated by the intense hospitality of the organized tour.

When travel to China was restricted to carefully controlled, meticulously organized guided tours, for example, Americans received glowing descriptions of the country. Now that Americans are able to stay longer but encounter the frustrations of dealing with a bureaucracy whose main purpose is something other than facilitating their particular enterprise, the public suddenly hears that China is "inefficient" and "disorganized." One suspects that, in both cases, one has learned more about the treatment of Westerners than about the average life of the ordinary Chinese. The fact that China does not "work" for foreigners does not necessarily

mean that it does not "work" for Chinese, just as China's attractiveness to the early "revolutionary tourists" said little about the
daily life of the ordinary Chinese.

Moreover, even longer-term visitors are denied access to important segments of the Chinese population—to peasants, to middle-
level cadres, to the military, or to leftists—and can forge real
friendships with few others.[76] And yet, the authors of the recent
journalistic accounts of China have rarely acknowledged the resulting contradiction between their claim to have new insights on
Chinese society, on the one hand, and their complaint that they
can form few candid relationships with ordinary Chinese, on the
other. They resent being isolated in their "foreign ghettoes" (a
description of which is placed at the beginning of virtually all
their books), and yet they insist that their experiences in Beijing
have enabled them to delve deeply into the heart of daily Chinese
life.

Even so, the reevaluation of China is rapidly becoming the
latest intellectual fad, expressed in the same self-righteous and
self-satisfied tones as in the early 1970s. Once it was "in" to
romanticize the PRC; now, it is equally chic to debunk it. The
message may be completely different, but the self-confidence of
the messenger is virtually identical. In fact, it is often the same
journals (and occasionally the very same people) that once glorified China that are now earnestly telling us that it's time to cast
aside the very illusions that they helped create.

Now, as then, Americans are told to expect novel new insights
about China. Once again, they are promised that they are about
to hear "the truth" about the PRC and that this new image of
China is going to surprise, even shock, them. As before, the
villains of the piece are said to be an earlier generation of Western
China watchers whose lack of objectivity produced only misunderstanding and illusion; and the heroes are the current breed of
objective observers who are ripping down every ideological and
institutional obstacle to bring us the truth.[77] In the early 1970s,
Americans were lucky to have a new wave of younger Sinologists
who were rejecting the anti-Communist and anti-Chinese biases
of their predecessors and gaining a sympathetic understanding
of the People's Republic. Today, they are equally fortunate that
yet another group of analysts has been able to get over the earlier
infatuation with Maoism, break through "China's great wall of
silence," and provide "uncensored stories and startling revelations" about the PRC.[78]

Finally, I am troubled by the degree to which, once again, Americans have fallen in line with official Chinese interpretations of their own society. When the Chinese said the Cultural Revolution was a good thing and that China had discovered a new path to economic development, most Americans readily agreed. Now that they say Mao made mistakes and that the Chinese economy is inefficient, Americans agree with that judgment too. Where they once idolized Mao for his noble attempt to revolutionize China, now they wish Deng Xiaoping well in his valiant battle to liberalize it.

Perhaps this is an innocent coincidence rather than a cause-and-effect relationship, but I would feel a lot better if, for once, Western observers would say something about China that differs significantly from what the Chinese are saying about themselves. Like the Ming and the Tang before them, the Mao and the Deng dynasties have both had their own official court historians. There is little need for Westerners to perform that task for them.

Let me not be misunderstood. I am not disputing the enormous contributions that the reassessment of China has made to American understanding of the PRC. Least of all am I calling for more apologies for the Communist Party. Rather, I am urging that, in their disillusionment with China, Americans avoid making the same mistakes that got them "illusioned" in the first place. The answer to uncritical acceptance of the official Chinese praise of the Cultural Revolution is not to accept, equally uncritically, the official condemnation. The remedy for fuzzy-minded idealism is not fuzzy-minded cynicism. Instead, Americans should strive for an independent, systematic, and comparative assessment of China in all its contradictions and complexity. Only such an approach can help dampen the pendular swings between unwarranted admiration and excessive denigration that have marred American understanding of China in the past.

Notes

1. Harold Isaacs, *Scratches on Our Minds: American Images of China and India* (New York: John Day, 1958).

2. Lucian Pye, "Building a Relationship on the Sands of Cultural Exchanges," in William J. Barnds, ed., *China and America: The Search for a New Relationship* (New York: New York University Press, 1977): 116–23.

3. *New York Times Book Review,* 25 April 1982, 18.

4. James Kenneson, "China Stinks," *Harper's,* April 1982.

5. Sheila K. Johnson, "To China, With Love," *Commentary,* June 1973, 37–45.

6. The trip reports of the 1970s are reviewed in Paul Hollander, *Political Pilgrims: Travels of Western Intellectuals to the Soviet Union, China, and Cuba, 1928–1978* (New York: Oxford University Press, 1981), chap. 7,; and in Johnson, "To China, With Love."

7. See, for example, Richard Baum with Louise Bennett, eds., *China in Ferment: Perspectives on the Cultural Revolution* (Englewood Cliffs, N.J.: Prentice-Hall, 1971); Victor Nee and James Peck, eds., *China's Uninterrupted Revolution: From 1840 to the Present* (New York: Pantheon, 1975); and John G. Gurley, *China's Economy and the Maoist Strategy* (New York: Monthly Review, 1976).

8. A prominent example is Michel Oksenberg, ed., *China's Developmental Experience* (New York: Praeger, 1973).

9. Some examples of the more critical works about China that appeared in the 1970s are Johnson, "To China, With Love"; Stanley Karnow, "China Through Rose-Tinted Glasses," *Atlantic,* October 1973; Simon Leys, *Ombres Chinoises* (Paris: Union Generale d'Editions, 1974), translated as *Chinese Shadows* (New York: Viking, 1977); Donald S. Zagoria, "China by Daylight," *Dissent* 22, no. 2 (Spring 1975): 135–47; Bao Ruowang, *Prisoner of Mao* (Harmondsworth: Penguin, 1976), 27–33.

10. Peter Moody, *Opposition and Dissent in Contemporary China* (Stanford: Hoover Institution Press, 1977); Amnesty International, *Political Imprisonment in the People's Republic of China* (New York: Amnesty International, 1978); and Susan Shirk, "Human Rights: What About China?" *Foreign Policy* 29 (Winter 1977–78): 109–27.

11. Nick Eberstadt, "Has China Failed?" *New York Review of Books,* 5 April 1979, 33–40; 19 April 1979, 41ff.; and 3 May 1979, 39–43. A revised and abridged version of this series appeared as "Did Mao Fail?" *The Wilson Quarterly* 4, no. 4 (Autumn 1980): 120–31.

12. The ones I have found most useful in preparing this essay include John Fraser, *The Chinese: Portrait of a People* (New York: Summit, 1980); Roger Garside, *Coming Alive* (New York: McGraw-Hill, 1981); A. M. Rosenthal, "Memoirs of a New China Hand," *New York Times Magazine,* July 19, 1981, 12–18ff., and 26 July 1981, 18–26ff.; Fox Butterfield, *China: Alive in the Bitter Sea* (New York: Times Books, 1982); and Kenneson, "China Stinks."

13. On inequalities in China, see in particular Butterfield, *China,* chap. 3; and Eberstadt, "Has China Failed?"

14. Both Luttwak and Fraser emphasize this point. See Luttwak, "Seeing China Plain"; and Fraser, *The Chinese,* chap. 7.

15. Atsuyoshi Niijima, "The Establishment of a New Commune State," *Chinese Law and Government* 4, nos. 1–2 (Spring–Summer 1971): 44, 49.

16. Richard M. Pfeffer, "The Pursuit of Purity: Mao's Cultural Revolution," *Problems of Communism,* November–December 1969, 25.

17. This aspect is emphasized in Leys, *Chinese Shadows,* and Luttwak, "Seeing China Plain."

18. Butterfield, *China,* 88.

19. Kenneson, "China Stinks."

20. Butterfield, *China,* 281.

21. James Reston, "China is Building a New Nation," in *The New York Times Report from Red China* (New York: Avon, 1971), 246–248.

22. Committee of Concerned Asian Scholars, *China! Inside the People's Republic* (New York: Bantam, 1972), 2. (Hereafter cited as *China!*)

23. Quoted in *New York Times Book Review,* 16 March 1975, 4–5.

24. The most scholarly analysis of this phenomenon is Lucian W. Pye, *The Dynamics of Chinese Politics* (Cambridge: Oelgeschlager, Gunn and Hain, 1981).

25. Kenneson, "China Stinks."

26. Fox Butterfield, "How the Chinese Police Themselves," *New York Times Magazine,* 18 April 1982, 54, 56.

27. Michel Oksenberg, "Mao's Policy Commitments, 1921–1976." *Problems of Communism* 35, no. 6 (November–December 1976): 1–26; and Edward Friedman, "The Innovator," in Dick Wilson, ed., *Mao Tse-tung in the Scales of History* (London: Cambridge University Press, 1977), 319–20. In an earlier article, however, Friedman attributed the "tragic losses" of the Cultural Revolution to Mao's deliberate inflammation of class struggle and to a "politics of destroying the old and tearing down established institutions." See Edward Friedman, "Cultural Limits of the Cultural Revolution," *Asian Survey* 9, no. 3 (March 1969): 188–201.

28. Harry Harding, "Reappraising the Cultural Revolution," *The Wilson Quarterly* 4, no. 4 (Autumn 1980): 132–41.

29. Richard Baum, "The Cultural Revolution in Retrospect," in Baum and Bennett, eds., *China in Ferment,* 177.

30. Rosenthal, "Memoirs," part 1, p. 14.

31. Ibid., part 1, p. 42; and part 2, p. 42.

32. Fraser, *The Chinese,* 51.

33. Edward Friedman, "Maoism, Titoism, and Stalinism: Some Origins and Consequences of the Maoist Theory of the Socialist Transition," in Mark Selden and Victor Lipsett, eds., *The Transition to Socialism in China* (Armonk: M. E. Sharpe, 1982), 207.

34. Butterfield, *China,* 19–20, 348–49.

35. Michel Oksenberg, "On Learning From China," in Oksenberg, ed., *China's Developmental Experience,* 6.

36. Eberstadt, "Has China Failed?"; and Jan Prybyla, "China's Economic Development: Demise of a Model," *Problems of Communism* 31, no. 3 (May–June 1982): 39–40.

37. Hollander, *Political Pilgrims,* p. 292ff. See also Michel Oksenberg, "Comments," in Ping-ti Ho and Tang Tsou, eds., *China in Crisis* (Chicago: University of Chicago Press), 2:493. As late as the winter of 1981–82, several of my undergraduate students told me that they found it difficult to understand why the Chinese would want to be any better off materially than they already are, since their quality of life was so much better than ours. Hollander calls this the "Noble Savage" myth—the admiration of the allegedly "simple, spontaneous, unregulated, and uncorrupted life" of the "Robust proletarian" and "earthly peasant." *Political Pilgrims,* 35–36.

38. Butterfield, *China,* 16–17.

39. Kenneson, "China Stinks," passim.

40. Johnson, "To China, With Love," 38.

41. *China!* 107.

42. Rosenthal, "Memoirs," part 1, p. 51; Kennson, "China Stinks."

43. Rosenthal, "Memoirs," part 1, pp. 45, 50–51.

44. *China!* pp. 107, 138.

45. Fraser, *The Chinese,* 36–37. A similar view of Beijing can be found in Leys, *Chinese Shadows.*

46. Hollander, *Political Pilgrims,* 279–80.

47. Louise Bennett, "Conclusion," in Baum and Bennett, eds., *China in Ferment*, 234.

48. Butterfield, "How the Chinese Police Themselves."

49. Shirk, "What About China?"

50. Butterfield, "How the Chinese Police Themselves." The quotation is from Fraser, *The Chinese*, 29.

51. Ross Terrill, ed., *The China Difference* (New York: Harper & Row, 1979).

52. Shirk, "What About China?" 111.

53. Fraser, *The Chinese*, 83.

54. Rosenthal, "Memoirs," part 2, p. 48.

55. Merle Goldman, "The Persecution of China's Intellectuals: Why Didn't Their Western Colleagues Speak Out?" *Radcliffe Quarterly*, September 1981, 13.

56. Hollander, *Political Pilgrims*, p. 280.

57. Rosenthal, "Memoirs," part 2, 39.

58. This linkage is stated explicitly in *China!* 2–3.

59. For a summary of the criticisms of refugee interviewing and a rebuttal, see Miriam London and Ivan D. London, "How Do We Know China? Let Us Count the Ways. . . ," *Worldview* 19, nos. 7–8 (July–August 1976): 25–26, 35–37.

60. Hollander, *Political Pilgrims*, chap. 8. For an earlier account, see Herbert Passin, *China's Cultural Diplomacy* (New York: Praeger, 1962).

61. Goldman, "The Persecution of China's Intellectuals," 13.

62. Fraser, *The Chinese*, 44.

63. Ibid., 278.

64. Kenneson, "China Stinks."

65. The dissidents play a central role in Fraser, *The Chinese*, and in Garside, *Coming Alive*.

66. Hollander, *Political Pilgrims*, 321.

67. For a slightly different interpretation of this phenomenon, see Jeane Kirkpatrick, "Dictatorships and Double Standards," *Commentary*, November 1979, 34–45.

68. Zagoria, "China by Daylight."

69. Eberstadt, "Has China Failed?"

70. Butterfield, *China*.

71. Kenneson, "China Stinks"; and Butterfield, *China*, introduction.

72. Goldman, "The Persecution of China's Intellectuals," 12.

73. The quotations are drawn, respectively, from Fraser, *The Chinese*, 17; Leys, *Chinese Shadows*, 51; and *China!* 268.

74. *China!* 100.

75. Leys, *Chinese Shadows*, 48.

76. I am indebted to Kenneth Lieberthal for this important point.

77. John Fraser's book has a number of unflattering references to Sinologists. See, in particular, *The Chinese*, 17 and 29.

78. Advertisement for Fox Butterfield, *China: Alive in the Bitter Sea*, placed by Times Books in the *New York Times Book Review*, 16 May 1982, 6.

Comparative Observations: American Images of Japan and China

HILARY CONROY

There is no single American opinion of China or of Japan, and Americans who think about East Asia from their varying perspectives and points of view do not always compare Japan and China. Nevertheless, stereotypes usually contain some grain of truth, and if one thinks as a big Uncle Sam looking westward across the Pacific during the nineteenth and twentieth centuries, he is first seeing a generalized "Oriental" type, which he is curious about but wants to keep at a distance; and then a differentiated Japan and China in which first one and then the other has the more favorable image.

Since the papers in this volume have dealt extensively and almost exclusively with American images of China at various periods in the history of American–East Asian relations, it is appropriate to begin with a few general remarks about American images of Japan. First, whether her overall image has been favorable or unfavorable, modern Japan has been regarded as an energetic, achieving society. This has been ascribed to various roots in traditional Japan: samurai drive, bourgeois mentality, natural entrepreneurship, peasant energy, and adaptability. However, Frances Moulder, while admitting the fact of the image, calls it untrue. This is because she feels that the relatively rapid recovery of Japan from the ravages of Western imperialism was due less to Japanese abilities or traditions than to the simple fact of less pressure from the West. In short, Japan was a small and relatively unimportant island country when China was the big juicy melon, which the various imperialist powers contemplated slicing up. Had Japan been more attractive to the imperialists, she would have been as easily and thoroughly disrupted and destroyed as China.[1]

We shall return to this theme later in this chapter, because it is in a sense the large overriding image of the long-range Ameri-

can mind on the Far East. Japan has been alternately admired
and detested but usually respected, while China has been both
loved and pitied but not generally admired or respected. First,
however, let us look at shorter-range alternating images of Japan
to get some idea of how that island appendage off Asia looked
in the American mind. If we begin with the visits of some of
the American voyagers of the mid-nineteenth century, we should,
of course, highlight the impressions of Commodore Matthew C.
Perry and his crew of note-takers, but first a word or two should
be said about the setting of the Perry encounter. For example,
the first American shipmaster to receive a message from Japan
took a look at the writing and concluded that "it looked as though
a chicken had walked across the page."[2] This was Captain Cooper
of the U.S. whaler *Manhattan,* who sought to establish contact
and possibly trade with Japan in March 1845, but who was informed (rather politely) that Japan's exclusion laws forbade this.

Cooper's remark about Japanese writing, the proud descendant
of centuries of Chinese and Japanese calligraphy—in which the
philosophical teachings of Confucius, Mencius, Chu Hsi, and their
Japanese counterparts, such as Hayashi Razan and other Shushi
scholars, were preserved—is most ironic in view of the depth
of the civilizations it represented and the crudeness of the American voyagers. But this is a good point from which to undertake
reflections on American images of Japan, for it should be remembered that however much Americans came to respect Japan and
the Japanese for their energy and efforts, it was from a position
of condescension. America in the nineteenth century, when the
first contacts were made, and far on into the twentieth was a
society of supreme self confidence.

By the middle of the nineteenth century, Americans were ener-
gized by what Stowe Persons called "the democratic faith," believing that there was a moral order, based on individualism,
Christianity, an idea of progress, and an American mission to
carry the torch of democracy.[3] There was not the slightest doubt
among Americans going to Asia, whether well or poorly educated
themselves, that their American civilization was vastly superior
to whatever might be found imbedded in the strange writing of
Eastern lands.

This sense of superiority was again revealed in the records
of the Perry expedition, the official ones authorized by the Commodore himself and the surreptitious ones kept, in defiance of
"the Como's" orders, by his underlings. According to his official

Narrative of the Expedition, Perry assumed that a firm attitude and insistence on heavy ceremonial courtesy toward himself and the president's letter he bore would impress the Japanese and bring about their compliance with his advice.[4]

Perry's subordinates expressed similar sentiments. For example, a junior officer, Edward Yorke McCauley, kept a diary that has been published under the title *With Perry in Japan,* edited by Allan Cole. McCauley's first observation on Japan was one that lasted with him and in the public mind. "One thing must be said about these people which can not be gainsaid, that they are without exception the most polite people on the face of the earth." McCauley, however also indicated that the Japanese had to be handled by force or threat of force. After the politeness notation, he says: "Nothing has astonished the natives so much as our impudence. Paixhan guns, electric telegraphs, steam and firearms all called for their admiration. These three steamers walking majestically up their bay, clearing mandarin and plebian boats out of the way without distinction, must have seemed to them a matter of doubt whether they would keep going on, over hill and dale into the water on the other side."[5]

On the occasion of the first visit of official Japanese envoys to the United States, in 1860, the American press had its initial opportunity to report impressions of Japanese in its dailies and weeklies. *Harper's Weekly* reported: "Few American ladies will be likely to fall desperately in love with the principal members of the Embassy in consequence of the striking beauty of their forms and faces. The first Ambassador is a man of small frame with a stoop across the shoulders. He has a long face and a peculiar nose not unlike the beak of a parrot. The second Ambassador is decidely worse looking."[6]

Despite their physical unattractiveness, the Japanese ambassadors made a good impression and their young apprentice interpreter, Tateishi Onojiro (Tommy), did indeed become a favorite with American "maidens and ladies." Newspapers that began by making fun of the Japanese came around to finding their deportment and demeanour most praiseworthy and in considerable contrast to that of the unruly American crowds who came out to see them. A month later *Harper's* reported: "The drollest part of the whole thing is that we speak of the Japanese as if they were barbarians and savages. But we have yet to read of the moment during these proceedings in which the Japanese gentlemen have not been quite as dignified, intelligent, and well-bred as any gentlemen in any country or time. The barbarism and savage behavior has been entirely upon our part," from the "shouting, staring, insulting mob."[7]

Akira Iriye in his introductory essay to the book entitled *Mutual Images: Essays in American Japanese Relations* (1975) argued that the idea of images as a conceptual tool in the study of foreign relations did not begin until as late as the 1930s. He saw Charles A. Beard's *The Idea of National Interests,* published in 1934, as an early example of the later trend in the study of images. He viewed such books as Harold Isaacs' *Scratches on Our Minds* (1958) and A. T. Steele's *The American People and China* (1966) and his own work in the 1960s and 1970s as bringing this study of images to a level of respectability. Nevertheless, whether scholars realized it or not, images were being formed.[8] If the Perry expedition and the first official Japanese embassy were the episodes that brought Japan dramatically to the minds of Americans, it was the general course of events in Japan's relations with the outer world over the next half century that built a somewhat conflicting but generally positive image of Japan in American minds. First there was Japanese general adaptability and willingness to learn. As the new Meiji government (post-1868) made clear its positive intentions in this regard in both words and deeds, American teacher-advisers to Japan were favorably impressed by the Japanese character. These teacher-advisers included William Elliot Griffis, who taught science; James Hepburn, who taught medicine and also devised a system for romanizing the Japanese language; William Smith Clark, agriculture; Robert Walker Irwin, business; Charles LeGendre, diplomacy; Ernest Fenolossa, philosophy; and Lafcadio Hearn, literature.

In addition several nationally prominent Americans who visited Japan, however briefly, helped to form a positive image. One of the first (1870) was William H. Seward whose stepdaughter, Olive, recorded her and his impressions, which were quite favorable: the Japanese were polite, friendly, and progressive, though in much need of American instruction. Ulysses S. Grant and his wife were wined and dined by the Emperor in 1879, and thereafter, back in America, Grant was known as a good friend of Japan. Those who contributed to building an appreciation of Japan in the United States included Percival Lowell; his famous poet sister Amy; John LaFarge, the artist; and the educator-historian, Henry Adams.[9] Also, American ministers to Japan "Judge" John A. Bingham and Richard B. Hubbard, whose terms at Tokyo together spanned the years 1873–89, were favorably impressed with Japan and reported home in that vein.[10]

In addition Japan's quite ardent participation in American "World's Fairs" at Philadelphia (1879), New Orleans (1885), Chicago (1893), and St. Louis (1903) delighted Americans. The combination of an exotic and artistic past with a progressive present made Japan seem both delightful and impressive. The only problem was a sense of worry, explicitly voiced by Lafcadio Hearn in his writings from Japan, that the present would overwhelm the past to rob Japanese civilization of its quaintness and charm. Its progress was respected, but Japan was not yet feared (at least in St. Louis) as a competitor.[11]

Chitoshi Yanaga, whose thick volume *Japan Since Perry* served as *the* standard text on modern Japanese history for many years, called the era that was inaugurated by the first (1860) official Japanese mission to America one of "cordial relationship unprecedented," and so it remained until approximately the turn of the twentieth century.[12]

The first faint cloud on the American image of Japan developed over the Hawaiian islands. There Japanese laborers were brought in great numbers by American planters to work their sugar and pineapple plantations. By the mid 1890s, more than twenty-five thousand had come, and the number was rapidly accelerating, to the alarm of the now vastly outnumbered American population that had controlled the islands through manipulation of the Hawaiian monarchy. The Japanese were hard workers, but too ambitious and too smart to suit their employers, who by 1897 feared a Japanese takeover.

By a combination of skillful lobbying and considerable luck, Hawaii's American leadership was able to obtain annexation of the islands from a formerly reluctant Congress; and Japanese leaders, unready and unwilling to provoke a quarrel, smoothed the matter over, leaving good images and relationships temporarily untarnished.[13]

However an era of "troubled encounter" (Neu) and "Pacific estrangement" (Iriye) was about to begin.[14] Victory in the Russo-Japanese war (1905) brought Japan, according to U.S. Navy Secretary H. A. Herbert, "to a place among the great nations of the earth."[15] By this time the American image of China and Chinese had been well established as a negative stereotype: weak country, undesirable people. The Chinese Laborers Exclusion Act (1882) with its several extensions and tightenings-up set the tone for

American attitudes toward and handling of Chinese immigration. And China, weak and inept, was being maintained as an "entity" through the goodness of American hearts and the Open Door Policy (1900).

Negativism about Japan was of an entirely different sort. Having become powerful as a nation, the Japanese were regarded as pushy and overbearing. Akira Iriye quotes Nevada Senator Francis G. Newlands as follows (1909): "The presence of the Chinese, who are patient and submissive, would not create as many complications as the presence of the Japanese, whose strong and virile qualities would constitute an additional factor of difficulty."[16]

While it is true that during the first brush with Japanese immigration on the West Coast a few ultraracist Americans had tried to denigrate the Japanese by placing them in the same category as the despised and pitied Chinese, this did not last long. The key word for this was "Mongolian," which could be applied indiscriminately to Chinese, Koreans, Japanese or other East Asians. The height of this approach came in 1906 when the San Francisco School Board decreed that Japanese children should attend what had heretofore been known as "the Chinese School" in San Francisco. During their discussions the board had used the term "pupils of the Mongolian race."[17]

Not only did the Japanese government protest this, but President Theodore Roosevelt forced the school board to rescind the offensive decree. After this the Gentlemen's Agreement of 1907, by which Japan voluntarily agreed to limit immigration to the United States, had the effect of requiring the United States government, at least, to treat Japan and Japanese with circumspection and respect and not to lump them with Chinese and other "Asiatics," "Orientals," and "Mongolians."

While there continued to be racist attitudes and anti-Japanese legislation in California and other western states, these now had to be expressed obliquely as pertaining to "aliens ineligible for citizenship" (e.g., in California's "Alien Land Law of 1913").[18] Indeed, an incensed spokesman for white Christian interests in California, one Montaville Flowers, M.A., felt impelled to write and warn of "The Japanese Conquest of American Opinion" (the title of his 272-page book).[19]

Flowers called Hawaii already a "Japanese colony," the Gentlemen's Agreement a "moral victory for Japan," and the alien land problem a question of "Who Shall Own the Pacific Coast." He saw powerful Americans as tools or allies of the Japanese in helping them establish areas of control in the United States.

Those included the Federal Council of the Churches of Christ in America, which employed Mr. Sidney L. Gulick, M.A., D.D., a native of the Marshall Islands and longtime resident of Japan, and Professor H. A. Millis, who wrote books and articles designed to "malign" the state of California "to put Japan over in states where she is not known, where there is no local interest, where the people are still asleep on this question, and to coerce the people of a section of the country."[20] Their message was spread not only by the Federal Council but by the World Peace Foundation of Boston, the American Peace Society of Washington, the Church Peace Union of New York, the Carnegie Endowment for International Peace, and the Japan Society of New York, which alone sent one thousand copies of Professor Millis's book "to presidents of American colleges and other."[21]

Obviously feeling on the defensive, Flowers claimed that the powerful pro-Japanese opinion molders had called Californians "rough, ignorant, prejudiced" and said that the legislation against Japanese was promoted by "boodlers, criminals, professional agitators, jingoes, demagogues."[22] Meanwhile, within less than a year, Japan had "launched ten war vessels" and "Japan's flag is flying from vessels in almost every trading post in the world." Her army had increased by 250,000 men, she had appropriated $400,000 for an aviation school, and "from January 1 to February 10, 1916 the excess of exports from Japan over imports amounted to thirteen million dollars."[23]

So argued an arch enemy of Japan, fearing and warning against her prowess. Her friends turned the argument around, admiring Japanese progress and restraint. Thus Lindsay Russell, president of the Japan Society of New York and one of Flowers's principal targets, had in 1915 "a symposium of papers by representatives/citizens of the United States on the relations between Japan and America and on the common interests of the two countries."[24] William E. Griffis was among the more rhapsodic contributors, even giving a "long live" for the Japanese emperor and empress.[25]

The same W. E. Griffis—a perennial writer and speaker on Japan following a teaching adventure there in his youth, 1870–74, and continuing through a latter-day return visit in 1926–27—credited Japan and the Japanese with great progress and achievements in almost everything: enlightened government, economic prosperity, and international brotherhood. Indeed, compared with American racists, the Japanese practised "real Christianity."[26]

In 1931, with the Manchurian Incident, the American image of Japan began to change for the worse. But again, even as the

war clouds thickened and American-Japanese relations moved toward Pearl Harbor, the tone was one of hatred but not of contempt.
During all these years, from 1900's Open Door proclamation days
to the end of the Pacific War China was always in the "help
needed" category, and although American missionaries loved
China (much more than Japan), it was certainly a love of condescension.

This situation almost reversed in the first decade after the Pacific
War. Defeated Japan lay prostrate; there was no longer any fear
of her in the American mind. The antagonism and hatred of the
war years soon dissipated. The author remembers riding around
Tokyo in army vehicles driven by vengeful veterans of Pacific
campaigns. For a month or two early in the occupation, they
took considerable delight in "Making Japs jump" out of the way
to avoid being run down. But this didn't last long. Before the
end of that first winter of occupation, Americans were experiencing positively friendly feelings for their Japanese charges. There
was a considerable degree of condescension in this, but the "pluck-
iness" of the Japanese in working their way through the hardship
of life in their shattered country mitigated that attitude. Occupation
memoir books like *The Conqueror Comes to Tea* and *MacArthur's
Japan* found the Japanese much less offensive and cruel than
the war and its propaganda had made them seem.[27] And their
evident determination to work hard toward recovery elicited respect from the conquerors. At home in America it was discovered
that the Japanese-Americans who had suffered wartime incarcera-
tion under the name of "relocation" had not been traitors at all;
rather, some of them, like the 442d infantry division from Hawaii,
had proved themselves heroes on the European front.

Meanwhile the China image was being further tarnished by the
increasingly obvious incompetence of the Nationalist government,
both in the latter-post-Stilwell days of the war and in the postwar
era of communist takeover of mainland China. Considerable sympathy (but certainly no admiration) went out to Chiang Kai-shek
(Jiang Jieshi) and his holdout forces on Taiwan. As for Mao and
his fellow communists on the mainland, they quickly lost whatever
admiration Americans had felt for them. As contributors have
shown in earlier essays, Edgar Snow's *Red Star Over China* and
the writings of other journalists and scholars who had sought
out the "Reds" at their wartime Yenan (Ya'nan) headquarters gave
Americans a glimpse of a "new China" of competence, courage,
and hard work—albeit ideological impurity—in contrast to the
worsening image of China under the Nationalists. But with the

establishment of the People's Republic at Peking (Beijing) in the fall of 1949, what from the general American point of view were unsavory happenings piled up so fast that China was soon being considered as bloody and bad as Japan in the 1930s—worse really because "they were doing it to their own people."[28]

Of course, it can be said that as with Japan in the 1930s there was some degree of "respect" for the power of Peking, but not enough to accelerate this to the level the Japanese militarists had attained, causing alarm and nervousness in the United States. Communist China wasn't *that* strong. It could damage her own people, but not the American homeland or Pacific area domain. While Americans did not believe that "unleashing" Chiang would topple the Communists, the argument about that had the effect of denigrating both Chinas. This situation continued through the 1960s, with increasing American irritation with (not fear of) what continued to be called "Red China." The Cultural Revolution, as proclaimed and promoted by Mao, seemed to most Americans so unrealistically absurd that they began to think of Red China as a self-destroying madhouse commanded by a madman. Only a few intellectuals even attempted to retain some shred of belief that China was following a course of future promise. Such books and Allyn and Adele Rickett's *Prisoners of Liberation* and Edgar Snow's *The Other Side Of The River* tried to explain China in a favorable light, and John Fairbank in the periodic updatings of his *The United States & China* tried to show that U.S.-China relations were not necessarily implacable, but these views were lost amidst general derision about little red books of *Quotations* from Chairman Mao.[29] Indeed, one of the most telling means devised by President Lyndon Johnson's political enemies to hit at him was their production of a little red book of *Quotations from LBJ*. Even the defection of China from the Soviet orbit went largely unnoticed until the end of this decade of the 1960s.

During the 1960s Japan almost became an American favorite, except with a few die-hard old soldiers left over from Pacific war days and some (though not many, as yet) auto industry people. The decade started badly, with cancellation of President Dwight Eisenhower's visit scheduled for June 1960. This was to have been to celebrate the signing of a new ten-year Mutual Security Pact, which (later on) was revealed to have permitted United States ships bearing nuclear weapons to visit Japanese ports. The clamor against the treaty—raised by student and antigovernment demonstrators covering a wide political spectrum who feared that the treaty would project Japan down a bad path to rearmament

and future war—led Prime Minister Kishi to ram the ratification
through the Diet and then resign to minimize the damage.[30] But
thereafter his successor, Ikeda, cooled the potential for antagonis-
tic feelings by lowering Japan's foreign politics profile, until it
was barely visible, and concentrating on economic recovery.

Then President John Kennedy sent Edwin O. Reischauer, a
Harvard professor of Japanese studies, to Japan as ambassador.
Not only did Reischauer mend the "broken dialogue," but he
put a friendly face on every aspect of American-Japanese relations.[31] Remaining through the Johnson years, he worked hard
to prevent troublesome issues from arising, and the American
press carried generally favorable "news" about Japan. Such things
as the "Bullet Train" (Shinkansen), which could travel at 150 miles
per hour from Tokyo to Osaka, a very competently run Japan
Air Lines, and well made Japanese products like Canon cameras,
Seiko watches, Shiseido cosmetics, Sony television sets, Honda
motorcycles, and of course, Toyota and Datsun automobiles became known favorably in the United States. A few Americans
"remembered Pearl Harbor" but most of them were avidly buying
Japanese imports. The Japanese did not help America in the Vietnam war "because of their peace constitution," which General
MacArthur had given them, but Americans knew the Japanese
were "on our side" against communism.

China remained a "problem," even though, despite the madness
of the Cultural Revolution, she did not, for reasons as yet not
understood by Americans, intervene against the United States
presence in Vietnam. Not even the China experts—only Henry
Kissinger, if scholars are to believe his memoirs—had any inkling
of the possibility of a thaw in United States relations with Peking
and the dawn of a new open door era in Chinese-American relations.[32] But Kissinger saw it, and told President Richard Nixon
(though according to Nixon, one of the most noted anticommunists
in American political life, he was the one who grasped the reality
of the opportunity presented by the Sino-Soviet split first). Whichever, Nixon ushered in a new era of American-Chinese relations
with his visit to Peking in 1973.[33]

During the 1970s roles reversed as China became an American
favorite with great numbers of well-guided American tourists seeing the Great Wall and the Peking opera and catching glimpses
of various clean and happy "workplaces" in China. Drugstore
became something of a favorite on the American avant-garde film
circuit, and Democracy Wall impressed many American visitors.

Meanwhile, Toyotas, Datsuns, and Hondas were too much for

the American auto industry. The oil shortage and scare of 1973 and thereafter, which American automakers took their time adjusting to, opened wide the American market to Japanese auto imports. Clever advertising and soaring gasoline prices brought a majority of American auto purchasers around to believing there was no "buy American" problem in purchasing a Datsun, distinctly small and foreign at first, from their "All American Datsun Dealer," as the TV advertising described them. But as layoffs hit Detroit and Reaganomics cooled and depressed the economy further, unemployed autoworkers began campaigns against Toyotas, Datsuns, and Japanese imports in general, even to the point of bashing windshields on a number of Japanese cars as a means of protest. Japanese autos and other Japanese products, however, were already owned by far too many Americans to make direct action feasible on any large scale. But reminders of Pearl Harbor and a subtle anti-Japanese tone began to enter the popular mood. Scholars and businessmen remained admirers of Japan in the sense that they were fascinated and intrigued by Japanese methods of production, even to the point of wishing they could somehow emulate Japanese no-strike and essentially nonunion working conditions. Ezra Vogel found "Lessons for America" in his very popular and influential book *Japan as Number One,* and *Time Magazine* in a special issue devoted to Japan (1 August 1983) tried hard to make Japan look good and especially to show there is no such thing as "Japan Incorporated"—that indeed Japan's Ministry of International Trade and Industry encourages competition at home to the point that inefficient companies lose out, leading to success abroad in the business world.[34]

But the prevailing American mood in the 1980s has been that Japan has become so successful that her sails should be trimmed a bit, either with some quotas or tariffs against Japanese imports or by forcing Japan to "pay the cost of her own defense."

Whether the argument is pro or con, there is still an element of respect for Japanese achievements. A century ago the Japanese educator-philosopher-journalist, Fukuzawa Yukichi, worried in the columns of his *Jiji Shimpo* newspaper that Japan would be linked with China and Korea in the minds of Westerners. "Datsu-A" he proclaimed. "Dissociate from Asia," or more stridently, "Get away from Asia." He did not want Japan to be associated with "backward" Asian countries, particularly with China and Korea. Although most Americans cannot tell a Japanese from a Chinese or Korean face in the physical sense, there has been no confusion with regard to the level of modernization of those countries. Whether liked or disliked, Japan since the Meiji period has been far ahead, and Fukuzawa would be proud of that.[35]

On the other hand, whether Japan deserves the respect she has enjoyed over China in her American image is far less certain. For all her achievements and progress, there is something superficial about Japan's eagerness to succeed in whatever may be the fashions of a given moment of world history, followed by sulking when the traditional structure is endangered by its achievements. Most Western historians, except the aforementioned Frances Moulder, give Japan high marks for achievement if not for deportment, but there may be deeper levels of analysis for examining levels of civilization, as Fukuzawa advocated.

Many students of the Vietnam War generation—including my son France, whose impressions of China are recorded in this volume—found much more of interest in China's history, both ancient and modern, than in Japan's. Beyond technology and trade (admittedly high), what has Japan to offer the cause of "the advancement of civilization"? Shinto, a not very deep religion; social hierarchy, too much; artistic genius, yes, but too narrow and refined. Why should poetry be limited to seventeen syllables and art to the diminutive and the meticulous? Bushido? Positively medieval. Whereas China has had everything, from Confucian humanism and Taoist individualism to Maoist concern for the masses, including much more science than Westerners thought possible before Joseph Needham's multivolume *Science and Civilization in China,* (1959–) no lack of entrepreneurial ability, a strong work ethic, and even a "Democracy Wall" (1979). "Modernization" may be slow but that is not the only measure of human achievement.[36]

So it may be argued, but unfortunately for China's image too many tragic excesses have clouded achievements, especially since America met China in the early nineteenth century: opium trade, Taiping rebellion, Boxer rebellion, warlords, Guo Min Tang collapse, Cultural revolution, and, of course, the massacre of student protesters at Beijing's Tian An Men Square in June 1989. Tragic, sad, pitiable are the words to describe these.

Tiananmen was especially poignant for my wife and for me. After visiting both the PRC and Taiwan in the summer of 1988 we had returned to our University of Pennsylvania full of optimism and hope for the future of both Chinas (or "one country, two systems" as was said in Beijing and not denied in Taipei). True, the PRC was bureaucratically inefficient as CAAC travel service, translated by our Chinese friends as "China Airlines Always Cancels" proved by bringing our 3 P.M. flight into Beijing at 3 A.M.

However, the signs of progress were everywhere. Riding through the country roads of South China had reminded us of Japan in the 1950s, with roads and bridges being built by human hands with three-wheeled equipment that might be characterized as "early modern." Beijing, busy and optimistic, was still bicycleland, but in Taiwan we could see how fast Chinese can modernize if they want to. The PRC seemed to be balancing the pace better, with less pollution.

Back at the University of Pennsylvania we worked during fall and winter to help set up a "Seminar on Economic Cooperation and Development in the Pacific Area" in cooperation with the Pacific Rim Economic Institute of China's People's University— "Seminar Pacific" as it was called—at the Friendship Hotel, Beijing, April 4–8, 1989.

It was, as expressed in our subsequent newsletter report "A week of Hope and Dialogue before the Deluge."[37] But once again, with the Tian An Men Square Massacre, American feelings for China were reduced to pity for the country and its people, in contrast to the respect and admiration accorded Japan for somehow pragmatically rebounding from the disasters it has encountered.

Notes

1. Frances V. Moulder, *Japan, China and the World Economy* (Cambridge: Cambridge University Press, 1977). A succinct presentation of Dr. Moulder's thesis may be found in her article entitled "Comparing Japan and China: Some Theoretical and Methodological Issues" in Alvin D. Coox and Hilary Conroy, eds., *China and Japan: Search for Balance since World War I* (Santa Barbara: ABC Clio-Press, 1978), 87–111.

2. Harry Emerson Wildes, *Aliens in the East* (London: Oxford University Press, 1937).

3. Stowe Persons, "Americanization of the Immigrant," in David Frederick Bowers, *Foreign Influence in American Life* (Princeton: Princeton University Press, 1944), 43–44. See also J. B. Bury, *The Idea of Progress* (New York: Macmillan, 1932).

4. Francis L. Hawks, comp., *Narrative of the Expedition of an American Naval Squadron to the China Seas and Japan*, 3 vols. (Washington, D.C.: Congress of the United States, 1856). See also Alfred Tamarin, *Japan and the United States: Early Encounters, 1791–1860* (New York: Macmillan, 1970), chaps. 2–3; George Henry Preble, *The Opening of Japan: A Diary of Discovery in the Far East*, edited by Boleslaw Szcesniak (Norman: University of Oklahoma Press, 1962); Arthur Walworth, *Black Ships Off Japan: The Story of Commodore Perry's Expedition* (New York: Knopf, 1946); and Edward Yorke McCauley, *With Perry in Japan: The Diary of Edward Yorke McCauley*, edited by Allan B. Cole (Princeton: Princeton University Press, 1942).

5. McCauley, *With Perry*, 85–88.

6. *Harper's Weekly* 178 (26 May 1860): 327.

7. *Harper's Weekly* 182 (23 June 1860), 386; see also Masao Miyoshi, *As We Saw Them: The First Japanese Embassy to the United States* (1860) (Berkeley: University of California Press, 1979), 28–52; Chitoshi Yanaga, "The First Japanese Embassy to the United States," *Pacific Historical Review* 9, no. 2 (1940): 113–38.

8. Akira Iriye, ed., *Mutual Images: Essays in American-Japanese Relations* (Cambridge: Harvard University Press, 1975): 1–23.

9. Foster Rhea Dulles, *Yankees and Samurai* (New York: Harper & Row, 1965), chaps. 9, 12.

10. Charles E. Neu, *The Troubled Encounter: The United States and Japan* (New York: Wiley, 1975), 18–19. For details on the U.S. Ministers to Japan in the Meiji era, see Payson J. Treat, *Diplomatic Relations Between the United States and Japan, 1853–1895,* 2 vols. (Stanford: Stanford University Press, 1932).

11. Lafcadio Hearn, *Glimpses of Unfamiliar Japan,* 2 vols. (Boston: Houghton Mifflin, 1894), and *Japan: At Attempt at Interpretation* (New York: Macmillan, 1904). On fairs see Neil Harris, "All the World's a Melting Pot," in Iriye, *Mutual Images,* chap. 2.

12. Chitoshi Yanage, "The First Japanese Embassy to the United States," *Pacific Historical Review* 9, no. 2 (1940): 137.

13. Hilary Conroy, *The Japanese Frontier in Hawaii, 1868–98* (Berkeley: University of California Press, 1953), 137–38.

14. Charles E. Neu, *The Troubled Encounter: The United States and Japan* (New York: Wiley, 1975). Akira Iriye, *Pacific Estrangement: Japanese and American Expansion, 1879–1911* (Cambridge: Harvard University Press, 1972).

15. William L. Neumann, *America Encounters Japan* (Baltimore: Johns Hopkins University Press, 1963), 103.

16. Iriye, "Japan as a Competitor," in Iriye, *Mutual Images,* 77–78.

17. See Walton Bean, *Boss Ruef's San Francisco* (Berkeley: University of California Press, 1952), 182; Thomas A. Bailey, *Theodore Roosevelt and the Japanese American Crises* (Stanford: Stanford University Press, 1934), 14; A. Whitney Griswold, *The Far Eastern Policy of the United States* (New Haven: Yale University Press, 1938), chap. 9.

18. Roger Daniels, *The Politics of Prejudice* (Berkeley: University of California Press, 1962), especially chaps 5–6.

19. Montaville Flowers, *The Japanese Conquest of American Opinion* (New York: George Doran Co., 1917).

20. Ibid., 78–79, 88–89.

21. Ibid., 88–89.

22. Ibid., 59.

23. Ibid., 236.

24. Lindsay Russell, ed., *America to Japan* (New York: G. P. Putman, 1915).

25. Ibid., 232.

26. See Griffis papers at Rutgers University, New Brunswick, N.J., especially box 20 and an unnumbered box for 1927.

27. John Lagerda, *The Conqueror Comes to Tea: Japan under MacArthur* (New Brunswick, N.J.: Rutgers University Press, 1946); Russell Brines, *MacArthur's Japan* (Philadelphia: J. B. Lippincott, 1948).

28. See Mark Tennien, *No Secret Is Safe* (New York: Farrar, Straus and Young, 1952).

29. Allyn Rickett and Adele Rickett, *Prisoners of Liberation* (New York:

Cameron Associates, 1957); Edgar Snow, *The Other Side of the River* (New York: Random House, 1962); and John F. Fairbank, *The United States & China,* 4th ed. (Cambridge: Harvard University Press, 1948, 1979).

30. George B. Packard III, *Protest in Tokyo: The Security Treaty Crisis of 1960* (Princeton: Princeton University Press, 1966).

31. Edwin O. Reischauer, "The Broken Dialogue with Japan," *Foreign Affairs* 39, no. 1 (October 1960): 11–26. In a real sense, it was with this article that Professor Reischauer began his goodwill ambassadorship toward Japan.

32. Henry Kissinger, *White House Years* (Boston: Little, Brown, 1979), 1049–96.

33. Richard Nixon, *R. N.: The Memoirs of Richard Nixon,* 2 vols. (New York: Warner Books, 1979). See especially 2:8–21.

34. Ezra Vogel, *Japan as Number 1: Lessons for America* (Cambridge: Harvard University Press, 1979). Herman Kahn anticipated Vogel's praise of Japan's success in his *The Emerging Japanese Superstate* (Englewood Cliffs: Prentice Hall, 1970). He modified this in his volume with Thomas Pepper, *The Japanese Challenge* (New York: Crowell, 1979). *Time Magazine,* 1 August 1983, especially 38–41. *Time*'s subheading was: "Fighting it out: Competition at home leads to success abroad."

35. Fukuzawa's "Datsu-A" argument was first published in *Jiji Shimpo,* 16 March 1885. See discussion in Bunso Hashikawa, "Japanese Perspectives on Asia: From Dissociation to Coprosperity," in Akira Iriye, ed., *The Chinese and the Japanese* (Princeton: Princeton University Press, 1980), 328–32. Sheila K. Johnson stresses a "situational approach" and "multiple images" in her *American Attitudes Toward Japan, 1941–1975* (Stanford, Calif.: Hoover Institution Studies, no. 51, 1975). See also Richard H. Minear commentary on "Orientalism and the Study of Japan," *Journal of Asian Studies* 39, no. 3 (May 1980): 507–817; and Matsuzawa Hiroaki, "Varieties of *Bunmei Ron*" (Theories of Civilization) in Hilary Conroy, Sandra T. W. Davis, and Wayne Patterson, eds., *Japan in Transition* (Cranbury, N.J.: Associated University Presses, 1984), 209–14.

36. Of course, this could be argued otherwise—that modernization and its accouterments are the all-important things. Perhaps the writer's comment here is in part a reaction to the strong put-down of China and praise of Japan in Lucian W. Pye's sophisticated analysis in *Asian Power and Politics: The Cultural Dimensions of Authority* (Cambridge: Harvard-Belknap Press, 1985); see especially chaps. 6–7. Reviewing Pye's study for the Annals of the American Political and Social Science Association, I suggested that Pye "seems too much inclined to admire Japan's orderly pragmatism and to denigrate China's lack of it," perhaps because as a political scientist, he keeps power always in focus, while I, as historian, must consider many other things as well. The Annals 488 (November 1986), 197–98.

37. IPS Newsletter (Petaluma, Calif.: Interchange for Pacific Scholarship), vol. 5, no. 1 (summer 1989).

Suggested Readings

This bibliography on American images of China and to a lesser extent of Japan was prepared in January, 1990, and is by no means comprehensive. It largely excludes literature on Asian immigrants in the United States—studies of assimilation—while including studies of diplomatic crises involving immigration. The bibliography is restricted to representative examples of pre-January, 1990, full-length memoirs by participants in American-East Asian relations, to anthologies, and to analytical works. It therefore includes, for example, Orville Schell's *Discos and Democracy, In the People's Republic, To Get Rich is Glorious,* and *"Watch Out for the Foreign Guests!"* but excludes Schell and Franz Schurmann's *The China Reader* and Schell and Joseph Esherick's *Modern China,* both historical works of far broader scope than Sino-American relations. This list also excludes popular and scholarly articles, even though many articles have played an essential role in shaping our understanding of American-East Asian relations, such as Michael H. Hunt's "Pearl Buck—Popular Expert on China, 1931–1941," in *Modern China* 3, no. 1 (January 1977): 33–64. The reader searching for popular or scholarly articles or works with a broader scope than American images of China or Japan up to January, 1990, is referred to the footnote references in articles in this volume, to annotated bibliographies in John K. Fairbank's *The United States and China* (1979) and Warren I. Cohen's *America's Response to China* (1990), and to current social science reference guides.

—JONATHAN GOLDSTEIN

Abend, Hallett, *My Life in China, 1926–1941.* New York: Harcourt, Brace, 1943.

Amnesty International. *Political Imprisonment in the People's Republic of China.* New York: Amnesty International, 1978.

Anderson, David L. *Imperialism and Idealism: American Diplomats in China, 1861–1898.* Bloomington: Indiana University Press, 1986.

Anderson, Irvine H., Jr. *The Standard-Vacuum Oil Company and United States East Asian Policy, 1933–41.* Princeton: Princeton University Press, 1975.

Bachrack, Stanley D. *The Committee of One Million*. New York: Columbia University Press, 1976.

Barnds, William J., ed. *China and America: The Search for a New Relationship*. New York: New York University Press, 1977.

Barnett, A. Doak. *Communist China and Asia: Challenge to American Policy*. New York: Harper, 1960.

Barrett, David. *Dixie Mission*. Berkeley: Center for Chinese Studies, University of California, 1970.

Battistini, Lawrence H. *The United States and Asia*. New York: Praeger, 1955.

Baum, Richard, with Louise Bennett, eds. *China in Ferment: Perspectives on the Cultural Revolution*. Englewood Cliffs, N.J.: Prentice-Hall, 1971.

Belden, Jack. *China Shakes the World*. New York: Monthly Review Press, 1970 [1949].

Bennett, Adrian. *Missionary Journalist in China: Young J. Allen and His Magazines, 1860–1883*. Athens: University of Georgia Press, 1983.

Bernstein, Richard. *From the Center of the Earth: The Search for the Truth about China*. Boston: Little, Brown, 1982.

Borg, Dorothy. *American Policy and the Chinese Revolution, 1925–28*. New York: Octagon, 1968.

—————. *The United States and the Far Eastern Crisis of 1933–38*. Cambridge: Harvard University Press, 1964.

—————, comp. *Historians and American Far Eastern Policy*. New York: Columbia University East Asian Institute Occasional Papers, 1966.

Borg, Dorothy, and Waldo Heinrichs, eds. *Uncertain Years: Chinese-American Relations, 1947–50*. New York: Columbia University Press, 1980.

Borg, Dorothy, and Shumpei Okamoto, eds. *Pearl Harbor as History: Japanese-American Relations, 1931–1941*.

Breslin, Thomas A. *China, American Catholicism, and the Missionary*. University Park: Pennsylvania State University Press, 1980.

Brown, Arthur Judson. *The Chinese Revolution*. New York: Student Volunteer Movement, 1912.

—————. *New Forces in Old China: An Unwelcome but Inevitable Awakening*. New York: Revell, 1904.

Buckley, Thomas H. *The United States and the Washington Conference*. Knoxville: University of Tennessee Press, 1970.

Buhite, Russell D. *Nelson T. Johnson and American Policy Toward China, 1925–1941*. East Lansing: Michigan State University Press, 1968.

—————. *Patrick J. Hurley and American Foreign Policy*. Ithaca: Cornell University Press, 1973.

Butterfield, Fox. *China: Alive in the Bitter Sea*. New York: New York Times Books, 1982.

Callahan, James Morton. *American Relations in the Pacific and the Far East, 1784–1900*. Baltimore: Johns Hopkins Press, 1901.

Campbell, Charles S. *Special Business Interests and the Open Door Policy*, Hamden, Conn.: Archon, 1968 [1951].

Carlson, Ellsworth C. *The Foochow Missionaries, 1847–1880*. Cambridge: Harvard University Press, 1974.

Ching, Frank, ed. *The New York Times Report from Red China*. New York: Quadrangle Books, 1972.

Clubb, Paul H. *United States Policy toward China: Diplomatic and Public Documents, 1839–1939*. New York: Russell and Russell, 1967 [1964 and 1940].

Clyde, Paul H., and Burton Beers. *The Far East: A History of the Western Impact and the Eastern Response, 1830–1975*. Englewood Cliffs, N.J.: Prentice-Hall, 1975.

Cochran, Sherman. *Big Business in China: Sino-Foreign Rivalry in the Cigarette Industry, 1890–1930*. Cambridge: Harvard University Press, 1980.

Cohen, Paul A. *China and Christianity: The Missionary Movement and the Growth of Chinese Antiforeignism, 1860–1870*. Cambridge: Harvard University Press, 1964.

——————. *Discovering History in China: American Historical Writing on the Recent Chinese Past*. New York: Columbia University Press, 1984.

Cohen, Warren I. *America's Response to China: An Interpretive History of Sino-American Relations*. New York: Wiley, 1990 [1971].

——————. *The Chinese Connection: Roger S. Greene, Thomas W. Lamont, George E. Sokolsky and American-East Asian Relations*. New York: Columbia University Press, 1978.

——————, ed. *New Frontiers in American-East Asian Relations*. New York: Columbia University Press, 1983.

Committee of Concerned Asian Scholars. *China! Inside the People's Republic*. New York: Bantam, 1972.

Conroy, Hilary. *The Japanese Frontier in Hawaii, 1868–1898*. Berkeley: University of California Press, 1953.

Conroy, Hilary and T. Scott Miyakawa. *East Across the Pacific*. Santa Barbara, Calif.: ABC-Clio Press, 1972.

Croly, Herbert. *Willard Straight*. New York: Macmillan, 1942.

Crossman, Carl. *The China Trade*. Princeton: Pyne Press, 1972.

Crow, Carl. *400 Million Customers*. New York: Harper, 1937.

——————. *The Traveler's Handbook for China*. Shanghai: Hwa-Mei Book Concern, 1913.

Cumings, Bruce. *The Origins of the Korean War: Liberation and Emergence of Separate Regimes, 1945–1947*. Princeton: Princeton University Press, 1981.

Curry, Roy W. *Woodrow Wilson and Far Eastern Policy, 1913–1921*. New York: Octagon, 1968.

Danton, George H. *The Culture Contacts of the United States and China: The Earliest Sino-American Culture Contacts, 1784–1844*. New York: Columbia University Press, 1931.

Davies, John Paton, Jr. *Dragon By the Tail*. New York: Norton, 1972.

Dawson, Raymond. *The Chinese Chameleon*. New York: Oxford University Press, 1967.

Dennett, Tyler. *Americans in Eastern Asia*. New York: Barnes and Noble, 1922.

Dulles, Foster Rhea. *American Policy toward Communist China, 1949–1969*. New York: Thomas Y. Crowell, 1972.

—————. *China and America: The Story of their Relations since 1784*. Princeton: Princeton University Press, 1946.

—————. *The Old China Trade*. New York: AMS Press, 1970 [1930].

Esherick, Joseph W., ed. *Lost Chance in China: The World War II Despatches of John S. Service*. New York: Random House, 1974.

Etzold, Thomas H., ed. *Aspects of Sino-American Relations since 1784*. New York: Franklin Watts/New Viewpoints, 1978.

Evans, Paul M. *John Fairbank and the American Understanding of Modern China*. New York: Basil Blackwell, 1988.

Fairbank, John K. *China: The People's Middle Kingdom and the U.S.A.* Cambridge: Harvard University Press, 1967.

—————. *China Perceived*. New York: Knopf, 1974.

—————. *China Watch*. Cambridge: Harvard University Press, 1987.

—————. *Chinabound: A Fifty Year Memoir*. New York: Harper and Row, 1982.

—————. *Chinese-American Interactions*. New Brunswick, N.J.: Rutgers University Press, 1975.

—————. *Trade and Diplomacy on the China Coast: The Opening of the Treaty Ports, 1842–1854*. Cambridge: Harvard University Press, 1953.

—————. *The United States and China*. Cambridge: Harvard University Press, 1979 [1948].

—————, ed. *The Missionary Experience in China and America*. Cambridge: Harvard University Press, 1974.

Feis, Herbert. *The China Tangle: The American Effort in China from Pearl Harbor to the Marshall Mission*. Princeton: Princeton University Press, 1953.

—————. *The Road to Pearl Harbor*. Princeton: Princeton University Press, 1950.

Fifield, Russell H. *Woodrow Wilson and the Far East: The Diplomacy of the Shantung Question*. Hamden, Conn.: Archon, 1965.

Flynn, John T. *While You Slept. Our Tragedy in Asia and Who Made It*. Old Greenwich, Conn.: Devin-Adair, 1971 [1951].

Foot, Rosemary. *The Wrong War: American Policy and the Dimensions of the Korean Conflict, 1950–1953*. Ithaca: Cornell University Press, 1985.

Forbes, H. A. Crosby; John Devereaux Kernan; Ruth S. Wilkins. *Chinese Export Silver, 1785 to 1885*. Milton, Mass.: Museum of the American China Trade, 1975.

Forsythe, Sidney A. *A Missionary Community in China, 1895–1905*. Cambridge: Harvard East Asian Monographs, 1971.

Foster, John W. *American Diplomacy in the Orient*. Boston: Houghton Mifflin, 1903.

Friedman, Edward, and Mark Selden, eds. *America's Asia: Dissenting Essays on Asian-American Relations*. New York: Pantheon, 1971.

Fuess, Claude M. *The Life of Caleb Cushing*. New York: Harcourt, Brace, 1923.

Gallicchio, Marc S. *The Cold War Begins in Asia*. New York: Columbia University Press, 1988.

Garrett, Shirley. *Social Reformers in Urban China*. Cambridge: Harvard University Press, 1970.

Garver, John W. *China's Decision for Rapproachement with the United States, 1968–1971*. Boulder, Colo.: Westview, 1982.

Goldstein, Jonathan. *Philadelphia and the China Trade, 1682–1846: Commercial, Cultural and Attitudinal Effects*. University Park: Pennsylvania State University Press, 1978.

—————, ed. *Georgia's East Asian Connection, 1733–1983*. Carrollton: West Georgia College Studies in the Social Sciences, 1983.

Greene, Felix. *A Curtain of Ignorance—China: How America is Deceived*. London: Cape, 1965.

Griswold, A. Whitney. *The Far Eastern Policy of the United States*. New Haven: Yale University Press, 1938. Gulick, Edward V. *Peter Parker and the Opening of China*. Cambridge: Harvard University Press, 1973.

Hao, Yen-p'ing. *The Commercial Revolution in Nineteenth Century China: The Rise of Sino-Western Mercantile Capitalism*. Berkeley: University of California Press, 1986.

—————. *The Comprador in Nineteenth Century China: Bridge Between East and West*. Cambridge: Harvard University Press, 1970.

Harding, Harry. *China's Foreign Relations in the 1980s*. New Haven: Yale University Press, 1986.

Harding, Harry, and Yuan Ming, eds. *Sino-American Relations, 1945–1955*. Wilmington, Del.: Scholarly Resources, 1989.

Hemenway, Ruth V. *A Memoir of Revolutionary China, 1924–1941*. Amherst: University of Massachusetts Press, 1977.

Hinton, William. *Fanshen: A Documentary of Revolution in a Chinese Village*. New York: Monthly Review Press, 1966.

—————. *Shenfan: The Continuing Revolution in a Chinese Village*. New York: Random House, 1983.

Hollander, Paul. *Political Pilgrims: Travels of Western Intellectuals to the Soviet Union, China, and Cuba, 1928–1978*. New York: Oxford University Press, 1981.

Hunt, Michael H. *Frontier Defense and the Open Door: Manchuria in Chinese-American Relations, 1895–1911*. New Haven: Yale University Press, 1973.

—————. *The Making of a Special Relationship. The United States and China to 1914*. New York: Columbia University Press, 1983.

—————, et al. *Mutual Images in U.S.-China Relations*. Occasional Paper No. 32. Washington, D.C.: Wilson Center, Asia Program, 1988.

Hunter, Jane. *The Gospel of Gentility: American Women Missionaries in Turn-of-the-Century China*. New Haven: Yale University Press, 1984.

Hyatt, Irwin. *Our Ordered Lives Confess: Three Nineteenth Century American Missionaries in East Shantung*. Cambridge: Harvard University Press, 1976.

Iriye, Akira. *Across the Pacific: The Inner History of East Asian-American Relations*. New York: Harcourt Brace, 1967.

—————. *After Imperialism. The Search for a New Order in the Far East*. Cambridge: Harvard University Press, 1965.

―――――. *The Cold War in Asia: A Historical Introduction*. Englewood Cliffs, N.J.: Prentice-Hall, 1974.

―――――. *Mutual Images: Essays in American-Japanese Relations*. Cambridge: Harvard University Press, 1975.

―――――, ed. *American-East Asian Cultural Relations*. Chicago: Center for Far Eastern Studies, University of Chicago, 1984.

―――――, ed. *U.S. Policy toward China*. Boston: Little, Brown, 1968.

Iriye, Akira, and Warren Cohen. *American, Chinese, and Japanese Perspective on Wartime Asia, 1931–1939*. Wilmington, Del.: Scholarly Resources, 1990.

Isaacs, Harold. *Scratches on our Minds: American Views of China and India*. Armonk, N.Y.: M. E. Sharpe, 1980 [1958].

Israel, Jerry. *Progressivism and the Open Door: America and China, 1905–1921*. Pittsburgh: University of Pittsburgh Press, 1971.

Jiang, Arnold Xiangze. *The United States and China*. Chicago: University of Chicago Press, 1988.

Jones, Dorothy B. *The Portrayal of China and India on the American Screen, 1896–1955*. Cambridge: MIT Center for International Affairs, 1955.

Kahn, E. J., Jr. *The China Hands*. New York: Random House, 1975.

Kalicki, J. H. *The Pattern of Sino-American Crises: Political-Military Interactions in the 1950s*. London: Cambridge University Press, 1975.

Karlgren, Joyce K. and Denis F. Simon, eds. *Educational Exchanges: Essays on the Sino-American Experience*. Berkeley: University of California Institute of East Asian Studies, 1987.

Kates, George N. *The Years that Were Fat: The Last of Old China*. Cambridge: MIT Press, 1967 [1952].

Kaufman, Burton I. *The Korean War: Challenges in Crisis, Credibility, and Command*. Princeton: Princeton University Press, 1986.

Koen, Ross Y. *The China Lobby in American Politics*. New York: Harper and Row, 1974.

Kubek, Anthony. *How the Far East Was Lost*. Chicago: Regnery, 1963.

La Fargue, Thomas E. *China's First Hundred*. Pullman: State College of Washington, 1942.

LaFeber, Walter. *The New Empire: An Interpretation of American Expansion, 1860–1898*. Ithaca: Cornell University Press, 1963.

Latourette, Kenneth S. *The History of Early Relations between the United States and China*. New York: Kraus, 1967 [1917].

Lauren, Paul Gordon, ed. *The China Hands' Legacy: Ethics and Diplomacy*. Boulder, Colo.: Westview, 1987.

Lewis, Bernard; Edmund Leites; and Margaret Chase, eds. *As Others See Us. Mutual Perceptions, East and West*. A special issue of *Comparative Civilizations Review* nos. 13–14 (1985–1986).

Li, Tien-yi. *Woodrow Wilson's China Policy, 1913–1917*. New York: Octagon, 1969.

Liu, Kwang-Ching. *Americans and Chinese: A Historical Essay and a Bibliography*. Cambridge: Harvard University Press, 1963.

―――――, ed. *American Missionaries in China: Papers from Harvard Semi-*

nars. Cambridge: Harvard East Asian Monographs, 1966.

Lutz, Jesse G. *China and the Christian Colleges, 1850–1950.* Ithaca: Cornell University Press, 1971.

McClellan, Robert. *The Heathen Chinee: A Study of American Attitudes Toward China, 1890–1905.* Columbus: Ohio State University Press, 1971.

McCormick, Thomas. *China Market: America's Quest for Informal Empire, 1893–1901.* Chicago: Quadrangle, 1967.

MacFarquhar, Roderick, ed. *Sino-American Relations, 1949–71.* New York: Praeger, 1972.

McKee, Delber L. *Chinese Exclusion versus the Open Door Policy, 1900–1906: Clashes over China Policy in the Roosevelt Era.* Detroit: Wayne State University Press, 1977.

MacLaine, Shirley. *You Can Get There From Here.* New York: Norton, 1975.

Mathews, Jay, and Linda Mathews. *One Billion: A China Chronicle.* New York: Random House, 1983.

Matray, James I. *The Reluctant Crusade: American Foreign Policy in Korea, 1941–1950.* Honolulu: University of Hawaii Press, 1985.

May, Ernest R. *The Truman Administration and China: 1945–1949.* Philadelphia: Lippincott, 1975.

May, Ernest R., and John K. Fairbank, eds. *America's China Trade in Historical Perspective: The Chinese and American Performance.* Cambridge: Harvard University Press, 1986.

May, Ernest R., and James C. Thomson, Jr., eds. *America-East Asian Relations: A Survey.* Cambridge: Harvard University Press, 1972.

May, Gary. *China Scapegoat: The Diplomatic Ordeal of John Carter Vincent.* Prospect Heights, Ill.: Waveland Press, 1982 [1979].

Mayers, David A. *Cracking the Monolith. U.S. Policy Against the Sino-Soviet Alliance, 1949–1955.* Baton Rouge: Louisiana State University Press, 1986.

Miller, Stuart C. *The Unwelcome Immigrant: The American Image of the Chinese, 1785–1882.* Berkeley: University of California Press, 1974 [1969].

Moody, Peter. *Opposition and Dissent in Contemporary China.* Stanford: Hoover Institution Press, 1977.

Moorsten, Richard, and Morton Abramowitz. *Remaking China Policy: U.S.-China Relations and Governmental Decision-making.* Cambridge: Harvard University Press, 1971.

Morse, Hosea Ballou. *The International Relations of the Chinese Empire.* 2 vols. London: Longmans, Green, 1910.

Morse, Hosea Ballou, and Harley MacNair. *Far Eastern International Relations.* Boston: Houghton Mifflin, 1931.

Nee, Victor, and James Peck, eds. *China's Uninterrupted Revolution: From 1840 to the Present.* New York: Pantheon, 1975.

Oksenberg, Michael. *Explorations in Sino-American Relations.* Boulder, Colo.: Westview, 1989.

————, ed. *China's Developmental Experience.* New York: Praeger, 1973.

Oksenberg, Michael, and Robert B. Oxnam, eds. *Dragon and Eagle: United States-China Relations: Past and Future.* New York: Basic Books, 1978.

Passin, Herbert. *Encounter with Japan.* New York: Kodansha, 1982.

Peck, Graham. *Two Kinds of Time.* Boston: Houghton Mifflin, 1950.

Pugach, Noel. *Paul S. Reinsch: Open Door Diplomat in Action.* Millwood, N.Y.: KTO Press, 1979.

Pye, Lucian. *Asian Power and Politics: The Cultural Dimensions of Authority.* Cambridge: Harvard University Belknap Press, 1985.

Rabe, Valentin H. *The Home Base of American China Missions, 1880–1920.* Cambridge: Harvard University Press, 1978.

Rea, Kenneth W., ed. *Early Sino-American Relations, 1841–1912.* Boulder, Colo.: Westview, 1977.

Reed, James. *The Missionary Mind and American East Asia Policy, 1911–1915.* Cambridge: Harvard University Press, 1983.

Reischauer, Edwin O. *My Life between Japan and America.* New York: Harper & Row, 1986.

Rickett, Allyn, and Adele Rickett. *Prisoners of Liberation.* New York: Cameron Associates, 1957.

Romanus, Charles F., and Riley Sunderland. *Stilwell's Command Problems.* Washington, D.C.: Office of the Chief of Military History, 1956.

—————. *Stilwell's Mission to China.* Washington, D.C.: Office of the Chief of Military History, 1953.

—————. *Time Runs Out in CBI.* Washington, D.C.: Office of the Chief of Military History, 1959.

Ross, Edward Alsworth. *The Changing Chinese: The Conflict of Oriental and Western Cultures in China.* New York: Century, 1911.

Schaller, Michael. *The United States and China in the Twentieth Century.* New York: Oxford University Press, 1989 [1979].

—————. *The U.S. Crusade in China, 1938–1945.* New York: Columbia University Press, 1979.

Schell, Orville. *Discos and Democracy: China in the Throes of Reform.* New York: Pantheon, 1988.

—————. *In the People's Republic: An American's Firsthand View of Living and Working in China.* New York: Random House, 1978 [1977].

—————. *To Get Rich is Glorious: China in the 80s.* New York: New American Library, 1985 [1984].

—————. *"Watch Out for the Foreign Guests!": China Encounters the West.* New York: Pantheon, 1980.

Service, John. *The Amerasia Papers.* Berkeley: University of California Press, 1971.

Shewmaker, Kenneth E. *Americans and Chinese Communists, 1927–1945.* Ithaca: Cornell University Press, 1971.

Smith, Arthur H. *China and America To-day: A Study of Conditions and Relations.* New York: Revell, 1907.

—————. *China in Convulsion.* 2 vols. New York: AMS Press, 1973 [1901].

—————. *Chinese Characteristics.* Port Washington, N.Y.: Kennikat, 1970 [1894].

—————. *Village Life in China.* Boston: Little Brown, 1970 [1899].

Snow, Edgar. *The Battle for Asia*. Cleveland: World, 1941.

——. *The Far Eastern Front*. New York: Smith and Haas, 1933.

——. *Journey to the Beginning*. New York: Random House, 1958.

——. *The Other Side of the River: Red China Today*. New York: Random House, 1961.

——. *Random Notes on Red China 1936–1945*. Cambridge: Harvard East Asian Monographs, 1957.

——. *Red Stars Over China*. New York: Grove Press, 1968 [1938].

Snow, Lois Wheeler. *China on Stage: An American Actress in the People's Republic*. New York: Random House, 1972.

So, Kwan Wai, and Warren I. Cohen. *Essays in the History of China and Chinese-American Relations*. East Lansing: Asian Studies Center, Michigan State University, 1982.

Spence, Jonathan. *To Change China: Western Advisors in China, 1620–1960*. Boston: Little, Brown, 1969.

Spurr, Russell. *Enter the Dragon: China's Involvement in the Korean War, 1950–1951*. New York: Newmarket Press, 1988.

Steele, Archibald T. *The American People and China*. New York: McGraw-Hill, 1966.

Stueck, William W., Jr. *The Road to Confrontation: American Policy toward China and Korea, 1947–1950*. Chapel Hill: University of North Carolina Press, 1981.

Sutter, Robert B. *China-Watch: Toward Sino-American Reconciliation*. Baltimore: Johns Hopkins University Press, 1978.

Swanberg, W. A. *Luce*. New York: Scribner's, 1972.

Swisher, Earl. *China's Management of the American Barbarians*. New York: Octagon, 1982 [1953].

Tamarin, Alfred. *Japan and the United States: Early Encounters, 1791–1860*. New York: Macmillan, 1970.

Tennien, Mark. *No Secret is Safe*. New York: Farrar, Strauss and Young, 1952.

Terrill, Ross, ed. *The China Difference*. New York: Harper and Row, 1981 [1980].

Thomas, John N. *The Institute of Pacific Relations*. Seattle: University of Washington Press, 1974.

Thomson, James C., Jr. *Sentimental Imperialists: The American Experience in East Asia*. New York: Harper and Row, 1981.

——. *While China Faced West: American Reformers in Nationalist China, 1982–1937*. Cambridge: Harvard University Press, 1969.

Thorne, Christopher. *Allies of a Kind: The United States, Britain and the War Against Japan, 1941–1945*. New York: Oxford University Press, 1978.

——. *The Limits of Foreign Policy. The West, the League and the Far Eastern Crisis of 1931–1933*. New York: G. P. Putnam's, 1973 [1972].

Tong, Te-kong. *United States Diplomacy in China, 1644–1860*. Seattle: University of Washington Press, 1964.

Tsou, Tang. *America's Failure in China, 1941–50*. Chicago: University of Chicago Press, 1967.

Tuchman, Barbara. *Notes from China*. New York: Collier, 1972.

—————. *Stilwell and the American Experience in China*. New York: Macmillan, 1971.

Tucker, Nancy B. *Patterns in the Dust: Chinese-American Relations and the Recognition Controversy, 1949–1950*. New York: Columbia University Press, 1983.

Utley, Freda. *The China Story*. Chicago: Regnery, 1951.

Van Alstyne, Richard W. *The United States and East Asia*. New York: Norton, 1973.

Varg, Paul A. *The Closing of the Door: Sino-American Relations 1936–1946*. East Lansing: Michigan State University Press, 1973.

—————. *The Making of a Myth: The United States and China*. East Lansing: Michigan State University Press, 1968.

—————. *Missionaries, Chinese, and Diplomats: The American Protestant Missionary Movement in China, 1890–1952*. Princeton: Princeton University Press, 1958.

—————. *Open Door Diplomat: The Life of W. W. Rockhill*. Champaign-Urbana: University of Illinois Press, 1952.

Vevier, Charles. *The United States and China, 1905–1913: A Study of Finance and Diplomacy*. New Brunswick, N.J.: Rutgers University Press, 1955.

West, Philip. *Yenching University and Sino-Western Relations, 1916–1952*. Cambridge: Harvard University Press, 1976.

White, Theodore, and Annalee Jacoby. *Thunder Out of China*. New York: Da Capo, 1980 [1946].

Wiest, Jean-Paul. *Maryknoll in China: A History*. Armonk, N.Y.: M. E. Sharpe, 1988.

Wildes, Harry Emerson. *Aliens in the East*. London: Oxford, 1937.

Wong, Eugene Franklin. *On Visual Media Racism: Asians in the American Motion Pictures*. New York: Arno, 1978.

Wright, Mary C. *The Last Stand of Chinese Conservatism: The T'ung-chih Restoration, 1862–1872*. Stanford, Calif.: Stanford University Press, 1957.

Young, Arthur. *China and the Helping Hand, 1937–1945*. Cambridge: Harvard University Press, 1963.

Young, Kenneth T. *Negotiating with the Chinese Communists: The United States Experience, 1953–1967*. New York: McGraw Hill, 1984 [1968].

Young, Marilyn. *The Rhetoric of Empire: American China Policy, 1895–1901*. Cambridge: Harvard University Press, 1968.

Contributors

DAVID B. CHAN has taught East Asian history and Sino-American relations at California State University at Hayward since 1963. In 1957 he received his Ph.D. in East Asian history from the University of California at Berkeley. Dr. Chan has published articles on medieval and modern China. He has served as executive vice president of the Institute of Pacific Studies and as resident director in Taipei of the California State Universities' Center.

Since 1967 PAOCHIN CHU has taught East Asian history and international relations at San Diego State University, where he has also directed the Center for Asian Studies. In 1970 he received his Ph.D. in international relations from the University of Pennsylvania. His dissertation concerned the diplomacy of V. K. Wellington Koo, also the subject of a book and several articles by Dr. Chu.

Since 1979 FRANCE H. CONROY has taught social science at Burlington County College, Cinnaminson, N.J., where he also directed the international studies program. In 1975 he received his Ph.D. in East-West political philosophy from Union Graduate School. He has written on China for *Peace and Change, The San Francisco Chronicle,* and *The Courier-Post* (Cherry Hill, N.J.). Dr. Conroy wrote for the "New Left" newspapers *The Guardian* and *The Call* before beginning his teaching career. In 1979 Dr. Conroy was invited to China by the Propaganda Department of the Central Committee of the Chinese Communist Party as a member of a writers and journalists delegation.

HILARY CONROY is Professor of Far Eastern History Emeritus at the University of Pennsylvania. He received his Ph.D. from the University of California and has been a Fulbright research scholar at Tokyo University, president of the Conference on Peace Research in History, and a senior specialist at the Institute of Advanced Projects at the East-West Center (Honolulu). The most recent of his publications are, with Alvin D. Coox, *China and Japan: Search for Balance* (1978); with Harry Wray, *Japan Examined* (1983); with Sandra T. W. Davis and Wayne Patterson, *Japan in Transition* (1984); and, with Roy Kim, *New Tides in the Pacific* (1987).

JACQUES M. DOWNS received his Ph.D. in American diplomatic history from Georgetown University in 1961. Since then he has taught American history at the University of New England, Biddeford, Maine. Dr. Downs coedited *The Thunder of the Mills: A New England Business and Economic History Casebook, 1690–1965* (1980) and *The Cities on the Saco* (1986).

JONATHAN GOLDSTEIN is an associate professor of East Asian history at West Georgia College and a research associate of Harvard University's John K. Fairbank Center for East Asian Research. In 1973 he received his Ph.D. in American–East Asian relations from the University of Pennsylvania, where he studied under Hilary Conroy. He wrote *Philadelphia and the China Trade, 1682–1846* (1978) and edited *Georgia's East Asian Connection, 1733–1983* (1983). He has published articles on nineteenth century Sino-American relations in *Ch'ing-shih wen't'i, Asian Cultural Quarterly* (Taipei), *American Studies* (Taipei), *New China,* and *The American Asian Review.*

HARRY HARDING is Senior Fellow at the Brookings Institution, Washington, D.C. He received his Ph.D. from Stanford University, where he has also taught political science. He is the author of *Organizing China: The Problem of Bureaucracy, 1949–1976* (1981); *China: The Uncertain Future* (1974); and *China and the United States: Normalization and Beyond* (1979). Dr. Harding edited *China's Foreign Relations in the 1980s* (1984).

SANDRA M. HAWLEY teaches history at San Jacinto College, Houston, Texas. She received her Ph.D. in American–East Asian relations in 1974 from Case Western Reserve University, where she studied under David van Tassel. She has published articles on American–East Asian relations and is working on *Asia in the American Imagination,* an examination of ideas and images in foreign policy.

JERRY ISRAEL is Academic Dean and Vice President of Simpson College, Indianola, Iowa. He has taught United States and modern Chinese history at Illinois Wesleyan University. He received his

Ph.D. in history from Rutgers University in 1967. Professor Israel is the author of *Progressivism and the Open Door: America and China, 1905–1921* (1971) and of articles about twentieth century American–East Asian relations and American images of China.

RAMON H. MYERS is the curator of the East Asian Collection and a Senior Fellow at the Hoover Institution on War, Revolution and Peace, Stanford, California. He received his Ph.D. in Economics at the University of Washington (Seattle) and has taught at the Universities of Hawaii and Miami (Coral Gables). He is the author of *The Chinese Peasant Economy* (1970) and, with Mark Peattie, coedited *The Japanese Colonial Empire* (1987). He coauthored, with Tai-chun Kuo, *Understanding Communist China: Communist China Studies in the United States and the Republic of China, 1949–1978* (1986).

RAYMOND G. O'CONNOR, University of Miami emeritus, has published in the fields of maritime and diplomatic history and American–East Asian relations. Most recently, Dr. O'Connor wrote the introduction and commentary for the second edition of *The Japanese Navy in World War Two* (1986).

MARK A. PLUMMER received his Ph.D. in United States and Asian history from the University of Kansas in 1960. Since then he has been a member of the history department at Illinois State University. He has spent extended periods of time in China (mainland or Taiwan) on five occasions since 1962 and has served as Fulbright professor of American history at National Taiwan University.

JAN S. PRYBYLA is Professor of Economics at The Pennsylvania State University. He is the author of, among others, *The Political Economy of Communist China* (1970); *The Chinese Economy: Problems and Policies* (1978, 1981); *Issues in Socialist Economic Modernization* (1980); and *Market and Plan Under Socialism: The Bird in the Cage* (1987).

MURRAY A. RUBINSTEIN teaches history of religion at Baruch College of the City University of New York. He received his Ph.D. in history from New York University in 1976 and has published articles and reviews about Christian missionaries in China in American and Taiwanese journals. In 1979–80 Dr. Rubinstein served as Fulbright lecturer in American Studies in Taiwan.

JONATHAN G. UTLEY has taught the history of the United States foreign relations at the University of Tennessee, Knoxville, since 1969. In 1970 he received his Ph.D. from the University of Illinois, Urbana. In addition to *Going to War with Japan, 1937–1941* (1985), he has written numerous reviews and articles on U.S.–East Asian relations.

RAYMOND F. WYLIE is Professor of International Relations and Director of the East Asian studies program at Lehigh University. He received his Ph.D. in political science in 1976 from the School of Oriental and African Studies, University of London. He has written *The Emergence of Maoism, 1935–1945* (1980); *China: The Peasant Revolution* (1972); *China Today: An Introduction for Canadians* (1972); and, with Immanuel C. Y. Hsu, "The China Hands in Historical and Comparative Perspective," in Paul Gordon Lauren, ed., *The China Hands' Legacy: Ethics and Diplomacy* (1987), 58–80.

Index

N.B. In preparing this text and index with many Chinese names for an American audience, I have been guided by Professor John Schrecker's advice to let common American usage dictate which transliteration should prevail. He asks rhetorically, "Do we use Firenze rather than Florence?" During two centuries of Sino-American relations several formal systems plus numerous arbitrary renditions have been used to convert Chinese words into Latin characters. In both the text and index I have entered Chinese names according to their commonest usage in American English, such as Chiang Kai-shek or Sun Yat-sen. Wherever feasible I have juxtaposed or cross-indexed transliterations less commonly used in American English, such as Jiang Jieshi or Sun Zhongshan.

—Jonathan Goldstein